Young **People's Leisure and Lifestyles**

... with the ...

... to be defined in the ... way.

... f a major seven-year longitudinal study
... 10,000 young people, the authors closely analyse issues con-
...ng young people in school, home, leisure and work settings. They
look, for instance, at young people in the context of the family and explore
the impact of parenting style on lifestyle development. Other important
topics considered in relation to young people's development include an
analysis of social class and occupational trajectories, 'risk' behaviours and
adolescent health and well-being, sports participation, and the formation of
friendship groups and the importance of peers across the adolescent years.

Importantly, the authors also assess whether class and gender relations
override youth culture, values and behaviour as the determining factors of
youth lifestyles. *Young People's Leisure and Lifestyles* will be of interest to
students of psychology, social work, sociology, education, youth and community work, and sport and leisure studies, as well as all those who work
professionally with young people.

Leo B. Hendry is Professor of Education at the University of Aberdeen.
Janet Shucksmith and **Anthony Glendinning** are Lecturers in the Department of Education at the University of Aberdeen. **John G. Love** is Lecturer
in Sociology at the Robert Gordon University in Aberdeen.

Adolescence and Society

Series editor: John C. Coleman
The Trust for the Study of Adolescence

The general aim of the series is to make accessible to a wide readership the growing evidence relating to adolescent development. Much of this material is published in relatively inaccessible professional journals, and the goals of the books in this series will be to summarise, review and place in context current work in the field so as to interest and engage both an undergraduate and a professional audience.

The intention of the authors is to raise the profile of adolescent studies among professionals and in institutes of higher education. By publishing relatively short, readable books on interesting topics to do with youth and society, the series will make people more aware of the relevance of the subject of adolescence to a wide range of social concerns.

The books will not put forward any one theoretical viewpoint. The authors will outline the most prominent theories in the field and will include a balanced and critical assessment of each of these. Whilst some of the books may have a clinical or applied slant, the majority will concentrate on normal development.

The readership will rest primarily in two major areas: the undergraduate market, particularly in the fields of psychology, sociology and education; and the professional training market, with particular emphasis on social work, clinical and educational psychology, counselling, youth work, nursing and teacher training.

Also available in this series

Identity in Adolescence
Jane Kroger

The Nature of Adolescence (second edition)
John C. Coleman and Leo Hendry

The Adolescent in the Family
Patricia Noller and Victor Callan

Young People's Understanding of Society
Adrian Furnham and Barrie Stacey

Growing up with Unemployment
Anthony H. Winefield, Marika Tiggemann, Helen R. Winefield
and Robert D. Goldney

Young people's leisure and lifestyles

Leo B. Hendry, Janet Shucksmith,
John G. Love and Anthony Glendinning

London and New York

First published in 1993
by Routledge
11 New Fetter Lane, London EC4P 4EE

Simultaneously published in the USA and Canada
by Routledge
29 West 35th Street, New York, NY 10001

© 1993 Leo B. Hendry, Janet Shucksmith, John G. Love and Anthony
Glendinning

Typeset in 10 on 12 point Times by
LaserScript Limited, Mitcham, Surrey
Printed and bound in Great Britain by
Biddles Ltd, Guildford and King's Lynn

British Library Cataloguing in Publication Data

A catalogue record for this book is available from the British Library

Library of Congress Cataloging in Publication Data

Young people's leisure and lifestyles/Leo B. Hendry . . . [et al.].
    p. cm. – (Adolescence and society)
    Simultaneously published in the USA and Canada.
    Includes bibliographical references and index.
    1. Youth – Social life and customs.   2. Leisure – Social aspects.   3.
Socialization.   4. Youth – Recreation.   I. Hendry, Leo B.   II. Series.
HQ796.Y5824   1993
305.23′5–dc20   92-45832
                                                                    CIP

ISBN 0–415–04349–2
ISBN 0–415–04350–6 (pbk)

Contents

Illustrations

FIGURES

TABLES

Acknowledgements

The authors gratefully acknowledge the support and co-operation of various individuals and organisations in carrying out the longitudinal study on which this book is based. We would like to thank trustees and executive officers of the Health Promotion Research Trust, in particular Professor Gary Love, Dr Fay Bendall and Mr Richard Wakeford; the Scottish Sports Council, in particular Mr Jon Best; all members of the advisory committee of the project under the able chairmanship of Professor John Nisbet; all the schools which took part and all the young people in Scotland and north-east England who collaborated with us and provided us with such valuable insights into their lifestyles and leisure as they grew up. Finally the project would not have been possible without the loyal supporting work at different times of Ms Janette McCrae, Ms Jeanette Scott and Mrs Gill West, along with other research associates and a host of fieldworkers. Within the Department of Education we also received superb administrative and secretarial assistance from Mrs Sheila Riach, Mrs Marjory Reilly and Mrs Margaret Sinclair.

1 Adolescence and adolescent lifestyles

INTRODUCTION

It has now become something of a cliché to talk about 'adolescence' as a twentieth-century creation. Adolescence, as a time set aside for waiting, developing and maturing and for accomplishing the rites of passage between childhood and adult status, is certainly an extended phase of life for today's young people.

A variety of social pressures and changes in child-rearing practices seem destined to foreshorten that period of life when the young person is truly a child. Maturing to puberty at an earlier age than their parents and grandparents young people become participants in domestic and global affairs through more open households and the omnipresent media. Thus today's child in some senses at least has entered upon adolescence long before leaving primary school. At the same time, however, compulsory schooling has been extended and the pressures on the workforce to become more highly skilled have put a premium on 'staying-on' at school or moving into tertiary education. The delay in acquiring an income is just one of the factors which seems to defer the passage to adulthood. Even for those who enter the world of work at an early age, independence and adult status is hard to achieve. Political changes resulting in the abolition of Wage Councils ensure that many young people end up on low salaries which do not enable them to live separately from their parents. Revised systems of social benefits are designed to force parents to remain responsible for the upkeep and welfare of their children in late adolescence. Whilst many adolescents may rail at the infantilising aspects of these changes, the prospects for independent life outside the family home are bleak for many, with a decline or halt in council house building, the disappearance of much of the private rented sector and the high interest rates which prohibit home-buying. Thus social and political changes extend the period of dependence on parents and residence in the parental household for many young people.

This rather gloomy picture of young people's prospects must be put into perspective. Not only might it be cyclical (with demographic changes producing a youth labour shortage and pushing wages up again for young people as we move towards the next century), but life as a prolonged adolescent may not be all that bad. Many young people benefit from the improvements in living standards that their parents have attained. The adolescent as a consumer of expensive designer casual clothes and of sports and audio equipment is not just a myth created by the advertising agencies. Such agencies know their markets too well; the quantity and type of advertising aimed at this age band is a useful surrogate measure of the quantity of available cash to be spent on or by this section of the community.

But more than all of these consumer goods, the one luxury bestowed on adolescents by this extended process of 'growing up' is leisure. To talk about adolescents as a leisured group perhaps conjures up rather classical pictures of young men and women at sport or improving activities, whiling away the golden hour until adulthood is thrust upon them. For many young people, nothing could be further than the truth. Old enough to assist their parents in the home, they are also sent home from schools with additional academic work, and many supplement or substitute parental allowances or pocket money by working in the evenings or at weekends, filling shelves, delivering leaflets, working tills and so on. For some girls in particular, whose 'skills' are more marketable in the world of casual labour and of whom much is demanded at home, the idea of limitless leisure as 'free time' may ring rather hollow.

Despite this process of gradual socialisation into the adult world of work and family commitment, the majority of adolescents maintain the luxury of putting their social interests first. Cognitive psychologists see early child-hood as the period of prime egocentricity. Many parents of adolescent children would re-define that model, watching their teenagers absorb resources, time and others' efforts. It is in that sense that young people are most truly 'leisured'.

One of the claims made in this book is that it is in the realm of leisure that young people truly become themselves. Leisure time is the period when different lifestyles can be tried and exchanged. Leisure activities provide the vehicle for socialising with peers and adults outside the family. Self-identity and group identity are explored and defined.

Within the study on which this book is based the temptation was simply to look at what young people 'did' in their free time. The truth is, of course, that these activities, be they sporting or otherwise, are but a tiny fraction of what leisure means to young people. Much adolescent leisure is about 'not doing', about 'hanging about', about 'talking to friends', about 'being alone to think', and this is a harder dimension to explore. Only the generosity of our survey and panel groups in being prepared to impart confidences about these things enables us to say something about the nine-tenths of the adolescent leisure iceberg that is hidden from view.

IMAGES OF ADOLESCENCE

Muncie wrote in 1984 that:

> By the turn of the century . . . the social construct of 'adolescence' had come to replace the social reality of class inequality as a major determinant in all youthful behaviour.
>
> (Muncie, 1984: 41)

He then went on to suggest that:

> While a stage of life untainted by adult pleasures was seen as desirable, it was also believed to expose the young to idleness and depravity.
>
> (Muncie, 1984: 41)

Earlier 'classical' theories of adolescence have established certain trends, emphases and biases which seem still to be reflected in modern views about the transition from childhood to adulthood. In an interesting and wide ranging book on adolescence, Lloyd (1985) has outlined a number of key historical theories which have helped to create public 'images' of adolescence. Amongst these significant theories Stanley Hall's view of adolescence as being a time of 'storm and stress' still maintains currency in the public's mind; as do Freud's ideas that human behaviour is motivated by unconscious psycho-sexual forces. The work of Benedict and Mead in primitive societies has also brought to public attention the differing effects of cultural forces on young people's development.

In a more recent book, Davis (1990) has shown, by tracing historically the general public 'images' of adolescents in society, that themes of rebellion, moodiness and 'angst', delinquency, 'sinfulness', energy, excitement and idealistic views of future society have been retained in adults' consciousness, and reinforced by the mass media, in creating stereotypic pictures of youth in Britain today.

Davis has traced the history of notions like 'youth as national (economic) asset', 'youth as minority stereotype' (positive as well as negative) and 'youth as a litmus test' (of the good and ills of the society). He demonstrated how these, though waxing and waning, have all (sometimes simultaneously) been key themes in the history of the concept. And he also illustrated how, alongside all this, and especially from the 1960s onwards, a 'youth culturalisation' of mainstream adult culture has taken place.

What makes this even more paradoxical is Davis's central theme: 'youth as continuity'. For he, like many others before him, provides ample evidence that, far from being revolutionary or even passively subversive, over many generations young people have been deeply committed to the basic values and institutions of their society. The problem (especially for them) has been that adult power-holders have needed to construct images and to accumulate 'data' which 'prove' the opposite in order to justify their requirement for controlling and highly oppressive responses to youth.

This chapter sets out to provide an overview of what adolescence is all about, as a context for some of the more specific concerns that follow in other chapters. It first looks at the different aspects of adolescence that have preoccupied theorists and researchers over the last half of this century. The agenda for youth research has clearly been driven as much by current social issues as by a need to fill gaps in knowledge. This has had a clear impact on the perspective from which we view adolescence as a period in the lifespan. The last half century has moved, however, to seeing adolescence principally as a transitional period between the protected and dependent status of childhood and the independence and freedom of adulthood. Psycho-social models of this transition emphasise the variety of 'tasks' that face adolescents. The number and type of these adjustments or challenges has often been seen to be at the root of the 'storm and stress' of the teenage years. More recent theorists challenge this view. Focal and ecological models are discussed as they point to the ways and mechanisms by which young people go through this period of adjustment in a staged way.

From a purely psychological viewpoint successful adaptation in adolescence is seen as utterly critical in generating success through the rest of the lifespan. The chapter looks at the development of self, with a particular focus on gender issues. Finally the development of self-esteem is examined, together with its relation to the development of so-called 'delinquent' patterns of behaviour.

ADOLESCENT ISSUES AND SOCIAL CHANGE

As G. Jones (1988) has suggested, it was during the 1950s that adolescents became truly 'visible'. In Britain, the post-war Education Act effectively extended the period of childhood dependence for young people. Older adolescents in greater numbers were congregated into formal institutions such as schools and colleges. But this was not just a British phenomenon. J.S. Coleman (1961), in his study of high school students in the United States, described the school as taking over the 'natural processes' of education in the family and setting the adolescent apart from the rest of society. The adolescent was consequently 'forced inwards towards his own age group', which 'maintains only a few threads of connections with the outside adult society' (J.S. Coleman, 1961: 3).

The 1960s created the climate for generational (rather than social class) conflict. We were living in an 'affluent society' and class distinctions were said to be disappearing. The student movements of the late 1960s appealed to the romantic imaginations of social commentators and apparently confirmed that the conflict was between generations rather than between the classes. Since the student movements were predominantly middle class, and apparently offered political and social alternatives to the existing order, the label 'counter culture' was applied to them. For some writers, the explanation of the counter culture lay in the concept of 'generational class'. Musgrove, for example, saw young people as a social class in themselves, 'relatively independent of the stratification system of adults' (Musgrove, 1969: 50). On much the same lines, Friedenberg considered the young to be oppressed by adult society, and concluded that adolescents were 'among the last social groups in the world to be given the full colonial treatment', adding that generational conflict was inevitable, since 'adolescence *is* conflict – protracted conflict – between the individual and society' (Friedenberg, 1973: 116). The young were thus seen as marginalised from 'adult' society and in inevitable conflict with it.

By the late 1960s, however, this analysis was being increasingly criticised for omitting the question of social class differences. Allen (1968) pointed out that it is not the relations between ages which explain change or stability in societies, but change in societies which explains relations between different ages.

During the 1970s social class was brought back to the forefront in studies of youth. Empirical work at this time, though, was limited to studies of subcultural youth groups with 'reasonably tight boundaries, distinctive shapes, which have cohered around particular activities, focal concerns and territorial spaces' (Clarke *et al.*, 1976: 14). According to this type of analysis, there is no such thing as a 'youth culture', standing in direct relation with the dominant culture of society. Instead there exists a system whereby youth subcultures are articulated to the dominant culture via their own particular cultures. Since social classes were the most fundamental groups in modern society, the major cultural forms will be 'class cultures'.

> Youth sub-cultures therefore co-exist within the culture of the class from which they spring.
>
> (Clarke *et al.*, 1976: 13)

For instance, Willis (1977) argued that the reproduction of the working class was an outcome not of occupational choice but of working class school culture. According to Willis, class culture mediated patterns of success and failure, making manual labour acceptable and ensuring the continuation of working class identity. Linked to these ideas, Murdock and McCron acknowledged that age was an important factor, since some experiences were seen to be youth specific. They agreed that:

> it is not therefore a question of simply substituting class for age at the centre of analyses, but of examining the relations between class and age, and more particularly the way in which age acts as a mediator of class.
>
> (Murdock and McCron, 1976: 10)

Jenkins has criticised Willis (1977) for omitting the issue of power relations in society, and sought to redress this deficiency in his own analysis of youth in Northern Ireland (Jenkins, 1983).

Murdock and McCron recognised that studies of youth subcultures should be more comprehensive and include previously ignored youth groups and adults; that empirical examination was needed of the work and non-work contexts through which class inequalities are mediated into everyday experience; and that a macro level of analysis was also needed, in the form of a structural and historical analysis of the relations between shifts in the social and cultural position of youth and changes in the structure of class relations and class-based meaning systems (Murdock and McCron, 1976).

At this time, in research terms, young women were reduced to the level of invisibility. McRobbie and Garber's (1976) work highlighted the 'culture of the bedroom' as the female equivalent of youth subcultures: a culture which exists, but from which male researchers would be excluded. Hall acknowledged that 'a theory of culture which cannot take account of patriarchal structures of dominance and oppression is, in the wake of feminism, a non-starter' (Hall, 1980). Other male researchers of youth subcultures followed suit (including Willis, 1981). The aim of a feminist perspective in studying female subcultures was:

> to combine a clear commitment to the analysis of girls' culture with a direct engagement of youth culture as it is constructed in sociological and cultural studies.
>
> (McRobbie, 1980: 37)

Griffin's (1985) study examined the way in which young women approach adult life and accept the reality of a gender-segregated labour market.

In studying youth subcultures, it is a dual lack of awareness which has permitted the relegation of women to near invisibility. On the one hand, the emphasis has been on the masculine culture of the street scene, with no consideration of the male at home. On the other hand, the emphasis on the female culture of the bedroom has allowed little room for the study of female delinquency. In between these two biases there exists a reality of youth, male and female, in the contexts of work, leisure and home, and in a close relation to the world of adults to which they will soon belong.

During the 1980s, the major emphasis of research on youth in Britain moved back to the study of transitions in youth in relation to the labour market. This was partly in response to the rapid increase in unemployment among school-leavers, and the government schemes aimed at keeping young people out of unemployment statistics. There were numerous studies of the effectiveness of different youth training schemes. Alongside these policy-related studies, however, there were studies of the consequences of unemployment in youth, which focused on the effect that extensive unemployment had on the transitions to adulthood (Hendry *et al.*, 1984; Hendry and Raymond, 1986). Concern about the effects of wide-scale youth unemployment led to interest in the transitions to adulthood, since it was considered that failure to achieve a successful transition into work might affect other areas of the lives of young people.

YOUTH AS TRANSITION

The realisation that adjustments in adolescence have critical implications for adult development has led to an increased academic interest in the adolescent years. There is now a preference amongst writers for viewing adolescence as a transitional process rather than as a stage or a number of stages. In this transitional period development seems to occur from the influence of a number of factors. Some of these, in particular physiological and emotional pressures, are internal to the adolescent, while others which originate from parents, teachers, peers and wider society are external to the adolescent. Sometimes these external forces 'push' the individual towards maturity faster than he or she would prefer, while on other occasions they act as a brake preventing the adolescent from gaining the freedom and independence which he or she believes to be a legitimate right. It is the interplay of these forces which contributes to the success or failure of the transition from childhood to maturity.

Erikson (1968) suggested that there are eight psycho-social crises extending through the individual's lifespan which establish stages in the development of personal maturity. He believed that the search for identity becomes especially acute during adolescence as a result of rapid changes in the biological, social and psychological aspects of the individual, and because of the necessity for occupational decisions to be made, ideals to be accepted or rejected and sexual and friendship choices to be determined. Erikson's view was that the chief task of adolescence is identity formation; while Laufer and Laufer (1985) believed that the development of sexual identity is what makes adolescence a psychological experience quite separate from childhood and the adult years.

From the pubertal changes that herald the teenage years, the adolescent has various personal and social 'learning' tasks to achieve. Havighurst (1972) proposed a range of tasks in adolescence and early adulthood (Table 1.1).

Two classical types of explanation concerning these psycho-social tasks within the transitional process of adolescence have been advanced. The psycho-analytic approach concentrates on the psycho-sexual psychological factors which underlie the young person's movement away from childhood behaviour and emotional involvement. The second type of explanation, the sociological or social-psychological, sees the causes of adolescent transition as lying primarily in the social setting, and concentrates on the nature of roles and role conflict, the pressures of social expectations and the relative influence of different agencies of socialisation, such as parents, peers, teachers and the media. The two approaches – the psycho-analytic and the sociological – differ mainly in emphasis. One accentuates internal forces and the other external forces, but they are clearly interdependent, and they share the view that adolescence is a stressful period.

Table 1.1   The personal and social learning tasks of adolescence

Adolescence (12–18 years)	*Early adulthood (18–30 years)*
1 Achieving new and more mature relations with the age mates of both sexes	1 Selecting a mate
2 Achieving a masculine or feminine social role	2 Learning to live with a marriage partner
3 Accepting one's physique and using the body effectively	3 Starting a family
4 Achieving emotional independence of parents	4 Rearing children
5 Preparing for marriage and family life	5 Managing a home
6 Preparing for an economic career	6 Getting started in an occupation
7 Acquiring a set of values and an ethical system as a guide to behaviour – developing an ideology	7 Taking on civic responsibility
8 Desiring and achieving socially responsible behaviour	8 Finding a congenial social group

Source: Based on Havighurst 1972

FOCAL AND ECOLOGICAL MODELS

In order to equate these dramatically different views of adolescence, we need to look for an integrated theory of adolescent development. Because of the complexities of modern society, children can reach physical adulthood before many of them are capable of functioning well in adult social roles. The disjunction between physical capabilities and socially approved independence and power, and the concurrent status ambiguities, can be stressful for the self-image of the adolescent. Many investigators, however, have claimed that for most youngsters the adolescent years need not be marked by stress or turmoil (Davis, 1990).

J.C. Coleman (1979) has presented a 'focal theory' arguing that the transition between childhood and adulthood cannot be achieved without substantial adjustments of both a psychological and social nature. Nevertheless, despite the amount of overall change experienced, most young people are extremely resilient and appear to cope with adjustments without undue stress.

Coleman's 'focal theory' offers a reason or rationale for this apparent contradiction. In it he proposed that at different ages particular sorts of relationship patterns come into focus, in the sense of being most prominent, but that no pattern is specific to one age only. Thus the patterns overlap, different issues come into focus at different times, but simply because an issue is not the most prominent feature at a particular age does not mean that it may not be critical for some individuals. These ideas, derived from empirical findings, combine to suggest a symbolic model of adolescent development where each curve represents a different issue or relationship. This is illustrated in Figure 1.1.

Coleman suggested that concern about gender roles and relationships with the opposite sex declines from a peak around 13 years; concerns about acceptance by or rejection from peers are highly important around 15 years; while issues regarding the gaining of independence from parents climb steadily to peak around 16 years and then begin to tail off. Such a theory may provide some insight into the amount of disruption and crisis implicit in adolescence and the relatively successful adaptation among most adolescents. The majority of teenagers cope by dealing with one issue at a time. Adaptation covers a number of years, with the adolescent attempting to solve one issue, then the next. Thus any stresses resulting from the need to adapt to new models of behaviour are rarely concentrated all at one time. Those who, for whatever reason, do have more than one issue to cope with at one time are most likely to have problems of adjustment.

We believe that most young people pace themselves through the adolescent transition. Most of them hold back on one issue, while they

Figure 1.1   The 'focal theory' model

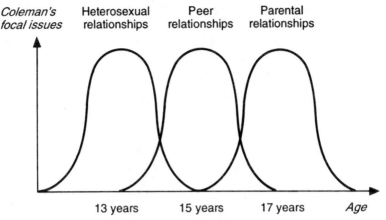

| Coleman's focal issues | Heterosexual relationships | Peer relationships | Parental relationships |

13 years   15 years   17 years   *Age*

Source: J.C. Coleman 1979

are grappling with another. Most sense what they can and cannot cope with, and will, in the real sense of the term, be an active agent in their own development.

(J.C. Coleman and Hendry, 1990: 205)

In producing an adaptation of focal theory Hendry (1983) has argued that the extent to which there is anxiety, fear or conflict in the various relational issues can be deduced by matching self-image with the ascribed role of significant others. Thus, if an adolescent girl sees herself as adult while her parents still see her as a child, or if an adolescent boy perceives himself as weak and skinny while acceptance by the peer group requires aggressive muscularity, then there is conflict or dissonance. This would suggest that external social factors are just as important as personal internal ones in determining social, relational behaviour. Feedback, on which self-concept is dependent, may be positive or negative and will consequently result in consonance or dissonance. It is this dimension which Coleman's focal model appears to omit. Feedback can lead to learning and subsequently to altered behaviour and to the development of a more stable self-concept via altered attitudes and beliefs (though of course in its turn feedback can be ignored or not acted upon!).

Coffield *et al.* (1986) have commented that Coleman's focal model makes no attempt to deal with disadvantage and deprivation. They have presented a different model (Figure 1.2) derived from their experience of carrying out research in the north-east of England with young people, many of whom were unemployed, all of whom were living at the very periphery of British society. In their model, social class and patriarchy are seen as all-pervading influences which determine to a large extent the options and choices available to young people in this under-privileged section of society.

Focal theory has to do with the *psychological* transitions of adolescence at a macro level, rather than with the economic and social circumstances of the *individual*. For example, all young people, irrespective of social background, attempt to negotiate increasing independence from their parents. The focal model suggests that it will be easier to handle the parental issue if the young person is not, at the same time, striving for greater acceptance within the peer group. Coffield is right to draw attention to the social circumstances of the individual, for these will obviously contribute in a substantial way to each adolescent's psychological adjustment. Gaining independence from parents has sociological and financial implications – as in unemployment – as well as being a psychological issue. There can be little doubt that in situations of economic hardship it will be more difficult to manage the adolescent transitions in a satisfactory manner. This point has already been made by Hendry (1983) in his argument that ecological

Figure 1.2 An attempt at an integrating model

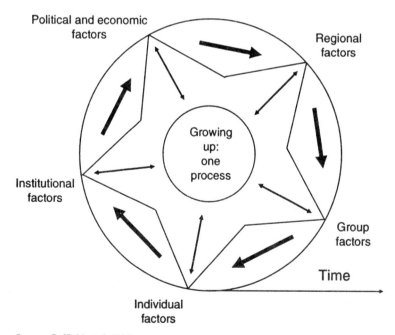

Source: Coffield *et al.* 1986

factors are as important as psychological ones in understanding the young person's development. Circumstances, many of them unpleasant, will be imposed on the individual, making it less likely that he or she will feel in control of events. This will in turn complicate relationships with friends and family, presenting the young person with a range of additional stress factors on top of all the normal burdens inherent in adolescent development.

At present we know far too little about the way in which the macro psychological models epitomised by focal theory interact with sociological models emphasising class differences and subcultures. Many of the following chapters begin to explore this interface through empirical data collected in the Young People's Leisure and Lifestyle (YPLL) project.

LIFESPAN PSYCHOLOGY

Lifespan developmental psychology has emerged as a powerful theoretical position over the last ten years. At its simplest, this approach to human development carries with it a number of fundamental assumptions.

Significant themes are the importance of a multi-disciplinary approach to studying development; the need for study of human ecology and contexts in human development (i.e. the geographical, historical, social and political settings in which the individual is living); a concern with the way in which individuals and their social groupings reciprocally influence each other; and the importance of individuals as 'active agents' in their own development.

This stress on dynamic interaction in the socialisation process draws attention to the adolescent in three modes: as stimulus (eliciting different reactions from the social environment); as processor, in making sense of the behaviour of others; and as agent, shaper and selector, by doing things, making choices and influencing events.

The ideas concerning reciprocal influences and individual young people as 'active agents' in their own transitional process from childhood to adulthood (Lerner, 1985) are important theoretical themes in gaining an understanding of young people in present-day society – hence the growing strength of lifespan developmental psychology. The approach as initiated in the field of social cognition (e.g. Selman, 1980) has had a profound effect on studies of adolescence by suggesting that adjustment in adolescence affects later development. Because there is so much change during adolescence, and because these changes require effective coping on the part of the individual, the processes involved in this period of the lifespan are also likely to be ones needed to respond to challenges throughout adult life. Furthermore, it could be hypothesised that adolescence differs from earlier years in the nature of challenges encountered and in the capacity of the individual to respond effectively to these challenges. If this is correct, adolescence will be the first phase of life requiring, and presumably stimulating, mature patterns of functioning and the development of a clear-cut personal and social identity that persists throughout life. Conversely, failure to cope effectively with the challenges of adolescence may represent 'deficiencies' in the individual's self-concept which will have negative consequences for subsequent development.

Lewin (1970) argued that adolescents, in passing through childhood to adulthood, are in a 'marginal' position and are entering a 'cognitively unstructured region'. Their sense of competence and ultimately their self-concept and future personal identity depend on how well expectations are accepted and processed into personal lifestyles at this stage of development. If these behaviour patterns fit the requirements of roles encountered at school, at work, in heterosexual relationships and in community life generally, then the outcome is satisfactory. Alternatively, if they fail to gain structure in their personal identity, confusion and conflict may result, as Erikson (1968) has proposed.

YOUNG PEOPLE AND THE DEVELOPMENT OF SELF

As far as self-concept is concerned, adolescence is usually thought to be a time of both change and consolidation. There are a number of reasons for this. In the first place the major physical changes which occur carry with them a change in body image and thus in the sense of self. Second, intellectual growth during adolescence makes possible a more complex and sophisticated self-concept. Third, some development of the self-concept seems probable as a result of increasing emotional independence, and the approach of fundamental decisions relating to occupation, values, sexual behaviour, friendship choices and so on. Finally, the transitional nature of the adolescent period, and in particular the role changes experienced at this time, would seem likely to be associated with some modifications of self-concept.

If the adolescent is comfortable in some environments, life-arenas and role-relationships, then discomfort in another arena can be tolerated and mastered. Teenagers are less able to cope if at one and the same time they are uncomfortable for example with their bodies, owing to physical changes; with family, owing to changes in the family constellation; with home, because of a move; with school, owing to great discontinuity in the nature of the school environment; or with peers, because of disruption of peer networks and changes in peer expectations and peer evaluation criteria, and because of the emergence of opposite-sex relationships as an important arena for success. There needs to be some arena of life or some set of role-relationships with which the individual adolescent can feel relaxed and comfortable, to which he or she can withdraw and have the self reinvigorated.

Nevertheless, with maturation, most adolescents begin to feel more competent and efficacious (Selman, 1980; Damon and Hart, 1982). Feelings of self-efficacy may, therefore, work to produce higher self-esteem even though other factors (such as the threat of unemployment as the school-leaving age approaches) may begin, at the same time, to attack self-esteem. Feelings of greater control and power relative to their social and physical environment have positive effects on self-esteem: further, adolescents may also improve their interpersonal skills with age and may be more capable of selecting peers and contexts that do enhance their self-esteem.

Elkind (1967) argued that while the attainment of formal operational thinking frees the individual in many respects from childhood egocentrism, paradoxically, at the same time it entangles him or her in a new version of the same thing. This is because the achievement of formal operational thought allows the adolescent to consider not only his or her own thoughts, but also the thoughts of other people. It is this capacity to take account of other people's thinking which is the basis of adolescent egocentrism. One example given by Elkind is that of the adolescent's appearance. To a large extent teenagers are preoccupied with the way they look to others, and they make the assumption that others must be as involved as they are with the same subject. Elkind ties this type of egocentrism in with the concept of what he calls 'the imaginary audience'. Because of this egocentrism adolescents are either in actual or fantasised social situations, anticipating the reactions of others. However, these reactions are based on a premise that others are as admiring or critical of them as they are of themselves. Thus they are continually constructing and reacting to their 'imaginary audience', a fact which, according to Elkind, explains a lot of adolescent behaviour – the self-consciousness, the wish for privacy and the long hours spent in front of the mirror. Conger and Petersen (1984) have provided strong corroboration for Elkind's views.

SELF-CONCEPT AND GENDER

Offer *et al.* (1984) have shown that there appears to be no increase in disturbance of self-image during early adolescence. They referred to their work as providing insights into 'current contradictions in adolescent theory'. Similarly Simmons *et al.* (1979) and Blyth *et al.* (1983) have studied the impact of two major changes confronting adolescents: the impact of the timing of pubertal development and the effects of transition into a new large, more impersonal school environment. Neither, apparently, had an impact on self-esteem for either adolescent boys or girls.

What factors, then, do disrupt the development of self-concept? Adjustment to gender roles seems to be one of the principal problematics. Douvan (1979) pointed out that for boys the major discontinuity occurs in the pre-school years where a discrepancy exists between passive, dependent babyhood and the independence and self-assertiveness that is expected of the male in his early contact with peers and the school situation. For girls, however, this discontinuity is seen in its most extreme form during adolescence. During these years females face, according to Douvan, the following situation.

> Socialised through childhood in a double system – in which the girl is allowed dependency but is also encouraged and supported through school to be independent, individualistic, competitive and achieving – she now finds that at adolescence she must abandon or disguise these individual competitive traits if she is to be acceptably feminine. Adults, and especially her peer group, expect her to shift from direct achievement to vicarious achievement, and to take as her major goals becoming a wife and mother . . . She is asked to give up established ways of being and behaving, ways practised throughout the primary school years. Abandoning established patterns represents her critical discontinuity . . .
> (Douvan, 1979: 90)

These patterns of identity may have their antecedents just prior to the adolescent years. Hendry and Percy (1981) found that by the upper stages of the primary school girls saw boys of their own age typically playing football, and this, together with playing 'space invaders', was the way boys most often saw themselves. On the other hand, quite a few boys saw girls as likely to play with dolls whereas no girl mentioned this for her own sex. Many girls said a typical 11-year-old girl would choose to go out with boys or go to a disco, but equally popular were going out with friends or parents, shopping and swimming or ice-skating.

Stanworth (1981) has also described the type-cast images created for girls within the context of the school. She found that more time, attention, affection and concern was given by teachers of mixed classes to boys than to girls. Boys dominated class discussion while girls, often described by teachers and by boys as 'faceless', were allowed to sit silent at the back of the class. Teachers were less likely to know girls' names, and tended to have low expectations of their job prospects. Furthermore, Stanworth found through interviews with teachers and pupils that both men and women teachers took more interest in their male pupils, asking them more questions in class and giving them more help. Asked which students they were most concerned about, women teachers named boys twice as often as girls. Men named boys ten times as often as girls. When asked which pupils they were most 'attached' to, teachers named boys three times as often as girls. Both boys and girls, asked to list their class in order of ability, tended to exaggerate the capacity of boys and to downgrade girls. The girls named as unpopular by girls were those who did speak out in class, refusing to accept the silent role played by other girls. They were accused by girls of 'hogging the limelight'. The girls most disliked by boys were the ones who 'sit at the back of the class and might as well be sucking lollipops all day'. The study led Stanworth to conclude:

> Girls may follow the same curriculum as boys – may sit side by side with boys in classes taught by the same teachers – and yet emerge from school with the implicit understanding that the world is a man's world, in which woman can and should take second place.

> (Stanworth, 1981: 58)

Such themes are also echoed in the work of Delamont (1984), who considered the important impact of sex roles and particularly sex-role inequalities in educational settings in the United Kingdom. It is clear, therefore, that within the socialisation process of adolescence the school creates stresses and ambivalence for young women in that they are caught up in the dilemma of achieving their academic potential and, at the same time, fulfilling and conforming to a stereotypic sex-role image of femininity involving 'passivity' to ensure popularity with their peers.

Both Wells (1980) and Keyes and Coleman (1983) have discussed the relationship between personal adjustment and sex-role identity conflicts in adolescence. In Keyes' and Coleman's study, though no sex differences were found for measures of personal adjustment, females appeared to experience more conflict over sex-role issues.

Data from a sample of young people aged from 12 to 18 years old were analysed by Streitmatter (1985) to examine the differences in gender-role perceptions across age groups. The results of the study indicated indirect support for Erikson's speculations about the importance of this as an issue in identity development. In other words, the youngest respondents showed the greatest disparity between male and female role perceptions. The older subjects, those in adolescence, displayed greater ambiguity toward their gender role, while the oldest respondents, approaching adulthood, indicated a stronger perceived gender identity.

The pattern found by Streitmatter indicated that male and female gender identification prior to adolescence is fairly distinct. Entry into adolescence seems to cloud the issue. This pattern indicated decreasing differentiation from 12 and 13 to 14 years and from 14 to 15 years. However, 15 to 16 year old comparisons reflected increasing differentiation. Apparently, the gender identifications which are adopted in childhood are reconsidered and reformulated during adolescence (this finding is similar to that of

Montemayor and Eisen, 1977). Gilligan (1990) contended that as girls enter adolescence they seriously confront the disadvantages of their gender and suffer from a lack of confidence and a confused sense of self. A second watershed appears to be the transition from school to work, when girls discover how limited their occupational prospects are in contrast to boys' prospects and begin to have to make hard choices about career and personal life that belie the notion of an easy combination of work and family.

SELF-ESTEEM DEVELOPMENT

The sources for the development of self-esteem rest primarily in reflected appraisals and social comparisons. Young people compare their competencies with those of their peers in order to discern their level of worth. A cross-sectional survey of nearly 2,000 schoolchildren by Simmons *et al.* (1973) identified early adolescents as experiencing the most difficulty with self-esteem. On the basis of this study they argued that the ages between 13 and 17 years are associated with sharp increases in anti-social behaviour, suicide attempts, drug and alcohol abuse, eating disorders and depression. Their results, although a little difficult to interpret because they included a number of different measures of self-esteem, seemed to indicate a major change between the years of 12 and 14. In their view:

> the early adolescent has become distinctly more self-conscious; his picture of himself has become more shaky and unstable, his global self-esteem has declined slightly, his attitudes towards several specific characteristics which he values highly have become less positive; and he has increasingly come to believe that parents, teachers and peers of the same sex view him less favourably.
>
> (Simmons *et al.*, 1973: 558)

Entry to a new period in the life-course may challenge the self-image, particularly individuals' self-evaluations, as they attempt new tasks in which they can succeed or fail, as they alter their values and the areas which are important for overall self-esteem and as they confront new significant others against whom they rate themselves and about whose judgements they care.

Rosenberg (1979) emphasised this importance of the reflected self and of social comparison in determining self-esteem, as well as the importance of doing well in the areas one values (the principle of 'psychological centrality'). It is possible to suggest that in adolescence girls show an increased tendency over boys to place high value on body-image and same-sex popularity. Thus, girls might be placed in increased jeopardy both because they value peer opinion more ('the reflected self'), especially at the point of transition to secondary school, and also because they value body-image more at a time when their body is changing dramatically and social comparisons along this dimension become more problematic.

In new and uncomfortable situations the adolescent may feel what Rosenberg has called 'recurrent transient depersonalisation' (Rosenberg, 1979). This self-detachment or feeling of depersonalisation may cause the adolescent to see himself or herself as generally ineffective. In other words, the inability to perform easily in a variety of important new contexts and roles may generalise to a low evaluation of self. Consequently, self-esteem may drop.

Within the principle of psychological centrality, Rosenberg (1979) hypothesised that specific self-evaluations have a greater impact upon global self-esteem if these evaluations are in areas about which the individual cares a great deal. This can be exemplified by the evidence on the effects of schooling on adolescents' self-esteem.

Given the need for adolescents to maintain or enhance self-esteem, they are likely to develop strategies for dealing with threatening situations. For example, Covington and Beery (1977) found that young people with low self-esteem adopted strategies such as avoiding group participation, not trying hard or setting unrealistic goals to create a situation whereby they could preserve what little sense of self-worth they possessed. In terms of attribution theory, the child with low self-esteem who experiences success will be likely to ascribe the outcome to luck or some other capricious factor as opposed to personal causation. Over time, adolescents with low self-esteem tend to adopt failure-prone strategies and attribute unsuccessful outcomes to lack of ability and successes to environmental causes beyond their control (Diener and Dweck, 1978; Dweck and Elliott, 1984).

Indeed Kaplan (1980) has stated that children turn to delinquency after a history of devaluing social feedback which has produced negative self-esteem. Delinquent behaviour is then adopted because it inflates self-esteem through behavioural rewards and psychological defences which allow the delinquent to reject general social feedback and to raise his or her self-perceptions. As a general principle, Kaplan has asserted that individuals who have experienced fewer devaluing experiences will require less self-enhancement. Related to the specifics of self-enhancement, Kaplan proposed three psychological defences: denial of personal responsibility for actions, reduction of aspirations and the disguising of deficiencies. Thus, according to Kaplan delinquents employ psychological defences to enhance self-esteem and to retain endorsement of socially accepted values. Denial and rejection of general social feedback and incongruencies between behaviour and self-perceptions appear to be the primary defences and such claims are supported in a study by Zieman and Benson (1983).

SUMMARY

This chapter has looked at the ways in which adolescence has been defined and redefined according to social circumstances in the last half century. That youth is essentially a period of transition dominates the viewpoint of this chapter and of the book as a whole. The idea that young people are faced with a variety of social and psychological tasks in establishing their adult identity and place in society is expounded and Coleman's focal theory examined as a vehicle for resolving some of the empirically observed contradictions. Young people do experience a great deal of aggravation and stress, yet the majority come to a reasonable resolution of their problems in relation to identity and the development of self-esteem. The suggestion is that this process is accomplished by a staged progression through a variety of age-related salient issues.

The social factors that impinge upon such macro transformations are examined in relation to the development of self-identity and self-esteem. Gender and social class are fundamental determinants in shaping the personality, the perspective and the lifestyle of young people as they move into adulthood.

THE BOOK

The rest of this book sets out to explore the activities and meanings of adolescent leisure. Chapter 2 looks at the YPLL Project itself. Some details about the inception of the study, the philosophy and research questions behind it and the research methods used are included. Whilst the study was carried out principally in Scotland, a case is made for the applicability of the results to a more general context.

Chapter 3 addresses the whole question of what is meant by leisure. Is it defined by its contrast with work? What characterises leisure for young people and how are obligatory duties like household chores, family visiting, homework and so on welded into the adolescent concept of leisure? The chapter explores the reasons for the claim that leisure is a justifiable focus through which to develop an account of other facets of lifestyle outlined in this book. A model linking patterns of leisure to the psycho-social transitions of adolescence is re-examined in the light of survey data. The information thus obtained reveals how adolescents of all ages and classes enjoy their leisure.

In Chapter 4 sport is considered. It forms a major part of young people's leisure lives, whether they are participants or spectators. The findings map out the extensiveness of sport among young people while at the same time highlighting the differential nature of such involvement according to age, gender and social class. Recognising that sport is learned behaviour, the reasons for involvement are looked at in terms of the input of the three major learning contexts in adolescence, the family, the school and the peer group. In addition, an examination of sports attitudes provides further insight into the type of sport played, recreative or competitive. Such an examination of attitudes when coupled with the findings on the amount of sport played, also reveals the curious position of women with respect to sport.

More general issues about school and what follows are addressed in Chapter 5. The experience of school is explored through an examination of academic attainment and attitudes towards school. The influence of social class background or school performance is noted and both class and gender differences emerge with respect to attitudes towards school. The chapter also goes on to look at young people's expectations on leaving school and examines the extent to which such hopes are realised in the early years of the labour market. The influence of social class is seen to be effective in reproducing the next generation of unskilled workers, tradesmen and professionals.

Chapter 6 looks at young people in the context of the family situation. A variety of family circumstances exist within which young people are brought up – the classic nuclear family being but a part of that variety. So much of the developing identity of the adolescent is focused upon changes in relations within the family that this is clearly an area of great importance. Comments from the young people in this study, however, do little to reinforce stereotypes about 'the generation gap' or indicate that there is any fundamental rift between adult and adolescent values, despite the clearly different leisure styles adopted by young people. Within families, the claim is that parental roles are changing. Little attention has been paid to the impact of this on adolescent development. We look at family relations in this context and at parenting styles generally. Do young people and their parents share leisure and, if so, what is the nature of it? Models of family functioning are explored.

Friends vie with parents as sources of influence on the adolescent's thoughts and behaviours. Chapter 7 looks at the types of friendships formed by young people and the purposes they serve. A clear distinction is made here between 'friends' and 'peers'. We ask what friends do for one another in adolescence. What qualities do young people look for in a friend, how do they make and lose friends and how do friends affect one's leisure life? The peer group does not necessarily bear connotations of friendship, yet the role of same-age adolescents in determining style, conferring acceptance and identity is well known.

In Chapter 8 issues relating to young peoples' health are brought into focus. Particularly controversial aspects of young peoples' health-related behaviour are rooted in leisure. Drinking, smoking, drug misuse and sexual behaviour are all examined here. Do some of these health behaviours represent particularly provocative demonstrations of youth subculture or are young people merely reproducing the habits of their elders? Paradoxically, despite the observed differentiation in young people's behaviour in this respect, previous studies have been unable to make the connection between health and social class noted in early childhood and again in adulthood. Data from the present study is used to dispute these other findings and to point to the clear links between class, lifestyle and health.

Chapter 9 attempts to draw together a composite picture. How does leisure contribute to the development of lifestyle? Has the idea of a youth subculture been supported by the data and views presented here, or do class and gender relations override youth as the determining factor of adolescent lifestyles? Can we say anything about life-types – about how young people will choose to spend the rest of their lives – from an analysis of their adolescent leisure?

Chapter 10 provides an overall review and summary of the material in previous chapters and looks at what conclusions can be drawn.

Finally it is perhaps worth mentioning that the volume of data collected during a seven-year study is immense. Only a fraction of what has been collected is reported here. In particular, although data from 1985 to 1991 is included in the ensuing chapters, the story of the longitudinal development of individuals and groups, their developing lifestyles and trajectories must be left to another volume.

2 The Young People's Leisure and Lifestyles Project

GATHERING INFORMATION AND VIEWS

In September 1987 over 10,000 young people in Scotland were invited to complete a questionnaire on their leisure habits, their feelings about school and family, their health and their hopes and fears for their future. The schools which took part ranged from tiny one-teacher schools on remote Scottish islands to the crowded inner city schools of Glasgow. Young people in new towns, in country towns and in city suburbs alike all took part in the survey, their ages ranging from 10 to school-leaving age. At the same time their predecessors, those who had left school in previous years, were receiving questionnaires through the post.

Their replies, when they were eventually collated and compared, painted a fascinating cross-sectional picture of the leisure lives and lifestyles of Scotland's adolescent population. This survey was repeated in autumn 1989 and again in 1991, thus yielding three comprehensive cross-sectional pictures of youth across the country and also a rich source of longitudinal information that had been absent up to this point in studies of young people's transition from childhood through the active and challenging years of adolescence to adulthood.

At the core of the project from the start was the belief that leisure was one of the prime vehicles within which young people developed expressions of lifestyle. Survey work alone could produce only a partial picture. Consequently a panel of 250 young people throughout Scotland was invited to become part of the project to give an in-depth and qualitative perspective on many of the issues raised in the questionnaires. Their contact with the research project on a number of occasions each year between 1986 and 1991 has produced a rich and vivid account of young people's feelings about their friends, their families, their relationships with school and their worries about work, and about why they chose to cleave to some leisure activities and drop others as they grew older. Sometimes the panel members met research workers in their own homes with their families contributing to the discussion; at other times they met in schools, community centres, coffee bars and so on. They met in groups for discussions and singly with a research worker for more confidential interviews. They talked on the telephone, kept diaries and reflected on their earlier lives, charting changes and trying to express reasons for personal, social and leisure decisions as they grew to maturity. Throughout, their willingness to help towards developing a more revealing account of adolescent leisure has been a driving force in the research. Some of their vivid comments are included here, and they breathe fresh life into the statistics.

RESEARCH INTERESTS

The research project arose from earlier work carried out by Leo Hendry with the Sports Council in preparing a state-of-the-art review of young people's sport participation (Hendry, 1981). Leo Hendry and the Scottish Sports Council approached the Health Promotion Research Trust for funding for a longitudinal project which would start to examine the broader context of involvement. This was granted and work began in 1986.

Although the study arose out of an interest in examining young people's involvement in sport and physical recreation, it was recognised early on that such an investigation would not be complete unless it embraced other aspects of young people's lives. The study therefore came to focus on leisure and the lifestyles associated with this domain. Leisure was explored as a social context in which a young person is afforded an opportunity for developing his or her own identity and as the social space in which a young person faces up to the developmental tasks of adolescence and negotiates independence from his or her parents. It was recognised that such lifestyles would be subject to the structural constraints of age, gender and social class.

The following six main research questions encompass the work of the study.

1 What are the general leisure interests of young people in adolescence and early adulthood?
2 What is the nature of young people's involvement in sport?
3 To what extent are young people influenced in their leisure and sport by the structural characteristics of age, gender and social class?
4 What are the roles of the family, the school and the peer group in influencing young people's leisure and sport participation?
5 Is it possible to identify healthy and unhealthy lifestyles in adolescence?
6 How do young people make the transition from school to work?

THE SURVEY SAMPLE

In 1987 a clustered stratified random sample of 10,000 young people was drawn from thirty Scottish secondary schools (clusters) and ninety-nine associated 'feeder' primary schools. In Scotland children generally start primary school in the August following their fifth birthday. Seven years of primary school (P1–7) are followed by transfer at age 12 (a year later than the English system) to secondary school. The young people in the YPLL sample came from six distinct age groups (cohorts) identified by stage within the educational system. The youngest two cohorts were aged 9–10 years (cohort one) and 11–12 years (cohort two) and were still in primary school (P5 and P7 respectively). The next two cohorts were aged 13–14 years (cohort three) and 15–16 years (cohort four) and were in secondary school (S2 and S4 respectively). The eldest two cohorts were aged 17–18 years (cohort five) and 19–20 years (cohort six) and were beyond the minimum school-leaving age (S4 plus two years and S4 plus four years respectively). The latter groups were sampled using school registers from two and four years previously. The study group thus approximated to a 1 per cent sample of the Scottish population aged 10–20 years (taken from the Census of 1981). The geographical spread of the sample embraced ten of the twelve regional and island authorities (Table 2.1).

For the first sweep of the study in 1987 cohorts one to four completed the questionnaire in school under the guidance of a field-worker, whilst cohorts five and six received the questionnaire by post. The response rates

Table 2.1 Regional breakdown of the YPLL sample in 1987

Region	n	%
Borders	–	–
Central	443	4.5
Dumfries and Galloway	145	1.5
Fife	1,046	10.5
Grampian	693	7.0
Highland	681	6.9
Lothian	1,488	15.0
Orkney Islands	–	–
Shetland Islands	156	1.6
Strathclyde	4,595	46.3
Tayside	578	5.8
Western Isles	91	0.9
Total	9,916	100

were high for the school-based cohorts but those completing the questionnaire at school were not compelled to provide their name and current address. For the second sweep in 1989 cohorts one and two again completed the questionnaire in school, whilst cohorts three to six completed it by post. Unfortunately, for technical reasons it was necessary to redraw two new cohorts to replace the original 'primary school' cohorts (one and two). These new cohorts were drawn from twelve of the original thirty secondary schools. Also for cohorts three and four only respondents from the same twelve schools were re-contacted in 1989. For the third sweep in 1991 the questionnaires were administered by post to all six cohorts. Questionnaires were sent to everyone with a valid address irrespective of whether they had responded to the second sweep in 1989 or not. Finally for each of the three survey sweeps cohorts one and two were given a different questionnaire from cohorts three to six.

Such was the survey design. Details of response rates to these three survey sweeps are given in Figure 2.1.

The original two 1987 cohorts one and two are omitted from the following discussion for the reasons given above. First, focusing on young people who completed questionnaires at school in either 1987 or 1989, 85 per cent of those sampled returned a 'usable' questionnaire and of these 20 per cent failed to provide a current address for future contact. Consequently this left 68 per cent of those sampled via school-based questionnaires available for further longitudinal study. Looking at young people originally contacted at school and followed up via postal questionnaires two years later, 54 per cent returned a completed questionnaire for a second time. Cohorts five and six were different from the other cohorts. They were contacted by post on all three occasions. Forty-seven per cent replied in 1987 and of these 47 per cent replied in 1989. Finally, cohorts three to six were contacted by post in 1989 and again by post in 1991. Of those responding in 1989, 59 per cent returned a completed questionnaire in 1991. In summary, an 85 per cent response rate was achieved using a school-based questionnaire whilst a 50 per cent response rate to a postal questionnaire was achieved in 1989 and 60 per cent of these postal respondents replied once again in 1991. Overall a longitudinal sample of over 725 young people in cohorts one and two and over 1,000 young people in cohorts three to six was delivered.

Given that attrition rates were running at roughly 50 per cent per sweep of the study the question naturally arises of how representative the YPLL sample is of Scottish youth. Comparisons of the class composition of the 1987 sample and 1987 General Household Survey data for Britain suggest that the initial YPLL sample is fairly representative of Scottish households (Table 2.2). But does it remain so with successive survey sweeps?

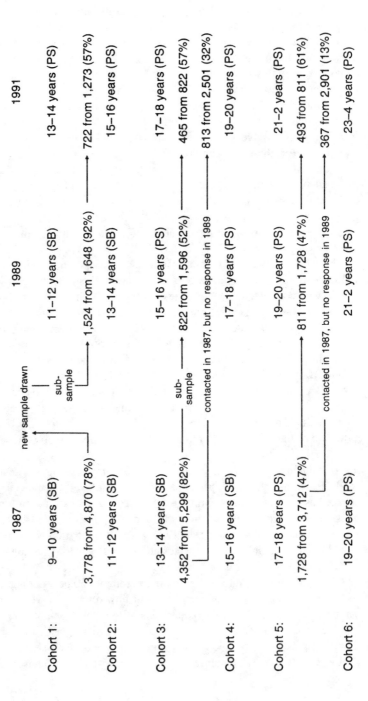

Figure 2.1 Sampling design and response rates for 1987, 1989 and 1991 (SB, school-based questionnaire; PS, postal questionnaire)

Table 2.2 Distribution of father's social class by cohort for the YPLL sample in 1987, 1989 and 1991

	Cohorts 1 and 2			Cohorts 3 and 4			Cohorts 5 and 6			Britain [a]
	1987 (%)	1989 (%)	1991 (%)	1987 (%)	1989 (%)	1991 (%)	1987 (%)	1989 (%)	1991 (%)	1987 (%)
Professional	–	6	7	9	8	8	9	9	9	7
Intermediate	–	25	28	26	28	32	27	27	32	28
Skilled (non-manual)	–	8	7	10	10	12	8	9	10	8
Skilled (manual)	–	41	38	35	34	32	36	35	33	38
Semi-skilled	–	15	16	16	15	13	16	14	12	14
Unskilled	–	5	4	4	5	3	4	6	4	5
Based on sample of size	–	1,273	535	3,169	645	362	1,222	574	328	9,190

Source: OPCS

Notes: These data were tested for cross-sectional and longitudinal differences in distribution of father's social class using log-linear analysis. The only significant differences found at the 0.05 level were cross-sectional. In both 1989 and 1991, the fathers of young people from cohorts 1 and 2 were more likely to be employed in skilled manual occupations than the fathers of respondents from cohorts 3 and 4 and from cohorts 5 and 6.

[a] 1987 General Household Survey figures for economically active men.

Intuitively we would expect biases to have been introduced into the sample at each successive sweep owing to the non-response of individuals from specific subgroups. This hypothesis was tested for young people's class of origin. Table 2.2 details the distribution of the social class of respondent's father by cohort for the three survey sweeps in 1987, 1989 and 1991. The data were analysed for cross-sectional and longitudinal effects using log-linear methods. Perhaps surprisingly there is no evidence for longitudinal effects on distribution of father's class. The YPLL team concluded that the class composition of the sample had remained stable throughout successive longitudinal sweeps. There are significant cross-sectional differences, however, at the 0.05 level. In both 1989 and 1991 the class composition of cohorts one and two was found to be consistently different from the class composition of cohorts three to six. Namely, in 1989 and 1991 the fathers of young people in cohorts one and two were more likely to be employed in skilled manual occupations than those in cohorts three to six.

However, there are biases present in the final sample. For example, young women are consistently over-represented within 'postal' cohorts after each survey sweep (Table 2.3). Amongst individuals contacted by postal questionnaire the number of young men in the sample consistently decreased by 4 per cent and the number of young women in the sample increased by 4 per cent.

Despite the fact that the longitudinal sample is biased in some respects, technically the issue of representativeness should not present any great difficulties to subsequent analysis. The final sweep of the study coincided with the 1991 Census. Consequently it will be possible to weight the sample using 1991 Census data and so ensure that the longitudinal data is representative of young people in Scotland.

Table 2.3 Distribution of the sexes by cohort for the YPLL sample in 1987, 1989 and 1991

	1987		*1989*		*1991*	
	Male %	*Female* %	*Male* %	*Female* %	*Male* %	*Female* %
Cohorts 1 and 2	–	–	50	50	46	54
Cohorts 3 and 4	50	50	46	54	42	58
Cohorts 5 and 6	48	52	45	55	41	59

THE PANEL STUDY

The panel study represents a major longitudinal element of the project. The intention in establishing it was to get beyond the general level of descriptive data afforded by questionnaire surveys to a methodology which would reveal more of the richness and complexity of the leisure *contexts* in which young people are involved.

One of the key focuses for the research was the desire to explore the changing facets of sport and leisure involvement as adolescents age. Simple correlational studies of the individual psychological or physiological characteristics and patterns of leisure participation are clearly inadequate. Complex social factors interact with these more individual factors to determine young people's decisions (conscious or unconscious) to join in, continue or cease certain activities. Coupled with this was the research team's desire to explore 'leisure' in its broadest definition. Leisure could not be seen as an easily identified set of activities or as a time allocation in young people's lives. Leisure was defined by each individual in relation to his or her perceptions of paid work, of duties, of responsibilities within the family, of demands made by school and so on. The panel studies, then, could easily be seen as an exploration of youth lifestyles. Clearly, a more qualitative investigation was necessary, and a decision was made to explore leisure contexts for a specific number of individuals by means of a series of interviews held two or three times a year over the life of the project.

The type of investigation that the project team had in mind and the resources of the project indicated that this 'panel' of young people should consist of approximately 200–250 individuals. The notion of a completely random selection of young people in Scotland was quickly rejected. Simple listings of the names and current addresses of adolescents do not exist for the whole of Scotland, besides which a random scatter of individuals throughout Scotland would have defeated the resources of the project if each child had required visiting two or three times a year.

Schools offered a clustered population which is comprehensively listed, and a similar clustered random sample based on the school grid had been the choice for the sampling framework for the questionnaire study.

Some thought was given to the idea of creating the panel as a subsample of the population used for the questionnaire, but external problems, in the form of an industrial dispute in schools at the start of the project, necessitated a re-scheduling of the research timetable. The panel investigation had to proceed before the questionnaire survey was undertaken.

At the same time it was realised that if the focus of interest was the leisure context which surrounded individuals there was no particular virtue in completely random sampling, but there was something to gain from highlighting specific types of context.

The eventual decision of the research team was to opt for a series of eleven study areas, each crudely described in terms of the built environment and the social class/life opportunities of its adolescent inhabitants. The team would be interested in the 'ecology' of each area, taking into account factors such as structure of population by age and social class, the patterns of local employment and unemployment, some consideration of the features of the built environment which determined leisure activities, the patterns of authority and government in each area which allocated or maintained facilities and the complex web of structural and personal relationships which encouraged or denied access to different types of activity for young people throughout their adolescent years.

The eleven study areas were clustered in three geographical regions (not coincident with political boundaries). This was to encourage ease of access for the field-workers but also to allow a more comprehensive picture of regional conditions to be built up. The appendix offers a brief portrait of each area. The distribution of the study areas reflects, in an approximate way, the general distribution of the population in Scotland.

In all areas a single secondary school was chosen as the focus of the catchment. Within this school a 13 and 16 year old sample cohort could be extracted. A cohort of 10 year olds was contacted from the feeder primary schools. In the case of the special and public schools, slightly different sampling arrangements were adopted to reflect the proportional difference in size between the communities under study.

In each school the panel sample was chosen randomly from registers of year groups according to date of birth.

The choice of 10, 13 and 16 year old cohorts resulted from pilot trials in one area of Aberdeen, where post-school samples contacted by letter had been reluctant to participate. It was felt that it would be more profitable and more manageable to start with three school-age cohorts, to establish a rapport and create a working relationship with them and then to follow their progress as they left school than to attempt to construct an artificial sample amongst the post-school population.

Anticipating from the pilot study that some parents/children would not respond or wish to participate, the research team originally sent invitations to about 300 children. The possibility of refusing to take part does, of course, raise the question of whether the panel should be seen as 'volunteers' and thus less typical or representative in some way. The research team felt that it was important to find out why some people had declined to co-operate and whether there was any particularly obvious bias such as social class, so some investigatory follow-up work on this group was undertaken.

When the sample was first taken from registers, the individuals chosen were gathered together at school and were asked to complete a brief question sheet which asked about father's job, family structure and family interests and activities. It was thus possible to make a crude comparison between the 240 young people who joined the panel and the sixty young people who declined. No significant differences were found.

MAKING COMPARISONS

Are Scotland's young people different from their peers in other parts of the United Kingdom in ways which would invalidate comparison or extrapolation of the findings presented in this book? The answer, of course, unsatisfactory though it might be, is that it is all a matter of perspective.

Scotland has a strong sense of national identity as a result of its historical relationship with its neighbours. But this identity rests in more than a fondness for tartan clothing or for certain brews. Scotland has a fundamentally different system of justice and policing, particularly in relation to juvenile crime for instance. Educational policy is derived from the Scottish Office in Edinburgh, not from a Whitehall department, and Scottish educational traditions are both respected and proudly defended. These are just two of the dimensions of difference.

That having been said, however, young Scots are participant in the full range of media-driven culture that their peers in England, Wales or Northern Ireland experience. Moreover, regional differences within Scotland (for instance between the heavily industrialised Central belt from Glasgow to Edinburgh and the more rural highland or upland regions to the north) may be as (or more) significant than English/Scottish differences. Such regional variations exist also in England, Wales and Northern Ireland of course.

We are confident that young Scots are sufficiently like their English counterparts to allow our findings to be generalised in painting a picture of various aspects of the adolescent transition and in offering insights into the development of adolescent lifestyles in Great Britain. Our study is doubly useful in offering a general interpretation of young people growing up in the United Kingdom and in allowing readers to consider differences which might obtain between 'our' young people within their transition to adulthood and those in other cultural settings.

G. Jones (1988) has emphasised the value of devising joint and complementary research strategies – utilising both survey and case study approaches – in gaining a better understanding of young people in the transition from childhood to adulthood. The reason for the values of this bi-partite research design has been effectively summarised by Aaro *et al.*:

The limitations, as well as the potential, of large-scale surveys deserve attention. There is a strong need for more qualitative and exploratory approaches as a supplement to data collections . . . The testing of new questions and of new ways of operationalising lifestyle . . . as well as other methodological innovations has to take place between the main surveys . . . Large scale surveys represent a conservative approach. Interviews with smaller groups . . . may increase the researcher's under-standing and interpretation of results, and permit closer examination of the validity and reliability of answers . . . Panel data offer opportunities to study processes of lifestyle development.

(Aaro *et al.*, 1986: 32)

Thus, linking the general findings described in this book with the insights and comments from the panel study may enable the reader to develop new insights into, and an understanding of, the development of adolescent lifestyles in modern British society.

3 Young people and leisure

INTRODUCTION

Findings from the YPLL Project provide us with some detailed insights into adolescent leisure and enable us to take a general look at theories of adolescent development from the perspective of up-to-date empirical data drawn from a large representative sample of young people. This chapter addresses the following three main research questions.

1 What changes occur in young people's leisure across the adolescent years?
2 Are there gender and social class differences in such changing patterns of leisure?
3 Do changes in young people's leisure coincide with relational focal issues?

A MODEL OF ADOLESCENT LEISURE TRANSITIONS

It is clear that different factors operate to influence leisure pursuits among young people over the adolescent years:

> In early childhood the behaviour of parents is of crucial importance; later friends, school, other adults and the mass media play an increasingly influential role. An attitude (towards leisure) develops, in interaction with other people. The individual develops norms, values and interests . . .
>
> (Engstrom, 1979: 34)

The middle years of childhood are a time at primary school when the sexes appear to draw apart in order to rehearse traditional and stereotypical sex roles in their play and leisure. During this time children seem to inhabit two cultures. A. Roberts (1980) suggested that parents and teachers encourage the child to absorb their values (and the values of wider society), while peers provide encouragement to join with subcultures containing like-aged children. According to Elkin and Handel (1978), this acceptance of peer culture has to be viewed as complementary to parental authority, and is an important step on the brink of adolescence. Hence Elkin and Handel propose that socialisation by peers supports the efforts of family and school and mediates the values of the adult world. The peer group gives the child contact with more egalitarian types of relationship, conveys information on taboo areas such as sex and passes on current trends and even fashions in the wider society. It expands the individual's social horizons, helps the development of a more complex personality and, finally, develops the ability to act independently of adult authority. Caught between two value systems, children on the brink of adolescence often use play as an expressive way of exploring and resolving the tensions between the two.

> Play is the principal business of childhood, the vehicle of improvisation and combination, the first carrier of rule systems through which a world of cultural restraint is substituted for the operation of impulse.
>
> (Bruner *et al.*, 1976: 20)

Thus, late childhood can be seen as a period of transition in rule-bound behaviour, where the individual child can experience the role of leader and follower by moving among various age-range groupings in leisure settings such as Scouts and Guides or youth clubs, exploring the alternative worlds of adult authority and peer norms.

Young people might well have acquired initial stereotypes and role knowledge in childhood, but during adolescence they have yet to explore the implications, opportunities, demands and constraints that fundamental social demarcations have for them, their social behaviour and their futures. It is important to understand the ways in which adolescents think about leisure, their attitudes towards leisure, the meanings and constraints they impose on it and the social forces which influence and shape their involvement.

Adolescence is a peak time of leisure needs. Young people have more free time and opportunities and perhaps less responsibility than at any other time of their lives. But young people at this age are restricted by lack of spending power, lack of transport and by legal and parental limitations. Although material and societal constraints are of great importance, psychological constraints may actually be of greater relevance. Iso-Ahola and Mannell (1984) have documented some of these constraints. They summarised the research evidence by pointing to three groups of constraint. The first related to perceived incompetence which, they argued, leads to reduced involvement and possible withdrawal from a range of leisure activities. The second group of constraints was related to attitudinal variables, including motives and needs. They proposed that lack of information is an important constraint in terms of what is actually available, in terms of what can be gained by participating and in terms of possible stereotypical images of particular activities. The third group of constraints related to social-cultural factors. They argued that certain types of social obligations turn play and recreation into work by changing intrinsic leisure motivation into extrinsic motivation. It is therefore necessary to stress the variability among adolescents in aspiration, motivations, attitudes and in the values they place on their leisure interests and pursuits.

Leisure activities may be chosen both for their personal meaning and for social expression. Further, these interests are coloured by influences such as the family, the educational system, peers, the media, leisure provision and leisure promotion industries, and social change such as a rise in youth unemployment. Thus adolescents' leisure can be seen as an interaction of underlying influences from within the individual and from the social environment (subculturally and in wider society).

J. Roberts (1981) has proposed a process by which people participate in leisure activities after consciously or unconsciously passing the idea through a range of 'social' and 'decision' filters. The social filters include age, sex, income, education, social class and social mobility; the decision filters include motivation, awareness of opportunity, free time and cost.

In considering how such determining factors interact to influence the development of particular leisure interests and activities amongst young people, a crucial point to stress is the way in which the interplay of factors influencing leisure choices varies as the focus of social interests changes across the adolescent years (J.C. Coleman and Hendry, 1990).

Figure 3.1 illustrates the changes and continuities in the adolescent's leisure preferences and behaviour (i.e. the shifting focus of leisure interests). The main factors influencing leisure choices are suggested by Hendry (1983) to be age, gender and social class. These are hardly surprising elements, but when linked to the shifting focus of relationships postulated by J.C. Coleman (1979) the model provides insights into a changing and differential pattern of leisure focus in the teenage years. It is argued that the focus generally shifts in stages from adult-organised clubs and activities, through casual leisure pursuits to commercially organised leisure, and that these transitions may occur roughly at the ages where the main relationship issues postulated by J.C. Coleman (1979) come into focus. The empirical evidence underlying Hendry's (1983) 'focal' theory of leisure was derived from a series of studies carried out by Hendry (1976, 1978, 1981, 1983) and by Hendry and his associates (Hendry and Percy, 1981; Hendry and Raymond, 1983).

The differential effects of sex and social class on leisure patterns can be

Figure 3.1 Focuses of interest and types of leisure pursuits

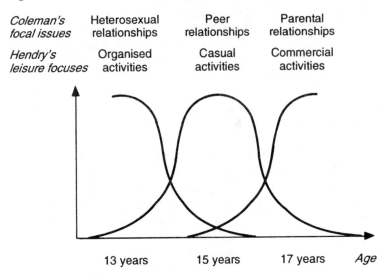

| *Coleman's* *focal issues* | Heterosexual relationships | Peer relationships | Parental relationships |
| *Hendry's* *leisure focuses* | Organised activities | Casual activities | Commercial activities |

13 years   15 years   17 years   *Age*

explained in relation to a dynamic interplay of factors. Looking at gender differences, the earlier physiological maturity of girls may enable them to be more readily accepted as 'adult' than adolescent boys in a variety of social-leisure contexts. This may allow young women to make earlier transitions towards peers and casual leisure pursuits (some appearing to miss out this stage entirely) and towards more exclusive courting dyads and commercial leisure provision. Turning to class-based differences, the continued allegiance of the middle classes, and particularly middle class boys, to games and organised pursuits may be indicative of Sutton-Smith and Roberts' (1964) conjectures about play-styles and their use as rehearsals for adult roles. It may also reflect the longer dependence on parents (often in conjunction with plans to pursue courses of higher education) which ensures a continuing (relaxed) relationship with adults and creates opportunities for further socialisation towards particular adult values. Other social, psychological and ecological factors beyond gender and social class will, of course, influence continuity and change in adolescents' leisure pursuits.

The coincidence of an interest in organised and structured leisure pursuits and clubs, with the focus on heterosexual relationships and gender identity in early adolescence, seems plausible. Conger (1979) has suggested that the increase in the sexual drive that accompanies puberty occurs when close social relationships and leisure activities are largely confined to members of the same sex. It is also a period, Conger pointed out, when the opposite sex can appear rather mysterious and anxiety-producing. Thus youth clubs and organised adult-led leisure pursuits can provide a 'safe' environment from which to observe and to interact with the opposite sex. Further, the adults present contain the social interactions among members, and the pervading values and norms are directed towards conventional socialisation (Hendry *et al.*, 1991b).

The second leisure focus concerns peer relationships in conjunction with casual pursuits. Because this focal leisure area involves not only peers and casual activities but also occurs at about the period when the minimum school-leaving age is reached, it contains perhaps the stage of greatest diversity of pattern. Nisbet *et al.* (1984), for example, in a study of both rural and urban locales in a Scottish region, found that over 70 per cent of pupils in their last year of compulsory schooling had been members of a sports club or team at some time in the past, but only 47 per cent were members at the time of investigation. With regard to non-sporting clubs, 80 per cent had been members in the past, but only 50 per cent were currently involved. This trend was most evident for uniformed organisations. In part, this conjunction of peer relations and acceptance of subcultural values with an interest in casual leisure may offer some additional insights into the anti-school subcultures described by Willis (1977) among others. The lure of the peer group in terms of behaviour is irresistible. Thus, while 'conformist' youths may continue to be more attracted to organisations and adult influence, such structured clubs do not touch many adolescents who pursue alternative subcultural leisure lifestyles. The general feeling among many young people is that official youth clubs are too tame or over-organised and that they are too much like school. Organised leisure facilities of necessity require supervision and this fact increases their resemblance to school. Thus, those activities are rejected by those adolescents who reject school, yet are accepted by those who accept school's values (Hendry, 1983). The significance of this is that whilst some young people will continue to have social contact with both adults and peers in their leisure, for many adolescents there will be an absence of adult influence in their lives outside the home.

At the next focal stage an interest in commercial leisure provision is linked to the peak of conflicts with parents, often over the adolescent's attempts to gain a degree of independence:

Perhaps indeed, (adolescents) have been kept in even longer subordination just because they *are* more mature and consequently threatening to the old . . . where society does not permit the adolescent to assume a social role compatible with his physical and intellectual development . . . adult maturity is come by with more difficulty.

(Musgrove, 1964: 162)

Emmett (1977) concluded that leisure interests in later adolescence reflect the fact that post-school years are courting years; that young people at work have more money and greater freedom in selecting their leisure pursuits; and that at 18 years of age they are legally entitled to drink in public houses. Adolescents in this period of their lives are close to being perceived as adults, and their leisure-time pursuits will be adult-oriented leisure interests closely matching their subcultural heritage. This fact alone will create a climate for inter-generational disagreements, as Musgrove (1964) earlier described.

What has been examined up to this point is largely a description of an empirically observed pattern. It is important to examine too the dynamics and processes involved in these transitions in leisure interests and lifestyle across the adolescent years. Is change gradual and are there identifiable 'triggers' that shift individuals on to new ventures and activities? Are the factors which precipitate change at the various stages in adolescent leisure mainly sociocultural, somatic or psychological?

If we look at the pre-adolescent period, we find that as children emerge from the middle years of childhood they are engaged in play patterns that are basically traditional, conformist and influenced by family background, but that these are slowly eroded by a more adult concept of leisure and recreation. In particular, Hendry and Percy (1981) found that by the upper stages of the primary school social pressures and the influence of the media were pushing boys and girls into much more gender-specific roles in terms of their leisure activities, whereas earlier on leisure lacked such a gender dimension.

Sociocultural factors would seem to predominate over physical and psychological ones at this juncture between childhood and adolescence. With these social triggers young people move towards the setting of organised adult-run activities as a context for slowly acquainting themselves with the opposite sex after a middle childhood where single-sex groupings are the norm. Such activities include youth clubs, sports clubs, school clubs, youth groups and Church groups.

Conversely, the process which triggers the transition from organised activities towards casual activities a few years later is one where physical and physiological factors may be brought to the forefront. For young women in particular, the relatively rapid changes in body shape and size and the onset of menstruation may well explain the rapid loss of interest in physical activity and organised games at this stage. The physiological and psychological changes experienced by all adolescents, however, require them to reappraise their self-images, and at this stage it is important for these self-images to be reinforced by peers.

Adults can play an important part in peer group interactions (adolescent clubs and groups are typically organised and supervised by adults) but many adolescents reject such leisure settings (J.C. Coleman and Hendry, 1990).

> The most significant factor is the pressure . . . to decide on leisure activities in relation to peers . . . which allow continued interaction with peers, and are highly valued within the peer group.
>
> (Hendry, 1976: 50)

Although such experiences of adolescent peer groups are integral to the definition of male subcultures at this stage, young women's experiences can be quite different. Young women tend to form small and intense friendship groups, with a 'best friend' being central to their experiences, but as they begin to form relationships with young men, these female subcultures based on supportive friendships may begin to break down (Griffin, 1981).

Women, especially young working-class women, have little access to leisure 'space'. Many social and leisure settings are predominantly male preserves (Scraton, 1986). For example, even when young women are found in groups hanging around shopping centres or street corners, their 'appearance on the street is always constrained by their subordination' to males (Cowie and Lees, 1981). It would seem that for many young women the answer is, as McRobbie (1978) suggested, to retreat to a 'home base' where they can meet with a few close friends. Frith (1978) described this as 'the culture of the bedroom'.

At the third focal stage the broad influencing factors are mainly socio-cultural: employment opportunities and disposable income, family commitments, associations with adult society, subcultural values, peers and the effects of the broad leisure interests developed in the previous stages.

Given the importance of these transitions, leisure in its widest sense can be significant in creating opportunities for self-agency, identity development and the development of social competence. Forms of self-presentation and social styles can be tried out without too many dire consequences should they fail to impress. At the same time these individualistic aspects of behaviour are carried out within institutionally defined roles, with relatively expected and predictable behaviours and rules.

EMPIRICAL EVIDENCE FOR LEISURE TRANSITIONS

Findings from the YPLL study suggest that adult-led organised leisure is popular with primary school pupils. For children at this pre-adolescent stage the most popular clubs are Brownies/Cubs, Girls'/Boys' Brigade, Sunday school and youth clubs. At 9–10 years of age 80 per cent of girls and 70 per cent of boys belong to at least one club. By 11–12 years of age, however, significant changes occur in the pattern of membership (Figure 3.2). Amongst the older age group 26 per cent of girls and 35 per cent of boys do not belong to any organised groups. As can be seen from these percentages, clubs are more popular with girls than boys.

The main reasons given for attending clubs or groups are 'going with friends' (54 per cent), 'learning different things' (48 per cent), 'doing different activities' (42 per cent) and 'it's better than staying at home' (38 per cent). Again, there are significant differences between members of 9–10 years of age and members of 11–12 years of age in the reasons given for membership. Although going with friends and learning and doing different things remain important, the emphasis shifts from the organised elements of clubs and groups (uniforms and rules) and the influence of adult figures (group leaders and parents) towards the more informal social aspects of group membership (meeting other girls and boys away from the family home). The social element of meeting other children is more import- ant for girls whereas the attendance of boys is more strongly influenced by their parents.

The children were also asked about a wide range of other leisure activities they pursued on a weekly basis. Hobbies and watching television and videos are the main preoccupations. Listening to records and tapes (71 per cent), reading books for pleasure (67 per cent), reading comics (59 per cent) and playing with toys (54 per cent) are also popular pastimes. Levels of involvement in hobbies, television viewing and reading do not change with age, but older children are more likely to listen to pop music and less likely to play with toys. This move towards adolescent pursuits and activities is more marked in girls. They are more likely than boys to listen to pop music and read books and they are less likely to read comics and play with toys. Further to this, at 9–10 years of age girls and boys are equally likely to play with toys, but by 11–12 years of age significantly fewer girls continue to do so. These findings are suggestive of the earlier maturation of girls which accelerates their transition from childhood leisure towards teenage culture.

Continuing with leisure activities, and considering the influences of family and peers, frequent visits to friends' homes are usual (62 per cent) whereas weekly family outings are much less so (19 per cent). There is in fact a decrease in family outings between 9–10 years of age and 11–12 years of age and an increase in visiting friends (see Figure 3.2). Both these activities figure more in girls' lives than boys'. Looking at the importance of family versus peers in relation to who children claim to spend most of their free time with when not at school, there is no evidence of movement away from the family towards the peer group between 9–10 years of age

Figure 3.2 Pre-adolescent leisure activities: (a) percentage belonging to an organised club or group; (b) percentage visiting friends' house on a weekly basis; (c) percentage spending most time with friends and percentage spending most time with family when not at school

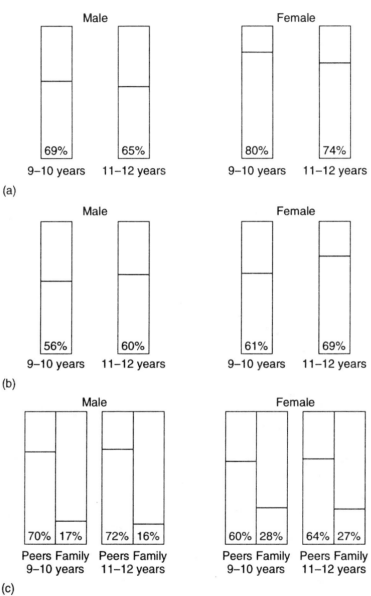

Source: YPLL survey 1987

and 11–12 years of age. There are, however, clear gender differences with girls spending more free time with their family than boys.

In summary, what is being suggested here is that the pattern observed towards the end of the pre-adolescent period anticipates the leisure transitions which occur across the adolescent years.

After the pre-adolescent years clear patterns begin to emerge in young people's leisure, which reflect gender, age and social class influences together with the grafting on of elements of adult leisure. While home-based leisure such as watching TV remains popular amongst most adolescents (aged 13–20 years), listening to music increases in popularity compared with pre-adolescent levels and interest in hobbies and reading books decreases. Gender differences are evident. Adolescent girls continue to be more involved in music, books and socialising with friends. By contrast, adolescent boys are more likely to maintain an interest in hobbies.

Turning to patterns of leisure activities outside the home, the most popular activities are visiting friends (85 per cent), hanging about in the street with groups of friends (56 per cent), discos (47 per cent), sports clubs (40 per cent), youth clubs or groups (31 per cent), cinemas (31 per cent) and pubs (29 per cent). Again clear gender differences emerge. Young women are more likely to visit friends and go to cinemas and discos whereas young men are more likely to be involved in sports teams and to go to sports clubs, youth clubs and youth groups. Again we note the impact of young women's earlier maturity on their leisure activities. Overall (where differences exist) adolescent girls are more likely to be involved in 'casual' and 'commercial' leisure whereas adolescent boys are more likely to be involved in 'organised' leisure.

In order to pursue some of these themes in more detail the YPLL data collected from the four older cohorts of young people (13–14 years, 15–16 years, 17–18 years and 19–20 years) was examined and a variety of questionnaire items relating to leisure selected. These included leisure activities and pursuits, membership of clubs, leisure spending, attitudes to leisure, the priority given to leisure and the availability of local neighbourhood facilities. Nine of the items were characterised as 'organised', seven as 'casual' and nine as 'commercial' elements. The twenty-five variables were then subjected to a principal components analysis. The aim of this analysis was to summarise a large and varied set of items by creating a small number of meaningful leisure dimensions. Eight factors were derived from the analysis. These were then rotated to produce a set of independent leisure dimensions, namely:

1 active involvement in sport and organised activities;
2 the adequacy of local neighbourhood sports facilities;

3 pub attendance and alcohol consumption;
4 visits to and by friends;
5 the importance of various aspects of youth-oriented culture
  (i.e. discos, pop music and clubs);
6 spectator sports;
7 entertainments (i.e. disco and cinema attendance);
8 hanging around in the street and the perception that there were few
  places to meet in the local neighbourhood.

A subset of these leisure factors was then selected for further analysis (1, 3, 4, 7 and 8 above). The five factors chosen were intended to represent adolescent transitions from 'organised' through 'casual' to 'commercial' activities as proposed by leisure focal theory (Hendry, 1983).

These five components of leisure were then examined for gender, age and social class differences using multivariate analysis of variance techniques. The aim of this analysis was to use the five factors to chart transitions in the types and levels of leisure involvement made by young people as they moved through adolescence and towards adulthood. A clear pattern of changes in leisure activities emerges across the adolescent years. There is a steady decline in sports participation and other organised activities from an initial peak at 13–14 years of age. Hanging around the local neighbourhood and the perception of a lack of places to meet declines rapidly after 16 years of age. Attending entertainments such as discos and cinemas increases steadily to a peak at 19–20 years of age. There is a corresponding but much more rapid increase in pub attendance. There are also clear gender differences. Young men are more likely to be involved in sport and organised leisure whereas young women are more likely to visit and be visited by friends and go to cinemas and discos. Further, at 17–20 years of age, young men are more likely than young women to hang around the neighbourhood and, at 19–20 years of age, they are more likely to go to pubs. Finally, there are few class-based variations in leisure, although young people from middle class homes are less likely to hang around their neighbourhood.

It is difficult to gain a picture of actual levels of involvement from the standardised mean factor scores analysed above. Therefore specific leisure items (from amongst those used in the principal components analysis) were selected to represent each of the five factors. The variables chosen all related to weekly participation in various leisure activities: attending youth clubs or groups; attending sports clubs; visiting friends; hanging around in the street with groups of friends; attending discos; and attending pubs. The variables selected as exemplars for the five factors were analysed using log-linear methods. As can be seen from Figure 3.3, the results confirmed

Figure 3.3 Adolescent leisure activities (weekly participation rates):
(a) percentage attending a youth club or group; (b) percentage attending a sports club;
(c) percentage visiting friends; (d) percentage hanging around the local neighbourhood
with friends; (e) percentage attending discos; (f) percentage attending pubs

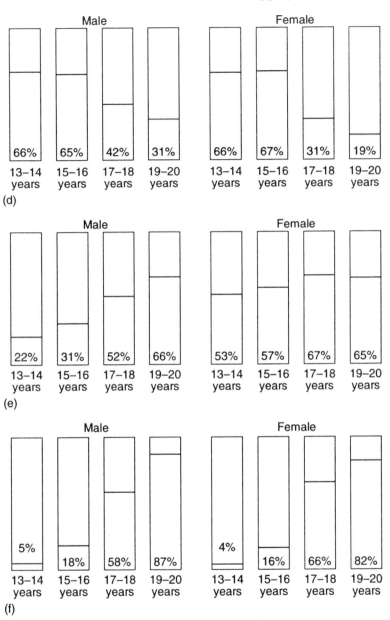

(d)

(e)

(f)

Source: YPLL survey 1987

in detail the more general findings outlined above. Involvement in youth clubs and groups shows a steady decline from a peak at around 13–14 years of age, whereas involvement in sports clubs, although highest at 13–14 years of age, shows a much more gradual decline than other types of organised clubs. Throughout adolescence young men are more likely than young women to attend organised clubs and in particular they are more likely to maintain their involvement in sports clubs. Visiting friends is most frequent at 15–16 years of age and is more common amongst young women. Hanging around the neighbourhood is most frequent at 13–16 years of age. There is a sharp decline in later adolescence which is more marked amongst young women. Also, young people from middle class backgrounds are less likely to hang around in groups. Disco attendance increases throughout the adolescent period but there are significant gender differences in the pattern of growth. In early adolescence to mid-adolescence young women are much more likely than young men to attend discos and it is only by late adolescence that young men reach the same level of involvement. Interestingly, there are also class-based gender differences. Young men from middle class homes are less likely to attend discos whereas young women from working class homes are more likely to do so. Finally, there is a dramatic increase in pub attendance between 15–16 years of age and 17–18 years of age which is clearly related to the legal drinking age. Interestingly, at 17–18 years of age, young women are more likely than young men to attend pubs, but by 19–20 years of age young men go to pubs more often than young women.

Interviews with panel members from the case study component of the YPLL Project provided a more personalised picture of adolescent leisure interests. These 240 or so young people came from eleven distinct socio-geographical areas. They were asked to complete diaries of weekday and weekend leisure activities. The diaries kept by panel members and the comments they made when interviewed confirmed in detail the more general findings derived from the large-scale questionnaire-based surveys:

> There is no life at night so most people end up at the pub, where they can meet friends in comfort, but they don't drink alcohol, only soft drinks. There are three restaurants open at peak season so we are spoilt for choice, but in winter there is only one open until 3 pm, so we can only go there on Saturday. Teachers don't bother about the pupils unless the police are involved and then all hell is let loose. They then start creating about what we do after school and at night and at weekends, and they moan because we do nothing positive, but they are not willing to sort it by starting up organisations.
>
> (Caroline, Mull)

There should be more places for 16 to 18 year olds to go. Between these ages there is nowhere suitable. When you're 16 you don't want to go to youth club discos any more especially if your boyfriend is old enough to get into nightclubs. The government don't seem to cater for the 16 to 18 year olds, as you are expected to carry on being a kid until your eighteenth birthday. You should be treated as an adult when you're 16. You are allowed to be married.

(Dianne, Inverness)

There is a very definite lack of places in town where young people (under 18) can meet, without going into pubs. This leads to many people illegally drinking and showing false ID. Why can't there be 'cafés', or something of that sort, open 'till late?

(Jane, Edinburgh)

At the weekends I usually go to pubs and nightclubs, and passing through the town centre to go to these places I have noticed large groups of say around 12–16 year olds, hanging around outside a burger place. This number has increased due to the closing of the only under 18's disco. It's sad to hear them all shouting, screaming and swearing at each other as well as staggering around. I know I'm not much older than most of them but at that age I don't remember getting into such a state through drink and boredom, 'cause at that time there was somewhere to go.

(Mairi, East Kilbride)

In summary, the findings of the present study are consistent with leisure focal theory. They reflect the changing patterns which the theory suggests occur across the adolescent years and clearly highlight the transitions made by young people from 'organised' through 'casual' to 'commercial' leisure. The results also support the claim that young women in general make these transitions earlier than young men, although by late adolescence young men attain similar levels of involvement in 'commercial' leisure.

EMPIRICAL EVIDENCE OF RELATIONAL TRANSITIONS IN ADOLESCENCE

Turning to relationships and relational issues in adolescence, the YPLL data was analysed using the same statistical strategies. Thirty-five relational items were selected. These included variables concerning gender identity, time spent with family and peers, peer acceptance, characteristics associated with popularity and unpopularity amongst peers, self-perceptions of sociability and friendship, attitudes to authority and parental control and, lastly, the importance attached to material independence. These variables were subjected to a principal components analysis and ten factors were identified. The resultant factors were then rotated to produce a set of independent relational dimensions:

1 perceived 'feminine' characteristics;
2 perceived 'masculine' characteristics;
3 the importance of social and material independence;
4 characteristics perceived as unpopular with the peer group;
5 being friendly and sociable;
6 popularity and attractiveness;
7 time spent with peer groups and friends;
8 time spent with girl-friend/boy-friend (as opposed to family);
9 appearance and behaviour is the individual's own business;
10 popularity and peer conformity.

Five of these relational dimensions were selected for further analysis (6–10 above). The factors were chosen to reflect the changing patterns of relational issues across the adolescent years (i.e. concerns with gender identity, relationships with peers and gaining independence from parents) as proposed by focal theory (J.C. Coleman, 1979).

The five relational factors were then examined for gender, age and social class differences. In general terms, issues relating to peer popularity by being pretty, good-looking or attractive steadily decline from a peak at 13–14 years of age, although these issues remain of greater concern to young men than to young women throughout adolescence perhaps as a feature of adolescent males' focus on physical attributes as a necessary component of peer popularity (Hendry and Jamie, 1978). Acceptance of and conformity to peer group norms also declines rapidly from a peak in early adolescence and again young men regard these issues as more important. Also, there are class-based differences in the perceived need to conform to peer group norms. Young people from middle class homes feel it is less necessary to conform. Spending time with peers is most common in mid-adolescence at 15–16 years of age and gradually declines in later adolescence. Again there are social class differences. In young adolescence, young people from working class backgrounds are less likely to spend a lot of spare time with peers. This finding may reflect the fact that working class adolescents are still likely to live at home, whereas middle class youths in higher education and away from home may spend a great deal of time with other students. Issues relating to adolescent concerns with independence in appearance and behaviour also peak at 15–16 years and show a marked decline thereafter. Finally, having girl-friends/boy-friends and spending a lot of time together (as opposed to with the family) increases rapidly from 13–14 years of age onwards and once more there are social class differences. Young people from middle class homes score less highly on this factor.

Individual items which were representative of each of the five relational factors were selected for further analysis. As noted previously, this was done because it is difficult to gain an impression of actual levels of concern with relational issues from standardised mean factor scores. The variables chosen were: to be popular with peers, need to be pretty/good-looking/attractive; to be popular with peers, need to be yourself/to be individual; to spend a lot of spare time with groups of peers; what young people do and how they dress outside their homes is their own business; and to spend a lot of spare time with the family. Using these variables as exemplars for the five factors, we confirmed in detail the more general findings outlined above (Figure 3.4). There is a steady decline across the adolescent years in the importance attached to attractiveness and a corresponding increase in the perceived need to be an individual. Young people spend most time with their family at 13–14 years of age whereas time with peer groups peaks at 15–16 years of age. Concerns with independence in dress and behaviour also peak in mid-adolescence at 15–16 years of age. There are significant gender differences. Adolescent boys are more concerned than adolescent girls with attractiveness and conforming to peer group norms but they are less tolerant of external controls on their dress and behaviour by authority figures outside the home. Young women are more likely than young men to spend time with peer groups and in later adolescence they are also more likely to spend time with the family. There are significant class-based differences across the adolescent years. With regard to time spent with the peer group, young women from middle class homes are more likely than other adolescents to spend their spare time with groups of peers. Interestingly, in later adolescence beyond the peak observed at 15–16 years of age, young people from middle class backgrounds are more likely than those from working class backgrounds to maintain the amount of time they spent with groups of peers. Finally, young people from middle class homes are more likely to view individuality as an important aspect of peer group popularity.

In conclusion, whilst the relational items used in the YPLL study were not identical to those in J.C. Coleman's (1979) original work, the present analysis yields similar results from a different perspective, and as such the findings are consistent with a shifting focus of relational issues throughout adolescence as proposed by focal theory. Taken together, the results of the analysis of young people's changing patterns of leisure involvement and relational issues across the adolescent years provide strong support for both of the original focal theories (J.C. Coleman and Hendry, 1990). They also support the claim that adolescent leisure transitions occur in tandem with relational issues as young people move towards adulthood.

Figure 3.4 Adolescent relational issues: (a) percentage perceiving 'being pretty/good-looking/attractive' as important to peer group popularity; (b) percentage perceiving 'being themselves, being individual' as important to peer group popularity (c) percentage spending a lot of 'spare' time with groups of peers; (d) percentage agreeing that what young people do and how they dress outside their home is their own business; (e) percentage spending a lot of 'spare' time with family

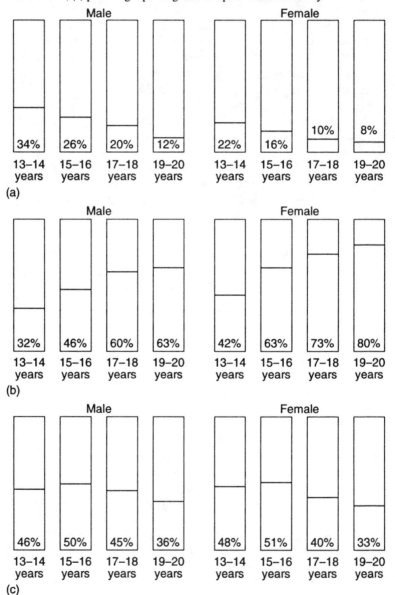

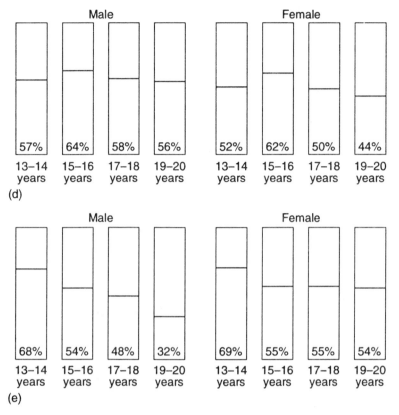

Source: YPLL survey 1987

LEAVING ADOLESCENCE BEHIND – LEISURE TRANSITIONS TO ADULTHOOD

At the beginning of this chapter young people on the brink of adolescence were examined in relation to their leisure choices. In this final section young men and women in late adolescence are looked at. Still defined as adolescent, they are, in their own eyes at least, young adults entering a new phase of life once school days are over.

It was suggested earlier that factors such as employment opportunities and occupational status were influential in later adolescence in relation to leisure choices. In order to pursue this theme attention was focused on the eldest two cohorts (17–18 years and 19–20 years) in the YPLL study. Young people in these two groups were beyond the minimum school-leaving age and therefore it was possible to examine how their current socioeconomic position might influence their leisure activities. The 17–18 year old age group was subdivided into those who were still at secondary school, those in further education, those in government training schemes, those in employment and those who were currently unemployed (there were very few non-employed persons at this stage of the study). Amongst the 19–20 year old age group, individuals were categorised as in further education, in employment or unemployed. Comparisons were then made between the leisure activities of these socioeconomic groupings of young people. It was found, for example, that the pattern of leisure involvement across the different groups was much the same for young women and young men. The results of the analysis are illustrated here by concentrating on three aspects of leisure: involvement in sports clubs; 'hanging around' the neighbourhood; and going to pubs. These three variables were selected as representative of 'organised', 'casual' and 'commercial' leisure.

Looking at the 17–18 year old age group (Table 3.1) it was found that those who are still at school are more likely to continue their involvement in sports clubs and less likely to hang around street corners and to go to pubs regularly. Those who are still within the educational system (but not at school) are also less likely to hang around. Those on training schemes or in employment are most likely to go to pubs. Unemployed young people are

Table 3.1   Types of leisure involvement in late adolescence by labour market position

	Current labour market position					
	At school	*Further or higher education*	*Training scheme*	Employed	*Un-employed*	*All*
	(%)	*(%)*	*(%)*	*(%)*	*(%)*	*(%)*
Percentage attending a sports club regularly						
17–18 years	43	25	32	40	25	37
19–20 years	–	41	–	37	27	36
Percentage 'hanging around' the neighbourhood regularly						
17–18 years	32	25	41	34	59	36
19–20 years	–	17	–	23	42	25
Percentage going to a pub regularly						
17–18 years	47	65	74	74	61	62
19–20 years	–	87	–	85	77	85

Source: YPLL survey 1987

less likely to participate in sports clubs and more likely to hang around the neighbourhood. Turning to the 19–20 year olds, those in further education are least likely to hang around. By contrast, unemployed young people are the most likely to hang around the neighbourhood and were least likely to be sports club members or to go to the pub regularly.

These findings illustrate the powerful effects of occupational status on young people's leisure pursuits in late adolescence. In particular, they clearly suggest that youth unemployment delays the general pattern of leisure transitions more usually found in adolescence.

> Leisure takes on a different quality when you are unemployed. It involves staying longer in bed, watching more television or just lazing about, but lacks the sense of restoration this brings when you have a 'meaningful' job. It is one thing to come home after a day's work and flop down in front of a television screen; but quite another to watch television during the day because you simply have nothing to do.
>
> (Hill, 1978: 118)

Such a comment reflects the profound impact unemployment has on day-to-day life. Amongst adolescents the ultimate effect of youth unemployment seems to be on the transition to adulthood. Being unable to find work appears to frustrate expectations of post-school patterns of work and leisure. A comment from one of the young people surveyed in the YPLL study illustrates this:

> When you are unemployed you are the most important person unemployed. You take it personally. It does not matter if you say: 'There are another 3.5 million'. Taking it from both sides of the counter. From experience. There is a total pessimistic outlook. Unemployment is a malignant growth on the whole of the east-end community with no short or long term cure.
>
> (Martin, Glasgow)

Unemployment creates a structureless state within which leisure with all its concomitant social opportunities vanishes. Hendry *et al.* (1984) found that pupils about to enter the job market tended to view future day-to-day living and leisure patterns in terms of the opportunities that only a job can provide. These 'school-leavers' envisaged a shift away from sports, hobbies and youth clubs towards more sophisticated 'adult' leisure interests. Hendry and Raymond's (1983) study of post-school adolescents showed that unemployed young people took part in cheaper forms of leisure, such as youth clubs and 'hanging around' on street corners. Many of these unemployed adolescents resented the fact that they could not afford the same entertainments as those who were working. They felt trapped in a limbo between youth clubs they had outgrown and 'adult' leisure provisions that were too expensive. The findings of the YPLL study support this picture of delayed leisure transitions. Thus a major consequence of unemployment is to deny young people entry to the 'package' of work and leisure which is integral to an 'adult' lifestyle. Two final comments from YPLL survey respondents illustrate this:

> I think unemployment is the most important issue facing young people. We worry about it more than people imagine. I think more support groups and clubs should be set up to help combat the alienation people feel and to point out that through sport and other leisure activities you can help alleviate the apathy and lethargy that undoubtedly set in.
>
> (Tracey, Edinburgh)

> I know how it feels to be unemployed, I was when I left college. I did supply work, but you never knew from one day to the next if you would be working. The boredom was dreadful. I had no money at all (I wasn't eligible for any benefit) so for 3 or 4 months I had nothing. It's a very depressing situation to be in. You feel the lowest of the low, and you get to the stage where you never think things are going to get any better, and you can't go out to buy anything – it's horrible!
>
> (Ann, Penicuik)

LEISURE SETTINGS

In the YPLL study there was an interest in the settings in which young people experienced leisure. This theme was pursued in the panel study. Young people were asked to describe where they 'hung around'. This produced some critical and 'distancing' comments, such as:

> The rough people in the area hang around outside the off-sales.

The majority, however, seemed to accept the inevitability of a 'hanging about' phase:

> People hang about the streets because there is nowhere else to go. Everyone who has nothing better to do goes.

Common venues were youth clubs, shopping centres, schools, waste ground, swing parks, cafés and chip shops, petrol stations and 'on the streets'. Particular areas clearly get a reputation as meeting places:

> In our area there is a path called the 'main path'. At weekends everyone meets there.

A number of respondents mentioned the territorial aspects of street life:

The streets-casuals. The park heavy metallers with carryouts in summer.

Hanging about was clearly seen as a phase, even by young people themselves. A number of respondents put ages on the 'types' of young people
who hung about (12–16) and it was clear that part of the territorial side of
'hanging about' had to do with age. Young people were almost allowed by
others to 'graduate' from setting to getting as they grow older. One boy
noted that at age 14–15 years you were allowed to hang around outside the
chip shop, and you were only allowed to hang around outside the pub at
16–17 years.

Sometimes particular groups of people were picked out as worth
avoiding – drug addicts in their favourite haunt, bikers assembled in the
local square and (mentioned several times) 'casuals' out looking for a fight.

Our study has shown clearly that up to mid-adolescence young women
do 'hang around' the local neighbourhood as Spencer *et al.* (1989) noted,
even though their venues may differ somewhat from those chosen by young
men.

A simple question, 'Is there anywhere in your area that your friends
would advise against going?', was revealing, showing young people's
complex understanding of leisure cultures and peer groups. Most perceived
'trouble' to themselves from gangs/groups of other young people.
Particular districts or areas were named or known as 'hanging about'
sectors (like schools or superstore car parks) within areas. It was seen to be
dangerous even to go near these places:

because if you don't look right then 'they' take an instant dislike to you.

Even rural towns had notable areas like this. Discos and pubs were mentioned frequently as places where trouble was so frequent that they were
better avoided. Drunkenness was mentioned in this context, but the
'bouncers' in many city centre discos or just the crowds of people inside
were seen as potentially dangerous.

At our local night club there is always trouble and the bouncers pick on
you for no reason. There are fights outside and people get jumped.

There are certain establishments you enter at your own risk (jokes about
such places include 'you wipe your feet on the way out' and 'go in for a
laugh and come out in stitches').

A large number of replies mentioned discos which they saw as out-of-
bounds because of rough behaviour. Drink was mentioned in the majority
of instances as the reason for bad behaviour:

there are various nightclubs and pubs I wouldn't enter due to undesirable people I would most certainly meet, and when they are drunk they can be very hard to handle.

This seems like a classic 'no-win' situation. A number of respondents claim that rules at leisure clubs, youth clubs and sports clubs were 'too strict'. On the other hand lack of supervision was clearly not appreciated. Several commented on the diminution of enjoyment by the majority where too lax control was used:

all the ruffians and smokers go there . . .

in a club round the corner they let anybody in – vandals, smokers, sniffers – and that put me off.

Spencer *et al.* (1989) have lamented the lack of an ethnography of adolescent life which would explore the complex way in which young people use and perceive their environments. This secret world of 'leisure nothings' as Wood (1984) has described it, becomes, if anything, even more impenetrable in adolescence. The work of urban anthropologists such as Gans (1968) and urban planners such as Banerjee and Lynch (1977) have indicated that though adolescents range further afield, physical settings continue to be important for providing meeting places and contexts for social learning and social experimentation. Spencer *et al.* (1989) described the 'alternative scripts' in use by adolescents who inhabit adult spaces but for different reasons. Fast-food cafés and bus shelters are not being used to buy food or to await transport. They are theatres for self-display, observation points for assessing the roles of others and of oneself, meeting grounds for establishing and maintaining solidarity with one's group. P. Marsh *et al.* (1978), for example, have looked at the finely regulated behaviour of those football supporter groups away from the match which, to other eyes, appears chaotic or anarchic; and Anthony (1985) described adolescents' use of shopping malls, young people spending up to five hours at a time watching each other, cruising round, playing video games and having occasional snacks. They capitalise to the full on what the planners euphemistically label 'public space', yet their very presence is often seen as subversive and threatening. Occasionally security guards will be employed to move them on or prevent them from 'capturing' territory by their presence. Van Vliet (1983) has coined the term 'the fourth environment' to describe such local contexts where aspects of growing up takes place. This fourth environment appears to fulfil important developmental functions for young people, yet surprisingly little is known about home range extensions and their importance as contexts for adolescent meetings and their social development.

SUMMARY

In this chapter leisure and psycho-social focal theories (J.C. Coleman and Hendry, 1990) have been used as a framework for looking at leisure transitions in adolescence, the influences of age, gender and social class on these changing patterns of leisure and at the role of leisure in young people's lives. Although these issues have been considered from a different perspective to that adopted in the original studies, YPLL results provide additional support for Coleman's and Hendry's models of leisure and relational transitions in adolescence. Of course, further questions need to be addressed regarding the personal and social factors which initiate – or fail to initiate – changes in individual adolescents. For example, socioeconomic factors such as unemployment have a major impact on leisure activities in later adolescence by selecting certain social and leisure transitions. Finally, there is a brief review of the contexts in which adolescents pursue leisure.

4 Young people and sport

INTRODUCTION

> On the one hand, sport is easily taken for granted . . . either as an enjoyable unserious activity which it would be unbearably pretentious even self defeating to subject to analysis . . . or, on the other hand, as an activity which is unquestionably good for the individual and society.
>
> (D.H. Hargreaves, 1982: 32)

As far as the United Kingdom is concerned, the European Sports Charter 'Sport for All' (1975) has provided a framework for the creation of a network of sports provision that runs from the school level, to the community level and to adult society at large (Sports Council, 1982, 1988; Scottish Sports Council, 1989). In particular, as part of a process of basing provision on a philosophy of lifelong leisure provision, the social, recreational and sporting needs of adolescents have been clearly recognised and acknowledged. Given the clear consensual framework within which sport is incorporated into society, we may ask to what extent young people are willing consumers of the opportunities thus provided? We might also query the simple assumptions that are made as to the positive benefits accruing from such involvement.

If the amount of time and money spent on the activity is anything to go by, then sport is one of the major interests of contemporary society. More than half of the population is believed to take part in a sport at least once each week (General Household Survey, 1991) and it is estimated that the sponsorship of sports goods and equipment involves hundreds of millions of pounds each year (Butson, 1983). The school curriculum still finds a place for sport amidst an increasingly crowded programme, while the government office of Minister for Sport testifies to the political significance of the activity.

There are some who argue that sport is all pervasive in advanced Western industrial societies. In the light of the growing international interest in such events as the World Cup or the Olympic Games, perhaps these claims need to be revised upwards. At the very least it would seem reasonable to concur with Kenyon's assertion that 'the cognitive world of most people includes sports' (Kenyon, 1969: 79–80). This chapter examines how such awareness is translated into attitudes and behaviour.

A useful starting point in examining participation in sport is Kenyon's classification of types of involvement. According to Kenyon (1969) involvement in sport can take place on two different levels. Primary involvement in sport includes all forms of participation while secondary involvement refers to both the consumption of sport (by coaches and fans) and the production of sport (by manufacturers of sports goods and sports promoters). Refinements to Kenyon's model are made by Edwards (1973). A new dimension is added to take account of the degree of involvement, direct and indirect. Thus, according to Edwards, primary involvement embraces the direct involvement of players and the indirect involvement of coaches and trainers, while secondary involvement includes the direct involvement of producers of sport such as the owners of clubs and promoters and the indirect involvement of consumers of sports such as fans and relations of those involved at the primary level. Clearly then there are a number of ways of being involved in sport. How then do we end up as players and fans?

SOCIALISATION INTO SPORT

Pathways to involvement in sport at whatever level can be understood as part of a process of learning. Although we often hear the phrase 'a born athlete', sportsmen and sportswomen are made rather than born. Our involvement as spectator or participant then can be traced to the 'assimilation and development of skills, knowledge, values, dispositions and self-perceptions' (Snyder and Spreitzer, 1978) that inform our adoption of a particular social role. In short, we are socialised into sport at whatever level.

The process of learning a social role takes place within a variety of contexts, the relevance of these settings varying according to our stage in the lifecycle. Three principal agencies of childhood socialisation have been identified: the family, the school and the peer group (Elkin and Handel, 1972). As the first and most immediate context of learning, the family's influence on our uptake of sport cannot be overestimated. Orlick (1972), for instance, has shown that the family is a significant factor in influencing participation. Two major elements appear to be directly related to attraction towards and avoidance of sports participation: the availability of significant role models (i.e. parents) for the young person; and sports-related reinforcement as evidenced by parental expectations, encouragement and support. Some studies have shown how gender-based sporting stereotypes are communicated by parents. For example, Snyder and Spreitzer (1976) found gymnastics the subject of more encouragement in relation to girls' participation than basketball because of the former's perceived 'lady-like' qualities. Parental influence has also been noted in sports participation among élite athletes with fathers acting as one of the main agents responsible for participation at this level (Kenyon and McPherson, 1973; Robinson and Carron, 1982). Similarly, 1991 YPLL survey data for the younger two cohorts (13–16 years) illustrate the differential impact of parental influence on young people's involvement in competitive and recreative sport (Table 4.1).

More than a third of males between the ages of 13 and 16 years in the YPLL study reported that they played competitive sport because 'My parents like me to do it', while less than a quarter of females were so influenced. Young males, aged 13–14 years, are particularly influenced by parents with respect to involvement in competitive sport. Overall, parental influence is stronger with respect to competitive sport, but in general the influence of parents on sport involvement declines with age.

In addition to exerting pressure on young people to play sport, parents are also found to promote sports participation through example. Evidence from the YPLL panel study highlights the extent to which parents provide role models for their children in sport (Hendry *et al.*, 1989). Thus the fathers of children in school sports teams are more likely either to play sport themselves or to be involved in the organisation of sport, compared with the

Table 4.1 Percentage of sport participants claiming influence of family on involvement (13–16 years)

	Males (%)	Females (%)
Competitive sport		
13–14 years	52	27
15–16 years	27	18
All	39	24
Recreative sport		
13–14 years	25	21
15–16 years	10	10
All	18	15

Source: YPLL survey 1991

fathers of children not in a school sports team. Also the influence of the family on sport is further confirmed by the finding that parents are second only to friends as fellow participants in sport played by children outside school. Finally, parental aid in the form of financial assistance to pursue sport, the provision of transport to and from sports events and simply making children aware of what sport is available in the area further testify to the importance of the family on young people's involvement in sport (Hendry, 1971).

The history of the role of the school in socialising children into sport is well documented. From early concerns with the development of the appropriate physical and social attributes befitting the children of the middle class (J. Hargreaves, 1979; Fletcher, 1984) to a concern with providing more general physical fitness and health among the population at large (Scraton, 1986) through to the more recent promotion of active lifestyles (Almond, 1983), the school has served to communicate the idea of physical education and sport as beneficial. As one of the major institutions in the lives of young people, often standing as the first agency outside the family with calls upon a child's loyalties and sentiments (Elkin and Handel, 1972), the significance of the school's ethos in relation to sport is considerable. Likewise, the role of individual teachers can affect a child's take up of sport. In a study of school sports carried out by Hendry (1978) the perceptions of physical education teachers as to certain social and physical characteristics among the pupils were seen to influence the pupils' sports attitudes and performance, both immediate and possibly in the long term. Thus pupils considered by the physical education teacher to be enthusiastic, friendly, popular, physically attractive and possessing physical skills were more favourably treated and consequently had more positive attitudes to sport, were more likely to play competitive sport at school and were more likely to maintain an interest in sport in their post-school lives. More recently Hendry (1992) has discussed the implications of a 'hidden curriculum' of school sport pointing out the negative effect of the over-emphasis on organisation and competitiveness surrounding school sport which 'may hasten the flight (away from sport) and into alternative youth cultures'. All this suggests that school sports will be most liked by pupils who are highly skilled, competitive and achievement oriented. Thus in the school setting evidence indicates (Reid, 1972; Hendry, 1978; Hendry *et al.*, 1989) that it is pupils who 'do well' academically who are by and large the pupils who take part in extracurricular sports activities.

Results from the 1991 YPLL survey for the younger two cohorts (13–16 years) provide further evidence of the link between school and sports involvement. First, the extent to which the school acts as a context or setting in which to play sport is examined (Table 4.2). Clear gender differ-

Table 4.2   Percentage of sport participants by context of involvement
(13–16 years)

	School (%)	Community sports centre (%)	Sports club (%)	Other setting (%)
Competitive team sport				
Males	22	8	38	32
Females	60	6	23	11
Competitive individual sport				
Males	17	6	41	36
Females	37	7	31	25
Casual team				
Males	34	12	7	47
Females	56	13	9	22
Casual individual				
Males	21	10	14	56
Females	26	19	14	42

Source: YPLL survey 1991

ences emerged with respect to the location in which a variety of (types of)
sports are played. In particular, young women who play competitive and
team sports are much more likely than their male counterparts to do so
whilst they are at school.

The differential use of sports settings by males and females may reflect
the lack of organised sport for women outside school. However, the fact
that two-thirds of young women who play competitive team sports do so
whilst at school may also reflect the coercion of females into male formulations of sport (competition and the 'team' game) within the school setting.
Historically such interpretations can be linked to the evolution of sport as a
male institution which specifically proscribed female involvement (Mason,
1988). Male formulations of sport continue to predominate in contemporary society and women continue to be under-represented within sport
(Scraton, 1985, 1986; Fasting, 1987).

Next, dividing the 1991 YPLL sample of 13–16 year olds into three
sporting subgroups based on the nature of their involvement in sport as
competitors, recreational players and non-participants, analysis showed
that competitors are more likely to have support in the sport they play from
teachers and other adults (beyond the family). Furthermore competitors are
more likely to seek outside (adult) organisation in their sport. This contrasts

with the desire to be left alone (to organise their own sport) expressed by recreational players. Finally, competitors were more likely to assess their school experiences as positive. The study shows, therefore, how the ethos of sport (consistent with the dominant school ethos) is internalised by a certain section of the school pupil population and hints at the role of teachers in shaping sports involvement among young people. Conformity and subordination of the self can be important elements of socialisation within sports contexts, and sport in general can be regarded as a primary means of conservative socialisation (Snyder and Spreitzer, 1978). Thus many young people who participate in organised sports associate closely with the values of their parents, teachers and coaches.

Hendry (1983) has suggested that for those pupils who are part of the 'pro-school' subculture, sport can be seen not only as an opportunity for recreation but also as an occasion for demonstrating a wide range of social skills and for further identification with school values. By contrast, the formation of a school-based subculture which is anti-sport and anti-school can be seen as a reaction to the tendency of teachers to label, grade and select pupils in their own image. In fact, there is a general decline in sports involvement across the school years. The constraints and opportunities offered within the school setting contrast with many young people's leisure interests where the emphasis is on informal social activities centred on friends and peers (J.C. Coleman and Hendry, 1990). As was noted in Chapter 3, sports involvement can be regarded as one aspect of the transition across the adolescent years from adult-led leisure groups and organisations through casual peer-oriented groups to commercial leisure contexts. The influence of the peer group on sports involvement is now considered.

Analysis of 1991 YPLL data for the younger two cohorts provides some insights into the relationship between peers and sport. To begin with these young people are more likely to play sport with friends compared with any other grouping, such as family members. The findings also show how friends promote involvement in sport simply by being fellow participants. Thus almost three-quarters of the males and just over half of the females (aged 13–16 years) played competitive sport because 'my friends play and we have a good time together'. Also, more than three-quarters of both males and females within these age groups played recreative sport for similar reasons (Table 4.3).

The influence of friends on participation in competitive sports is seen to increase between the ages of 13–14 years and 15–16 years for both males and females, while influence on participation in recreative sport remains relatively unchanged. Such a trend contrasts sharply with the decline in parental influence on sports involvement. These findings are consistent with focal theories of adolescent development which cite the growing

Table 4.3   Percentage of sport participants claiming influence of friends on involvement (13–16 years)

	Males (%)	Females (%)
Competitive sport		
13–14 years	66	50
15–16 years	76	55
All	71	52
Recreative sport		
13–14 years	76	78
15–16 years	80	77
All	78	77

Source: YPLL survey 1991

influence of peers at this age (J.C. Coleman and Hendry, 1990). Interestingly, when young people of a similar age (13–16 years) from the 1989 YPLL survey were asked why they had given up playing a particular sport in the past two years, the main reasons cited were a lack of time to practice, loss of interest and the fact that other activities had assumed more importance. Again these findings are consistent with focal theories of adolescent development which propose a shift in emphasis from organised through casual and towards commercial leisure interests.

Collectively then, the three principal agents of socialisation in the lives of young people – the family, the school and the peer group – serve to orient the young person towards new beliefs and practices. As was demonstrated, however, these agents are not necessarily consistent in the messages they convey. Hence the outcome is sometimes confusing and contradictory.

INFLUENCES ON YOUNG PEOPLE'S INVOLVEMENT IN SPORT

So far the influences of family, school and peers have been explored, but other (often related) factors may be just as important. Attention is now turned to an examination of three of these: namely, gender, age and social class. The findings presented here are based on 1991 YPLL survey data which is drawn from a core of longitudinal cases (number of cases n = 1,666). These young people were between 13 and 24 years of age in 1991. Individuals in the younger two cohorts (13–14 years and 15–16 years) were still at school, while those in the older four cohorts were beyond the minimum school-leaving age.

Looking at the previous research, measures of involvement in sport have in general been study specific, making comparisons difficult if not impossible. Thus some studies adopt an 'open-ended' approach to sports involvement, allowing respondents to report on as many activities as they wish, while others have limited reporting to specific types of sport. Some studies define time-limits for involvement, for example being interested only in sport played 'over the last four weeks', while others are less specific. Finally some studies are sensitive to seasonal factors in involvement, while others do not take account of such variation. In summary, therefore, caution is required in interpreting reported levels of sports involvement and careful attention should be paid to the (specific) parameters involved.

Two general measures of sports involvement were derived from the 1991 YPLL survey questionnaire, although the level of detail in the questionnaire allows for considerable refinement of these measures. The first was frequency of involvement, which was assessed in terms of weekly participation in at least one of an inventory of thirty-nine sports or physical activities. The second was type of involvement and this was assessed in terms of a threefold categorisation: namely, those who currently play competitive sport, those who currently play sport for recreation only and those who are currently non-participants. The categorisation was constructed from items relating to current monthly participation in competitive individual, competitive team, casual individual and casual team sport.

First a general picture of the sports involvement of the YPLL sample of young people in 1991 (aged 13–24 years) is given. Overall this picture is in line with national statistics (General Household Survey, 1987). The YPLL data shows that three-quarters of young men play sport on a weekly basis while only two-thirds of young women do so. Focusing on team sport, two-thirds of young men currently play team sports while only one-third of young women do so. In terms of the type of sport played, amongst young men one-half play competitive sport, one-third play sport for recreation alone and one-sixth are currently non-participants, while amongst young women one-quarter are competitive players, one-half are recreative players and one-quarter are non-participants. These and other findings relating to gender are discussed in detail below, but it is worth noting here that in general young women play sport less frequently than young men, and they play less competitive sport and less team sport. For them, the emphasis where sport is played at all is on sport for recreation.

Next, broad sociocultural background influences are considered. The YPLL study was based on school catchment areas which reflected a wide diversity of socioeconomic and cultural backgrounds. Nevertheless, a detailed examination of ten different catchment areas in 1991 provides little evidence for consistent differences in patterns of sports involvement between areas. As Rodgers (1974) notes, individual differences in young people's perceptions may be of more importance. Indeed evidence from the same respondents' comments at the time of the 1989 questionnaire highlight the importance of perception in relation to sports involvement. For example, young people living in one of the new towns studied differed in their assessment of the sporting amenity of the area:

> There is not enough sports facilities in New Town, other than that it's a great town.
>
> (Steven, aged 12 years)

> the sporting facilities in New Town are good.
>
> (Lorna, aged 12 years)

> I think the sports facilities will be all right in New Town when it has all been done up (i.e. ice rink).
>
> (Michele, aged 12 years)

Turning to the influences of gender and age on sports involvement, the findings show that young men play sport more frequently than young women across adolescence and that for both sexes weekly involvement in sport declines prior to leaving school (Table 4.4). This decline continues beyond the end of compulsory schooling (at 16 years of age) and the largest drop occurs at the minimum school-leaving age. This is true of both young men and young women, but it is more marked for young women.

The type of sports involvement of young men and young women is also different (Table 4.4). Young women are less likely than young men to be competitors and are more likely either to play sport for fun or not at all. For young men, while there is a gradual increase in non-participation with increasing age, involvement in competitive sport remains relatively stable. By contrast, for young women the emphasis shifts from competitive to recreative sport with increasing age, and this shift is already present prior to leaving school. Further, the pattern of decreasing participation is repeated for young women but this decrease begins earlier. Patterns of involvement in team sport in general echo those observed for competitive sport (Table 4.4). Team sport is a predominantly male activity and there is a general decline in involvement with age. This decline is very gradual for young men, while amongst young women the decline is much more marked and begins before the end of compulsory schooling at 16 years of age with the largest drop occurring at the minimum school-leaving age.

Looking at the influence of social class background (as characterised by parental occupation) there is little evidence for significant class-based

Table 4.4 Sport involvement by gender and age group

	Age group					
	13–14 (%)	*15–16 (%)*	*17–18 (%)*	*19–20 (%)*	*21–2 (%)*	*23–4 (%)*
Weekly involvement in sport						
Males	96	89	77	67	65	59
Females	87	77	52	53	49	42
Type of involvement in sport						
Males						
Non-participant	12	10	16	17	21	22
Recreative only	35	37	32	38	34	26
Competitive	53	53	52	45	45	52
Females						
Non-participant	18	22	31	27	32	33
Recreative only	36	46	51	61	58	56
Competitive	46	32	18	12	10	11
Involvement in team sport						
Males	76	79	71	67	61	57
Females	66	54	30	25	22	20

Source: YPLL survey 1991

differences in sports involvement. There are neither significant differences in frequency nor type of involvement (although overall 5 per cent fewer young people from semi-skilled and unskilled social class backgrounds play sport on a weekly basis).

However, when the analysis is extended to consider young people's own socioeconomic position (i.e. in full-time education, unemployed, employed full time in a skilled occupation etc.) clear class-based differences emerge. As can be seen from Table 4.5, type of involvement is related to current labour market position. Amongst young men, those in semi-skilled or unskilled manual jobs are more likely to be non-participants, while amongst young women, those in semi-skilled or unskilled manual jobs and housewives are more likely to be non-participants. Young women in full-time education and those who are currently unemployed are more likely to play sport, although such involvement among unemployed young women is mainly recreative.

Table 4.5   Sport involvement by current socioeconomic status (17–24 years)

	Full-time education (%)	Employed 1/2 (%)	Employed 3 (%)	Employed 4/5 (%)	Un-employed (%)	Non-employed (%)
Males						
Non-participant	16	18	14	38	25	–
Recreative only	32	30	34	28	26	–
Competitive	52	52	52	32	49	–
Females						
Non-participant	23	32	33	45	23	41
Recreative only	58	59	56	39	68	56
Competitive	19	9	11	16	9	3

Source: YPLL survey 1991

Notes: 1/2, Registrar General's professional and intermediate classes; 3, Registrar General's skilled non-manual and manual classes; 4/5, Registrar General's semi-skilled and unskilled classes.

SPORTS ATTITUDES

By way of offering insight into the differential nature of sports involvement among the young people, an index of sporting attitudes was derived from a principal components analysis of seven questionnaire items (Table 4.6).

Looking first at the distribution of scores on the index with respect to age, gender and the type of sport played (Table 4.7), the results show how competitors are generally positive and non-participants negative about sport. Positive attitudes decline between the ages 13–14 years and 15–16

Table 4.6   Questionnaire items relating to 'attitude to sport' index

Attitudes to sport

Sport gives you a healthy, fit body
Sport keeps you mentally fit and alert
There's no point in doing sport unless you've got a natural talent
You give up too much if you go on with sport once you leave school
It's a shame that employers don't give time for sport
Sport is a good way of meeting and keeping up with friends
Sport is only for those who can afford it

Source: YPLL survey 1991

Table 4.7 Mean score on 'attitude to sport' index by type of sport involvement

	Age group					
	13–14	*15–16*	*17–18*	*19–20*	*21–2*	*23–4*
Males						
Non-participant	–0.2	–0.5	–0.5	–0.8	–0.8	–0.6
Recreative only	0.0	–0.2	0.1	0.0	–0.2	0.0
Competitive	0.4	0.4	0.4	0.6	0.2	0.4
Female						
Non-participant	–0.1	–0.4	–0.5	–0.6	–0.5	–0.6
Recreative only	0.0	–0.1	0.0	0.0	–0.1	0.0
Competitive	0.3	0.2	0.5	0.7	0.3	0.5

Source: YPLL survey 1991

years, although thereafter no further deterioration occurs. Thus sporting attitudes are 'set' prior to the minimum school-leaving age being reached. Given the earlier findings which suggest that females generally play less sport than males, it is perhaps surprising that overall there are no significant differences in the sports attitudes of young men and young women. Hence young women are apparently as positive as young men about sport and its benefits and yet they are less likely to be participants. However, the earlier findings also show that female sport is predominantly recreative and male sport is predominantly competitive and that young women are notable by their absence from team sports. Taken together these results suggest that for young women opportunities for participation are more limited and that male formulations of sport predominate.

Finally, a similar analysis was carried out in terms of sports attitudes and social class. The lack of association noted earlier between social class of origin and the type of sport played was manifest again with respect to sports attitudes. However, as previously, differences were noted in terms of the current socioeconomic position of the young people themselves (Table 4.8). Thus, young people of both sexes in full-time education and those employed in 'middle class' occupations are more likely to be positive about sport, perceiving it to be beneficial in terms of its association with both mental and physical health and the opportunities it affords for making friends, while unemployed males and full-time housewives are more likely to hold negative attitudes about sport, seeing it as the preserve of those with natural talent and as costly in time and effort if engaged in beyond the school years.

Table 4.8 Mean score on 'attitude to sport' index by current socioeconomic status (17–24 years)

	Full-time education	Employed 1/2	Employed 3	Employed 4/5	Un-employed	Non-employed
Males	0.2	0.2	0.0	–0.2	–0.7	–
Females	0.2	0.1	–0.1	–0.3	–0.1	–0.6

Source: YPLL survey 1991

Notes: See Table 4.5.

In sum, therefore, age, gender and current socioeconomic circumstances can be understood as three principal dimensions of sports involvement, according to which differential patterns emerge. Taken together they suggest that sport, at the direct primary level, is enjoyed more by young people in early rather than late adolescence, by males rather than females and by young people currently in full-time education rather than young people in semi-skilled and unskilled jobs. These findings are once again consistent with leisure focal theory. As was argued in the previous chapter, the adolescent's leisure focus generally shifts from adult organised, through casual peer-oriented activities, towards commercially organised leisure; with sports involvement being a part of this general transition. Within this framework the differential effects of gender and social class can influence patterns of leisure involvement. For example, the earlier physical, psychological and social maturity of young women may mean that they make these transitions earlier than many young men.

BEING A FAN

Are influences on young people's primary involvement (as a player) also important to involvement at the secondary level (as a fan) and is there a connection between the player and the sports fan? Various explanations have been offered for the phenomenon of the 'fan'. Beisser (1966) suggested that being a fan is associated with a need to 'belong' to a group (which he regarded as particularly acute in contemporary urban societies) while Thompkins (1973) proposed that being a fan provides a socially sanctioned outlet for emotion. Such explanations can only be part of the story (Edwards, 1973), as findings from the 1991 YPLL survey show. Young people who are sports fans tend also to be players. Thus for most young people being a fan would appear to be another expression of their acceptance of the dominant (sports) culture.

Looking at the results in detail, a third of young people could be described as fans since they attend a sports fixture at least once a fortnight. When asked about attitudes to sport, the fan (irrespective of gender or age) displays a more positive attitude to sport (in terms of physical, psychological and social benefits) compared with those who are not fans. Reflecting on earlier findings, those who play sport show the same favourable disposition. As with primary involvement, fans are more likely to be males rather than females (42 per cent and 27 per cent respectively) and to be younger rather than older (42 per cent and 28 per cent respectively). Indeed, looking further at the sporting profile of the fan, it is found that fans are more likely to play sport frequently and to be competitive in their involvement (Table 4.9). Further, fans maintain their allegiance to primary involvement with increasing age, although they play sport less often and there is a shift in emphasis from competitive to recreative involvement which is much more marked amongst female sports fans. It would appear then that fans in general are drawn from those young people already favourably disposed towards sport and to the values, such as competitiveness, associated with sport.

SPORT AND HEALTH

There has been recent concern within society – and the national sports councils in particular – about young people's levels of involvement in physical activity and sport. This concern has been motivated by factors such as the high incidence of cardiovascular disease in the adult population. There is a desire to inculcate active lifestyles in the young as a means of prevention. In fact, various empirical studies (Balding, 1986; Currie *et al.*,

Table 4.9 Type of sports involvement of those who attend a sports fixture more than once a month

	Non-participants (%)	Recreative only (%)	Competitive (%)	All (%)
Males				
13–16 years	4	25	71	100
17–24 years	4	30	66	100
Females				
13–16 years	11	32	57	100
17–24 years	11	64	25	100

Source: YPLL survey 1991

1987; Macintyre *et al.*, 1989) have indicated a relatively high involvement of school-aged children in regular physical activity, although some caution needs to be expressed in relation to the fact that physical education remains a compulsory part of the school curriculum for most children and this fact is built into most measures of physical activity. Hence these high levels of physical activity may in fact be illusory and in the longer term young people may fail to be socialised into the behaviours associated with healthy lifestyles.

The evidence of many researchers points towards an association between sport, exercise and physical health (Astrand, 1987; Cox, 1989) and sport, exercise and psychological well-being (Moses *et al.*, 1989; Gratton and Tice, 1989; Steptoe, 1989). Healthy and unhealthy lifestyles are discussed in detail in Chapter 8. Findings from the 1987 YPLL survey show that in mid-adolescence young people can indeed be characterised as leading relatively healthy or unhealthy lifestyles and that such 'ways of living' are associated with levels and types of involvement in sport.

A number of measures of general physical and mental health were included in the 1991 YPLL survey. All of them, however, relied on the young person's self-assessment of their own condition. A measure of self-assessed general health was based on the General Household Survey (OPCS, 1989) question: 'Over the last 12 months how has your health been?' Respondents were also asked if they had a 'disability or long-standing illness' and whether this 'limited' their activities. Finally, a measure of psychological well-being was derived from the General Health Questionnaire (GHQ12) (Goldberg and Williams, 1988).

Using these subjective measures of health status it was found that the associations between self-assessed health and type of sport played (competitive, recreative or non-participant) are markedly different for young men and young women (Table 4.10). Amongst adolescent males, non-participants are less likely to report 'good' general health, while competitors are more likely to do so. Finally, amongst males non-participation is associated with psychological stress. By contrast, amongst young women in general there is little evidence to suggest a consistent pattern of associations between self-assessed health and type of sport played. These findings are consistent with male formulations of sport as essentially competitive team games. From this perspective, males link participation with self-perceptions of physical and mental health.

SUMMARY

In drawing this chapter to a close it is worth re-emphasising the three major points that have been made. First, sport is learned behaviour. The

Table 4.10 Self-assessed health status by type of sports involvement

	Non-participant (%)	Recreative only (%)	Competitive (%)	All (%)
Percentage reporting general health as good in last twelve months				
Males	70	73	82	77
Females	67	69	67	68
Percentage reporting limiting disability or long-term illness				
Males	11	6	6	7
Females	7	6	6	6
Percentage reporting psychological ill health (GHQ12 > 2)				
Males	33	24	24	25
Females	35	34	31	33

Source: YPLL survey 1991

knowledge, motivation and opportunity needed to play sport are made available through a process of socialisation. Such a process takes place in a variety of settings which variously promote and discourage participation. It was shown how parents are particularly influential in providing role models, 'pressure' and concrete assistance which affect the sporting behaviour of young people. Such influence, however, was also shown to decrease as young people grow older, so that by the age of 15–16 years it was friends who were promoting involvement or influencing non-participation. Having friends as fellow participants was a major factor in encouraging involvement in both recreative and competitive sport at this age. School was also shown to be an important factor in the sports involvement of young people. Traces of the 'hidden curriculum' were to be found in the link between positive school attitudes and the likelihood of playing competitive sport. Further it was noted that young women's participation in competitive and team sports was often limited to the school context. This may reflect both the lack of facilities for women outside the school setting and the coercion of women into male formulations of sport whilst at school.

Second, sport participation was shown to be widespread among young people, although age, gender and social class differences were also noted. While highlighting the decline in sports involvement with age, the findings drew attention to the timing of such a process, which, it was shown, clearly begins prior to the minimum school-leaving age being attained. This is consistent with leisure focal theory which suggests that the transition from adult-organised leisure clubs and activities towards more informal peer-oriented pursuits occurs at this stage of adolescent development. Combined with other results which show how positive attitudes to sport decline between the ages of 13–14 years and 15–16 years but remain fairly stable thereafter, the results call attention to the strategic importance of schools in the promotion of sport. Also, it was noted that within the overall decline in sports involvement across the adolescent years significant differences exist between males and females with respect to the type of sport played. Thus, again between the ages of 13–14 years and 15–16 years, a significant shift in sporting behaviour occurs: young women move from being competitors to being recreative sport players around this time. By contrast, young men remain relatively stable in their sporting subgroups across the adolescent years and into early adulthood. If ways are to be found to promote greater sports involvement among females, recognition of this fact must be acknowledged in any policy initiatives. The findings also highlight the fact that the majority of young people who are sports fans also play sport. In other words, for most young people being a sports fan reflects a more general interest in and commitment to sport.

Finally the chapter examined the relationship between sport and self-assessed health. Amongst young men perceptions of health are linked to type of involvement in sport. By contrast, there is no clear evidence for such a link between health and sport amongst young women. However, a more detailed examination of adolescent lifestyles in Chapter 8 shows that sports involvement is associated with relatively healthy and unhealthy lifestyles.

5   School and work

INTRODUCTION

In this chapter we examine young people's transition from school into the youth labour market and post-compulsory education. This transition towards adult status is a complex and often difficult one for many young people in contemporary British society. Evidence as to the importance of labour market position in the lives of older adolescents is presented elsewhere in the book: in Chapters 3 and 4, for example, we found that patterns of leisure involvement and sports participation were clearly related to labour market position; and it will be shown in Chapter 8, for example, that young people's health and health behaviours are also linked to their present labour market position. In this chapter, however, we prefer to examine the transition itself in some detail, rather than focus on the impact that career trajectories and current socio-economic circumstances may have on young people's lives.

To this end the chapter first examines young people's attitudes towards their school experience. The future educational and employment intentions of young people in mid-adolescence are then considered. We next look at the distribution of school level qualifications amongst young people in later adolescence. Following this, we shift the focus of the chapter away from the school context and towards young people's labour market involvement. The relationship between labour market position and school qualifications is analysed, as are the links between young people's current labour market position and their social class of origin. Finally we analyse attitudes to work amongst older adolescents. In other words, the chapter examines the educational and occupational transitions young people make between mid-adolescence and late adolescence.

SCHOOL VALUES

The two decades of the 1970s and 1980s saw Britain move away from selective education to a system of comprehensive schools which were supposed to contain a mixture of social backgrounds and abilities. Thus by 1990 almost all young people of secondary school age in the public sector were in comprehensive education (in 1990 only 7 per cent of British secondary school children attended independent fee-paying schools).

Despite the stated aims of the comprehensive system, in the past such schools have often contained two groups of pupils with markedly different values, attitudes and aspirations 'under the one roof' (Hendry and McKenzie, 1978). Pupils' pro-and anti-school subcultures appeared to be as firmly entrenched within comprehensive schools as they had been in selective and non-selective schools (e.g. D.H. Hargreaves, 1967; Ball, 1981). Thus it was argued that within the comprehensive system there remained a substantial core of young people who dismissed the idea of staying on at school and also that this was based on a subculture and social system which rejected both the values promoted by school and the process of schooling itself (Carter, 1972). The 'inappropriate' nature of much of what was taught in many secondary schools was well illustrated by the aspirations and awareness of future prospects displayed by working class pupils in Willis's (1977) and Corrigan's (1979) case studies. These working class pupils saw secondary education as a 'confidence trick' and were totally disengaged from it. More recently Meighan (1986) has pointed out that links between social class, educational attainment and life chances have been consistently established in research studies in the United Kingdom.

There appear to be gender differences in the ways in which anti-school subcultures are expressed. Resistances to schooling for young women often take on a different form: for example, they may reject the formulation of girls as neat, polite, passive and hard-working (McRobbie, 1978); or they may resort to the 'silent sullen stare' used in classroom encounters (Griffin, 1981). However, in general, young women apparently display more overt conformity to the values promoted by school: but for some young women such conformity may simply mask a rejection of school as irrelevant.

Changes in the youth labour market in the 1980s have also had an impact on young people's attitudes towards school. The removal of the prospect of employment may encourage some adolescents to reject both an academic and a vocational school curriculum. Justifications of schooling in vocational terms are met with the response that school-based qualifications are no guarantee of employment (Hartley, 1985). Yet, as Coffield *et al.* (1986) have pointed out, leaving school, starting work and associating with adults are often judged by young people as central to the process of growing up. For some adolescents there is a clear conflict between the values of schooling and the social and economic 'signs and symbols' of approaching adulthood. From this perspective many school-leavers regard the education system as having completely failed to equip them for what they see as the demands of adult society (e.g. Keil, 1978; Youthaid, 1979; Pollock and Nicholson, 1981; West and Newton, 1983).

EDUCATIONAL – OCCUPATIONAL TRANSITIONS

Until the last decade the majority of young people travelled along well-signposted career trajectories (K. Roberts, 1984). Their home background and educational streams enabled them to anticipate their initial occupations and, realistically, the types of adult employment to which these early jobs would lead. With the re-emergence of youth unemployment in recent years the transition to adult society has become more problematic (Wallace, 1986).

In 1986 the UK Economic and Social Research Council launched a major longitudinal study of young people in four British labour markets (Bynner, 1987). 'Career trajectories' were identified by K. Roberts (1987) as a central organising concept in this study. Such career trajectories were regarded as being very much related to opportunity structures within local labour markets. There has been much debate, however, concerning the relative influence of individual choice and of opportunity structures in shaping young people's entry into labour markets (K. Roberts and Parsell, 1988). What is clear is that by the late 1980s – in comparison with previous generations of young people – entry routes were both diverse and complex (K. Roberts and Parsell, 1990).

At the time of the 1987 YPLL survey – despite a background of uncertainty within a contracting labour market – just under half of all Scottish young people still left school at the minimum leaving age of 16 years (Raffe and Courtenay, 1988), although the trend through the 1980s and into the 1990s has been towards staying on at school and then going on to further and higher education. Within this overall picture of expansion of the post-compulsory secondary and tertiary education sectors there exist important class-based differences. National data sets confirm that young people from the middle classes are more likely than working class adolescents to stay on to gain better qualifications and that they are more than twice as likely to enter higher education.

Associations between duration in (secondary) education and post-school careers do not guarantee, however, that 'more' qualifications can be equated with 'better' employment opportunities (Ashton and Maguire, 1986). A combination of structural arrangements within youth labour markets and wider normative constraints – in relation to gender for example – serve to mitigate the potential effects of additional years in school. For some staying on at school leads to 'downward status mobility' in terms of eventual post-school careers, with many moving from 'academic school courses to non-advanced further education . . . [or] from school to Youth Training Schemes' (Raffe and Courtenay, 1988) or to low status clerical and shop work (Dex, 1987).

The British government's response to current labour market conditions – and in particular youth unemployment – attempts to address an alleged mismatch between school-leavers' capabilities and occupational requirements in areas such as the service and high-technology sectors. These sectors – it is claimed – contain the best hopes for future job creation. Hence the case for the Technical and Vocational Education Initiative, the Youth Training Scheme (now called Training, Enterprise and Education) and the Sixteen to Eighteen Action Plan. However, attempts to tighten the bonds between schooling and job requirements and to strengthen young people's vocational orientations seem problematic. Educational solutions to the disappearance of jobs for adolescents produce diminishing returns (Bates *et al.*, 1984) and the vocational skills of today may well be outdated for use in future society (Holt, 1983). J.S. Coleman and Husen (1985) have pointed out that these educational practices may simply be helping to create a new underclass. They claimed that, within secondary schools, a tail-end abandons hope and effort, and sometimes attendance, long before the official leaving date.

ATTITUDES TO SCHOOL

The 1987 YPLL survey questionnaire for the 13–20 age range included a nine item inventory concerning young people's attitudes towards their school years. Those young people who had already left school were asked to provide a retrospective assessment of their experiences. Data relating to three of these items are considered here: an overall assessment of school as a positive experience; responses to teachers' authority; and attitudes towards truancy. As can be seen from Table 5.1 most young people regarded school – on the whole – as an enjoyable experience. This generally positive attitude towards school was tempered, however, by the fact that around half of the young people surveyed resented teachers' authority, and for a substantial minority disaffection with school was translated into truancy.

Looking at the data in Table 5.1 in more detail, variations in attitudes towards school were found with respect to both gender and age. In general, young women were more positive about school, they were less resentful of authority (or had less experience of direct conflict with authority) and they were less likely to consider truanting from school than were their male contemporaries. The changing pattern of attitudes towards school with

Table 5.1 Attitudes to school by gender and age group

	Age group			
	13–14 (%)	15–16 (%)	17–18 (%)	19–20 (%)
Males				
On the whole I like (liked) being at school	69	58	66	65
I get (got) fed up with teachers telling me what to do	51	54	45	44
I am (was) delighted to find an excuse to stay away from school	31	36	35	36
Females				
On the whole I like (liked) being at school	82	69	78	78
I get (got) fed up with teachers telling me what to do	40	44	37	35
I am (was) delighted to find an excuse to stay away from school	17	25	24	25

Source: YPLL survey 1987

increasing age was much the same for both sexes however. Both young men and young women were in general least positive about school in mid-adolescence. Disaffection with authority also peaked at this time. As was noted above young people's attitudes towards school in late adolescence were largely retrospective. This may explain why attitudes towards truancy amongst young people at this stage of adolescence were similar to those reported by young people in mid-adolescence, whereas problems related to authority were regarded by older adolescents as less of an issue.

Turning to class-based differences in school attitudes, the data in Table 5.2 highlight the presence of significant social class gradients. Young people from non-manual social class backgrounds were less likely to report conflict with authority and they were also less likely to contemplate truancy. In summary the above findings suggest that young women were more likely than young men to conform to the dominant school culture. This would also appear to be true in general of young people from the middle classes. Finally disaffection with school was most marked in mid-adolescence at a time when young people were beginning to make the break from the compulsory educational system.

Table 5.2   Attitudes to school by gender and social class of head of household (13–20 years)

	Occupation of head of household		
	---	---	---
	Non-manual (%)	Manual (%)	Unemployed (%)
Males			
On the whole I like (liked) being at school	69	62	57
I get (got) fed up with teachers telling me what to do	45	52	55
I am (was) delighted to find an excuse to stay away from school	28	36	40
Females			
On the whole I like (liked) being at school	80	74	74
I get (got) fed up with teachers telling me what to do	36	42	45
I am (was) delighted to find an excuse to stay away from school	18	24	24

Source: YPLL survey 1987

FUTURE INTENTIONS

The future intentions of young people from the 13–14 and 15–16 year old age groups in relation to education and employment were then examined. These young people were still within the statutory education system. Four items relating to education and employment were considered: the useful-ness of the school experience; confidence and ability to secure employ-ment; the priority given to securing employment as soon as possible; and the intention to go on to further or higher education before entering employment. These four items were chosen in order to examine young people's attitudes to the impending divide at the age of 16 between continuing in full-time education and early entry into the youth labour market.

There were significant gender- and class-based differences in relation to education and employment as can be seen from the data presented in Table 5.3. Young men were more likely than young women to place a high priority on starting work as soon as possible and they were less prepared to defer entering the labour market in order to extend the period spent in

Table 5.3 Attitudes to education and future employment by gender and social class of head of household (13–16 years)

	Occupation of head of household		
	Non-manual (%)	Manual (%)	Unemployed (%)
Males			
School should stick to the basics – the rest is a waste of time	17	25	28
I lack the confidence and ability to get a job	15	24	30
I regard it as very important to start work as soon as possible	26	40	51
I'll go to college or university, then get a job	49	27	17
Females			
School should stick to the basics – the rest is a waste of time	10	19	23
I lack the confidence and ability to get a job	16	23	29
I regard it as very important to start work as soon as possible	17	29	42
I'll go to college or university, then get a job	61	40	33

Source: YPLL survey 1987

full-time education. Males were also more likely than females to regard much of their school experience as a waste of time.

A similar pattern of differences was found with respect to social class background. Young people from non-manual backgrounds were least likely to regard school-based education as largely a waste of time and they were most likely to intend continuing on to further or higher education. Interestingly they were also more likely than any other group to be both confident about and to consider themselves to have the abilities needed to secure employment. By contrast almost half of the young people who came from a home background where the head of the household was unemployed regarded starting work as soon as possible as a priority, although they were more likely than any other group to feel they lacked the confidence and ability to do so. They were also more likely to feel that 'schools should stick to the basics'.

In summary, it would appear that young women at this stage of adolescence were more likely than young men of the same age to perceive education as both relevant and as a priority in terms of their future plans. This would also appear to be true of young people from middle class backgrounds. These findings complement the gender- and class-based differences reported above on more general attitudes towards school and may well anticipate the patterning of school level qualifications by gender and social class observed amongst young people in later adolescence.

SCHOOL QUALIFICATIONS

Next, the educational qualifications attained at school level by the 17–18 and 19–20 year old age groups in the 1987 YPLL sample were analysed for gender- and class-based differences. Before considering the results of this analysis some aspects of the Scottish examination system for secondary education are briefly reviewed. At the time of the first YPLL survey in 1987 young people in Scotland typically sat 'ordinary' grade Scottish Certificate of Education (SCE) examinations at the end of the fourth year of secondary school at 16 years of age. On reaching their sixteenth birthday young people could then leave school. For those who chose to stay on at school for a further year of study more advanced 'higher' grade examinations were usually attempted at the end of the fifth year. It was then possible to enter a sixth year of study in order to pursue still more advanced school level qualifications or to supplement and strengthen the qualifications already obtained. In the 1987 YPLL sample of 17–20 year olds about one-third had left secondary school without passing an SCE examination, whereas around one-quarter had passed three of more SCE higher grades (which could be regarded as the minimum requirement for entry to higher education).

Table 5.4 clearly shows that there was a notable gap between the qualifications obtained by young women and those obtained by young men. The findings suggest that overall young women performed better at school than young men although this gap disappeared as the level of qualifications obtained increased. Table 5.4 also demonstrates marked class-based differences in educational attainment. Young people from non-manual backgrounds were much more likely to obtain better qualifications at both ordinary and higher grade. For example, they were twice as likely as young people from manual backgrounds to attain the minimum requirement for entry to higher education. It is even more important, however, to note that almost half of the young people who came from a home background where the head of the household was unemployed had left secondary school with no SCE passes.

Table 5.4 Educational qualifications (school level courses) by gender and social class of head of household (17–20 years)

	Scottish Certificate of Education (SCE) examinations		
	No SCE passes *(%)*	*Five or more 'Ordinary' grades passed* *(%)*	*Three or more 'Higher' grades passed* *(%)*
Males			
Non-manual	17	65	41
Manual	36	43	17
Unemployed	54	26	15
All	35	44	24
Females			
Non-manual	13	71	42
Manual	27	46	18
Unemployed	48	34	16
All	27	51	25

Source: YPLL survey 1987

THE YOUTH LABOUR MARKET

We turn now to entry into the labour market beyond statutory secondary education. Table 5.5 details the current labour market position of young people in later adolescence amongst the 1987 YPLL sample. At 17–18 years of age, 45 per cent of young people were in full-time education (with 35 per cent still at secondary school), whilst a further 30 per cent were in full-time employment (but not on training schemes). The remaining 25 per cent were on the periphery of the labour market in youth training schemes, in part-time employment, seeking paid employment or non-employed. There was a marked drop between 17–18 and 19–20 years of age in the proportion of young people in full-time education and a corresponding increase in the proportion in full-time employment, but the proportion of young people who where neither in full-time education nor in full-time employment remained relatively static. Amongst 19–20 year olds, 25 per cent were in full-time education, whilst 50 per cent were in full-time employment. The remaining 25 per cent were on the fringes of the labour market in part-time employment, unemployed or non-employed. These

Table 5.5 Current labour market position by gender and age group for young people beyond the statutory period of secondary education

	At school	Further or higher education	Youth training	Employed full time	Employed part time	Unemployed	Non-employed
	(%)	(%)	(%)	(%)	(%)	(%)	(%)
Males							
17–18 years	37	8	8	29	1	16	1
19–20 years	–	24	–	50	3	20	3
Females							
17–18 years	34	10	11	30	3	10	2
19–20 years	–	25	–	50	7	14	4

Source: YPLL survey 1987

results highlight the diversity of routes through which early entry to the youth labour market may occur. It is also of note that there was little difference in the overall proportions of young men and young women in full-time education or in full-time employment. However, on the periphery of labour market involvement gender differences were evident. Males were more likely than females to be unemployed, whereas females were more likely than males to be in part-time employment or not seeking paid employment.

A general picture of the relationship between school qualifications and labour market position is provided by Table 5.6. In the table SCE ordinary grade passes are used to characterise the level of educational qualifications attained by young people in the YPLL sample. Ordinary grades were chosen because at the time of the 1987 YPLL survey these examinations were in general attempted at the end of the compulsory period of secondary education. The findings show that school level qualifications clearly differentiate between young people with respect to labour market position. At 17–18 years of age, it was found that those remaining in full-time education were best qualified; whereas those in training schemes and manual employment tended to be less well qualified; and the young unemployed were most likely to have poor qualifications. A similar pattern was evident for males and females at this age. It is notable that, for both sexes, poorer school qualifications would appear to present a 'choice' between lower status employment and training schemes, whilst for young people with very few qualifications unemployment seemed likely.

Two years on, at 19–20 years of age, differentiation with respect to qualifications was even more marked: those young people in full-time education were best qualified; whilst those in non-manual occupations were now also better qualified; and young people in manual employment, unemployed or non-employed were more likely to have poorer qualifications. Gender differences were apparent at this age amongst young people in paid employment. However, these differences would appear to reflect gender-based structural arrangements within the labour market: for young women non-manual jobs cannot necessarily be identified with higher status (and better qualifications). In other words, for early female entrants to the labour market occupational mobility between 17–18 and 19–20 years of age may mean moving from a low status manual job to a lower status non-manual job. To summarise the above findings, despite the diversity of routes into the youth labour market, school qualifications remained strongly linked to labour market position.

The attitudes of young people in later adolescence towards work were also examined. Data drawn from eight attitudinal items relating to work were subjected to a principal components analysis (Table 5.7). Three

Table 5.6 Percentage of young people with five or more SCE Ordinary grade passes by current labour market position, gender and age group

	Full-time education (%)	Youth training (%)	Employed non-manual (%)	Employed manual (%)	Unemployed (%)	Non-employed (%)	All (%)
			Current labour market position				
Males							
17–18 years	74	30	53	28	10	–	45
19–20 years	88	–	72	27	18	25	47
Females							
17–18 years	74	30	49	25	10	–	50
19–20 years	89	–	62	10	20	23	53

Source: YPLL survey 1987

underlying factors were identified: (i) a factor associated with the material benefits of work; (ii) a factor associated with the social benefits of work; and (iii) a factor associated with the status conferred by work. These factors were then analysed for variations with respect to gender, social class background and current labour market involvement. Looking first at gender differences it was found that males were more likely than females to identify work with material benefits. By contrast females were more likely than males to identify work with social benefits, such as maintaining friendships. Social class differences were evident with respect to the second and third factors. For example, young people who came from homes where the head of household was unemployed were more likely to consider that 'people look down on the unemployed'. Looking lastly at current labour market involvement significant differences were evident with respect to all three factors. By way of an example, young people who were neither in full-time education nor employment were more likely to perceive work as conferring status.

Finally we considered the connection between young people's social class background and their current labour market position in late adolescence, at 19–20 years of age (see Table 5.8). Before proceeding it is worth noting that, amongst young people in full-time employment, males were more likely to occupy manual positions, whereas females were more likely to occupy non-manual positions. Despite this segmentation of the labour market into 'male' and 'female' occupations, a similar patterning of differences with respect to social class of origin was found for both sexes. Young people from non-manual backgrounds were more likely than their contemporaries to be in full-time education, they were more likely to be employed in non-manual occupations, they were less likely to be employed in manual occupations and they were less likely to be unemployed. In

Table 5.7 Factors underlying attitudes towards work (17–20 years)

Factor	Attitudes to work
1 Material	Provides you with money
	Allows you to be materially independent of parents
	Makes you appreciate leisure time more
	Provides the resources to be fashionable and go out
2 Social	Is a place where you meet and make friends
	Enables you to be with other people
3 Status	People look down on the unemployed
	Provides self-worth

Source: YPLL survey 1987

complete contrast, young people from homes where the head of household was out of work were less likely than other young people to be in full-time education, they were less likely to be employed in non-manual occupations and they were more likely to be unemployed. Clearly processes of sorting in terms of eventual socioeconomic position are far from complete by late adolescence. Nevertheless, the above results suggest that, in general, young people maintain the socioeconomic position associated with their social class of origin, although there is some exchange across class boundaries.

SUMMARY

In this chapter we have examined young people's educational and occupational contexts in some detail. The findings show that, for the present generation of adolescents, the transition from school towards adult society can be a complex and difficult one. An examination of the secondary school context suggests that there remains a core of young people who reject the school process and the values promoted by school as largely irrelevant to their future role in adult society. Within the 1987 YPLL sample this anti-school culture was, in general, associated with young people from

Table 5.8   Current labour market position by gender and social class of head of household (19–20 years)

	Current labour market position				
	Full-time eduction	*Full-time non-manual employment*	*Full-time manual employment*	*Unemployed*	*Other*
	(%)	*(%)*	*(%)*	*(%)*	*(%)*
Males					
Non-manual	42	19	21	14	5
Manual	19	16	45	16	4
Unemployed	16	11	26	42	6
All	24	16	33	20	5
Female					
Non-manual	35	48	6	5	6
Manual	21	35	19	16	9
Unemployed	19	28	13	26	14
All	25	38	13	14	10

Source: YPLL survey 1987

working class backgrounds, but was most marked among young people from homes where the head of the household was unemployed. Although class-based rejection of school applied equally to both sexes, overall young women were apparently more conformist than young men. It may simply be, however, that young women express their disaffection with school in different ways.

For young people in mid-adolescence, attitudes towards school were found to be consistent with their future educational and occupational intentions. Differences in future intentions were most marked across the social classes. In this, the class-based differences in career goals found among young people in mid-adolescence anticipated well the class-based differences in labour market position found among older adolescents. It was also notable that many of those in the mid-adolescent age group who intended to enter the labour market early, felt that they lacked the confidence and abilities to make the transition successfully.

The distribution of school level qualifications among older adolescents was also consistent with the patterning attitudes towards school observed among the mid-adolescent age group. There were, for example, clear class-based differences across the range of school level qualifications. On the whole, young people from middle class homes obtained significantly better qualifications, whilst young people from homes where the household head was unemployed fared particularly badly. A strong link between labour market position and school level qualifications was also noted.

A more detailed examination of young people's labour market position in later adolescence showed that, at 17–18 years of age, entry into the labour market was often complex and uncertain and that two years on, at 19–20 years of age, the process of sorting into adult employment roles was well under way. At 17–18 years of age, a significant proportion of young people were on the fringes of the labour market – neither in full-time paid employment nor in full-time education – and amongst early entrants into the labour market who secured employment, it was found that young males tended to be in lower status manual jobs whereas employment opportunities for young women were often focused on lower status non-manual occupations.

The above picture of young people's differing educational and employment contexts was further confirmed by an examination of the relationship between social class of origin (i.e. parental class) and current socio-economic position in later adolescence (i.e. present class). It was found that young people's present labour market position was clearly related to their social class of origin. In conclusion, it would appear that there are strong links between social class background, educational–occupational trajectories and young people's life chances. Thus, any consideration of adolescent lifestyles must take account of emergent differences in young people's socioeconomic position as they make the transition from statutory schooling to non-compulsory education and the youth labour market: and it is particularly important to note the strong links between educational–occupational trajectories and social class background. We return to the relationships between young people's life chances and their behaviours, attitudes and values in Chapter 9.

6 Young people and families

INTRODUCTION

A comment I would like to make is, people don't realise how young people's parents treat them and how it makes life harder having parents that always disagree with them and pick on them.

(Elizabeth, Airdrie)

I think parents should be more informed on today's problems so they can advise their children on how to stay clear and choose for themselves . . . The problems kids have is not being able to communicate with their family. I was lucky and have understanding parents . . . I am far from being 'straight' and have been in trouble and involved in everything. I am lucky and have pulled myself out of it and have discovered there is more to live for. If all kids had more people to talk to then the teenagers today would be far better off.

(Ingrid, Aviemore)

Statements like the two above (volunteered by young people who filled in the 1987 YPLL survey) illustrate an area of adolescent life which causes much angst to both young people and their parents alike. Adolescence is typically a time when the childhood relationships with parents are re-assessed and re-negotiated as young people move towards independence and adulthood. During this period of transition, families can be both a source of strain and support.

This chapter looks at the overall role that families play in adolescent life and assesses whether changes in family structure and circumstances may be important to young people's development. The formalised structure of schooling in the Western world ensures that most family interaction occurs in so-called 'leisure time'. How do parents and their adolescent children interact in this sphere? What are the typical and enjoyed interactions between young people and their parents and what is their significance?

How are activities chosen and acceptable limits to behaviour defined and used in the leisure sphere? Are parenting styles reflected in family leisure behaviour? How are the adolescent's needs for both independence and affection worked out in balancing leisure relationships with parents and peers?

FAMILY TYPES

The family is acknowledged to be the social institution that has the most significant influence on the development of the individual. Parents act as role models, standard setters and reward dispensers in cognitive and self-concept development, in identity achievement and in sex-role identification.

We must not make the mistake of envisaging the family either as a static social institution or of consisting of one standard form. Cross-cultural studies of family arrangements and relationships show a wide diversity of roles and functions for family members, and historical analysis of our own culture shows equally obvious differences. Extended families now rarely exist within single households in our culture, and even neighbourhood networks of relatives are being gradually broken down by changed housing patterns, the need for job mobility and so on. Birth control on the scale practised since mid-century has seen a rapid diminution too in the size of family units, and altered patterns of divorce and re-marriage have brought attention to the different needs and patterns involved in 'reconstituted' families. Changing patterns of education and career expectation as well as economic necessity have brought increasing numbers of women into the workplace with significant implications for family incomes and expenditure patterns and childcare roles.

The data from the 1989 YPLL survey shows that amongst the children still at school, 14 per cent were living with a single parent and 6 per cent with a step-parent. A further 2 per cent lived in another type of family (for example, with grandparents or foster parents). Thus nearly a quarter of this sample – which is representative of the adolescent population of Scotland as a whole – were living in a family situation other than the traditional nuclear family.

In some of the study areas the proportions of children living in single parent or 'reconstituted' families were much higher. Figures for the proportion of YPLL respondents living in families falling into the categories 'nuclear', 're-combined' and 'single parent' was checked with ACORN codes for the areas they lived in. (ACORN is a census-derived index of quality and type of housing and environment.) This analysis showed nuclear families to be more likely to exist amongst those recorded as living on the better council or private housing estates and, conversely, less likely to exist amongst those living on the poorest council estates. Recombined families (those with a step-parent) seem evenly spread across all ACORN groups. Single-parent families are more likely to live on the poor council estates and less likely to live on the better council estates and private estates. Not enough of the sample resides in rural areas to make it easy to see whether there is a rural–urban distinction. Since there are also clear social class patterns amongst the distribution of family types, we could speculate that the prevalence of single parent and reconstituted families in many of Scotland's urban areas reflects the distribution of semi-skilled and unskilled workers living on housing schemes in these areas. This is borne out by analysis of the data which shows nuclear families being more likely amongst young people living in households where the father was in a manual occupation, with most single-parent families amongst the unemployed or economically inactive. However, it must be recognised that there is a certain tautology about this. Households affected by marital breakdown often consist of a single mother with no resources for childcare who is therefore unable to work.

How is this diversity of family experience reflected in young people's personal and social development? The evidence from previous studies is ambiguous and contradictory. The popular and intuitive view would be that children who undergo some trauma in terms of the break-up of the family or the effective loss of a parent will suffer in numerous and varied ways. The empirical evidence for this, however, is not easy to find. One reason is the inadequacy of data about what family circumstances adolescents actually live in. Adults cohabiting but not married are rarely recorded in surveys. Thus many of the so-called single-parent families may in reality be mis-classified. Few surveys record the recency or otherwise of marital or family break-up, and this muddies the analysis when researchers are attempting to assess whether family trauma of this kind affects young people's self-concepts or developing identity. In addition, most studies which rely on survey-type data find it impossible to establish the *quality* of relationships that exist within families. Commonsense tells us that there will be 'good' single-parent families just as there will be 'bad' intact families in which to grow up. Leo Tolstoy makes a famous remark on the pages of *Anna Karenina*, indicating that all happy families resemble each other, but that each unhappy family is unhappy in its own way.

A further problem that confounds researchers is whether the problems popularly associated with single parenthood, for example, are caused by that state itself or by the fact that such families frequently find themselves in financially straitened circumstances. In other words, it is not the problem of being a mother alone which can affect the child's emotional and social development, but the problem of being a mother with an inadequate maintenance allowance, no childcare provision, poor housing provision and all the accompanying stress.

It is for all these reasons that research has so few clear messages to tell us about family type and adolescent development. For example, some studies report that adolescent self-concepts are negatively affected by divorce (Young and Parish, 1977; Parish and Taylor, 1979; Parish and Dostal, 1980), but others have not found this to be true (Raschke and Raschke, 1979; Parish, 1981; Parish et al. 1981).

The immediate and short-term effects of divorce are often quite distressing for children and adolescents, producing feelings of fear, anger, guilt, depression and shame (Wallerstein and Kelly, 1976; Hetherington, 1979). But other work has shown that young people are often better off living with one supportive parent than with two who bicker and disagree continually (Landis, 1970; Ahlstrom and Havighurst, 1971).

Some studies have highlighted the fact that it is foolish to expect all adolescents to react in the same way to such trauma. Thus Hetherington (1979) discerned gender differences amongst children adjusting to family circumstances that had changed as a result of divorce. He speculated that boys may be exposed to more stress and aggression and may have fewer emotional supports than girls.

At another level, individual differences in coping strategies are now being explored as a better explanation of the way in which some young people seem to survive such traumas whereas others clearly suffer a great deal. There is still a need for research to address the debate about the impact of social forces versus individual differences in looking at the links between childhood adversities and adult functioning.

It seems likely that the shorthand of classifying families as 'intact' or otherwise, with the implication that the 'otherwise' is in some way problematic, does very little to advance our understanding of the dynamics of family relationships. Moreover, it may serve to perpetuate the stigmatisation and stereotyping of children and adolescents from single-parent or divorced families. Lloyd (1985) describes a study in which teachers were shown a videotape of a boy engaging in various social interactions. Half of the teachers were told that the boy was from an intact home and the other half were told that his parents were divorced. Teachers in the latter group rated the boy more negatively on two of eleven personality traits (happiness and emotional adjustment) than did teachers in the former group. Also, teachers who believed the boy's parents to be divorced rated him more negatively than the intact-family boy on his ability to cope with stress, one of five behavioural predictions teachers were asked to make.

In analysing both data and young people's comments then, we may refer to family types, but it behoves us to bear in mind all the inadequacies of data collection and all the dangers of relying on a uni-dimensional classification of young people's experiences.

FAMILY LIFE

There is some dispute about the *amount* of time young people spend with their parents as they pass through adolescence. A general perception is that the teenage years see young people spending more of their leisure time with peers and less with their families. Montemayor (1982) carried out a study in which a number of young people in America were asked via a telephone interview to account for their movements and activities over a three-day period. Adolescents spent significantly more free time with their peers or on their own than they did with their parents. However, in relation to time spent doing tasks, more time was spent with parents and less with peers.

A diary exercise with the interview panel group in the YPLL study illustrates how gradual is this transition from a childhood pattern to that of the near-adult. Young people in the panel were asked to keep a diary for a week detailing their activities hour by hour and stating what activities were undertaken and with whom for each time period.

Table 6.1 shows that leisure time spent with family halves between the 12 year olds and 18 year olds from 48 hours per week to an average for boys and girls of 23 hours per week. The amount of leisure time spent with peers consequently increases so that by 18 years of age around half the time is spent with peers. At this age boys spend more leisure time with parents than peers. The fact that girls seem to spend more leisure time with peers reinforces the claim made by Montemayor that males and females follow very different developmental pathways in the process of separating from parents and developing an independent identity. Males seem to base their identity on instrumental competence and knowledge about the external world. In pursuit of these intra-personal goals, adolescent males spend less time with parents and an increasing amount of time engaged in hobbies, sports, work and school. In contrast, females base their identity on inter-personal competence, which is more easily and appropriately achieved through interaction with peers than with parents. Females therefore take time away from parents to spend it with peers.

As with the Montemayor (1982) study, the panel data reveal that it is not just the *amount* of time spent with families that alters – it is also the type of activity involved. For example, amongst the youngest group (11 year olds) shared family activities included family outings, visits to relations and shopping trips, but by age 14 most time spent with families was restricted to meal times and television watching.

Table 6.1   Amount of leisure time spent with family versus peers over the course of one week

Panel respondents	n	Proportion of leisure time spent with family as compared with peers	
		Family (%)	*Peers* (%)
12 years			
Females	63	76	24
Males	61	79	21
15 years			
Females	54	67	33
Males	51	69	31
18 years			
Females	48	42	58
Males	47	55	45

Source: YPLL panel 1987

Such results confirm the findings of studies done by Csikszentmihalyi and Larson (1984) using time-sampling. However, an important point is made by Youniss and Smollar (1985) that this type of information, fascinating though it is in terms of illustrating the transition that young people make, does not lend itself to structural analysis – one cannot make any inferences about the characteristics of the relations detailed or assess the level of satisfaction involved in each one. They note that time *per se* may be deceptive. A more telling variable may be the quality of the interactions in the available time, a point that has been stressed in the study of mother–infant relationships.

Not everyone would accept the premise that a fundamental part of family life is the sharing of activities. Families come in all forms, some heavily committed to close domesticity and shared leisure, others using the family home as a stopping-off point on the way to individual activities. Data from the YPLL surveys are interesting, however, in demonstrating the impact of age, gender, class and family type on the sorts of domestic situations young people experience.

Young people in the 1987 under-16 YPLL sample were asked about four particular sorts of activities – eating together in the evening, working together on jobs around the house, going out on trips together and playing games or sports together. Of the four listed, eating together and going on trips together were most often shared with their family. Not surprisingly perhaps girls were more likely to record sharing jobs around the house whilst boys more often played games and sports with a family member. The differences between age groups are more striking, however.

Whilst 62 per cent of 11 year olds regularly share an evening meal with their family, only 35 per cent of 15 year olds would do so. 27 per cent of 11 and 12 year olds regularly share outings with their family compared with only 6 per cent of the 15 year olds. Shared activities in the form of games and sports undertaken with the family are a regular occurrence for 19 per cent of the 11 year olds but, again, only for 6 per cent of the 15 year olds. The dramatic fall-off in shared activities between the ages of 11 and 15 thus demonstrates the growing independence of the adolescent from the parent or family.

Family type does seem to have some impact on shared activities. Children in single-parent families were less likely to share an evening meal with their parent or to share outings. In single-parent families characterised by low income, domestic tasks may overwhelm the eldest children, especially girls. They and their parents may be deprived of leisure.

Perhaps the most important aspect of adult–adolescent relationships is the fact that adult status is looming for the young person. They must grow up and become independent of their parents. Their parents must decrease their emotional hold on their children whilst continuing to support them. It is hardly surprising that problems occur in accomplishing these difficult transitions. Analyses of the problematic behaviour of young people at this stage often overlook the important point that the process is a two-way one. Letting go can be equally difficult for parents. The need to change parental behaviours is as problematic, and the need to do so may come at a time when other factors in parents' lives cause anxiety. Interlocking identity crises for parents and adolescents increase the likelihood of disagreements between them. Issues of sexuality, life choices and achievement, changes in communication and power, changes in attachment and clashes in values provide the focus around which adolescents and their parents may find interaction difficult. Despite the potential minefield that thus exists, most adolescents and parents make the transition through adolescence and remain on good terms.

Young people in the YPLL study were asked about the quality of their relationships with parents. The results for the 1987 survey show an overwhelming percentage of young people claiming to get on well with their parents, but there are significant differences between girls and boys across the age cohorts in terms of that claim. A higher proportion of boys generally claim to get on well with their mother. Girls' relationships with their mothers clearly improve by age 19–20 years. Good relationships with father were claimed by a consistently high proportion of boys across all age groups. Girls seem to get on better with fathers in the youngest age group, and then again at age 19–20, with a slight dip in the middle years of adolescence.

Enquiries were made through the panel study in the YPLL project into what things upset happy relations within the household. On the topic of conflict and arguments both boys and girls were aware that their behaviour sometimes upset other members of the family, but a much larger proportion of boys (81 per cent) than girls (57 per cent) felt that other members of the family did things to upset them.

Young people in the 1989 YPLL survey were also asked what kind of things upset their parents. Overall, the major sources of disagreement were clearly trouble or poor performance at school, closely followed by domestic disagreements about doing chores or staying out late. However, of more significance are the figures which separate out the perceived response of mothers and fathers. Mothers were perceived to be far more likely to be upset over chores not done at home, youngsters staying out late or not confiding their problems. Fathers were seen to be less concerned/upset overall, with few indeed being involved in hearing their children's problems. Girls perceived their parents being far more worried if they were not told where their adolescent child was going than did boys.

What conclusions then are we to draw from these data? A theory that fathers are less neurotic or irascible is not really tenable. Youniss and Smollar (1985), whose figures reveal a similar pattern, indicate that it places the mother as the law-giver and arbiter of the family in most instances, thus locating her also at the source of conflict whenever there is any challenge to family norms or rules.

Further analyses were carried out to examine the effect of social class background on such domestic disputes. The children of those families in the (intermediate) social class were most likely to perceive parents (particularly their mothers) being upset by chores not done. Mothers from the (unskilled) social classes were perceived as most likely to be upset over poor performance at school, though fathers from this group were least worried. Fathers in lower socioeconomic groups were more likely to object to the friends of their adolescent children. The messages that came through from this about family cultures related to class are not clear, although the concern expressed by working class mothers about poor school performance might reflect the belief in the possibility of upward social mobility through education held by some.

Family type had some impact on how family disagreements were perceived. Children in single-parent families felt parents were less likely to be upset over chores not done than young people in other family situations.

Children in step-family situations were most conscious of the problems this raised. Mothers in step-family and single-parent situations were perceived to be considerably more upset over poor school performance than mothers in intact families, but the inverse was true for fathers. Clearly mothers take over the worrying role in the absence of the second parent. This is also borne out in the data on the topics of disagreements over adolescents not telling parents where they were going and of going about with friends that parents disapproved of. Like Lloyd (1985) we found that major conflicts seem to occur over minor issues in most families. These include such things as style of dress, hair length and musical tastes. Perhaps this may reflect the displacement of anger to issues which are less likely to disrupt family relationships.

FAMILIES TALKING

Young people under the age of 16 years were asked in the 1989 survey to reveal who they talked things over with. A list of topics was suggested and young people could nominate for each either their mother, father, a close friend of the same sex or a close friend of the opposite sex as the person they were most likely to confide in.

Parents were a first choice over friends in such areas as discussing progress at school, careers, problems at school, but not necessarily in areas relating to more personal matters. Mothers were preferred over fathers as confidantes in all areas except that of careers and sex as far as boys were concerned, and, not surprisingly, for both sexes where problems with mother were concerned. Even in the latter instance 54.8 per cent of girls preferred to talk about problems with their mother with a best friend of the same sex and only 19.6 per cent chose their father for the same purpose. Once again mothers emerge as the central figure in family life.

The most startling differences between boys and girls were in the realm of discussions about the more intimate matters, such as problems with friends, self-doubt, views about sex and so on. Nearly 70 per cent of all girls chose to confide in their mother over problems with friends, and 41.2 per cent of the boys preferred to speak to their mother about such matters. Fathers were the choice of only 3.9 per cent of the girls and 11.1 per cent of the boys in this matter. Doubts about their own abilities would be voiced to their mother by nearly half the girls and 33.2 per cent of the boys. Only 16.1 per cent of girls and 26.5 per cent of boys would speak to their fathers about a similar concern. Figures like these point to a disengagement by fathers from the affairs of most concern to many adolescents in these years of critical development.

Analysis by social class of data on these issues reveals some interesting points. Girls from professional backgrounds were the only ones as likely to talk with their father as with their mother on the subject of how well they were doing at school. Similarly girls in this class were the only ones more likely to talk through 'problems with their mother' actually with their mother (rather than with their father as was the case in all other social classes). The converse of this is that boys from this class were much less likely to perceive their father as an appropriate confidante in discussing 'problems with mother' than boys from other classes.

In single-parent families (most of them lone mothers with children) mothers, not surprisingly, become the principal confidante of their children. Thus single parents in a sense became both mother and father in discussing matters like progress at school. Where 'problems with mother' were concerned, more young people from single-parent families were likely to discuss things openly with their mother, but there was also a greater reliance on a close friend of the same sex in discussing such matters.

Some of this centrality of the mother and the marginality of many fathers comes through again in a question which aimed to look at the 'situated' aspect of young people's emotions. Thus the young people were invited to associate a humour or disposition, such as being playful or relaxed, with a family member or other person. This produced responses indicating that fathers were most often the person with whom young people felt 'distant', 'serious', 'careful what they said'. Nearly a third of young people recorded that they felt most 'relaxed' with their mother, as opposed to 9.2 per cent with their father. Over two-thirds recorded feeling most 'loved' with their mother, as opposed to 10 per cent with their father. Lest this paints altogether too rosy a picture of children basking in a warm motherly glow, we should add the corrective that mothers generally brought on the sensations of argumentativeness and selfishness in their children more than fathers did. What it all points to, as Youniss and Smollar (1985) have noted, is that mother's role in enforcing family rules brings her into conflict with her children more readily, but she is still viewed as being supportive and tender, not distanced in the way that fathers are seen.

The effects of social class on family roles and personalities are unclear. One finding of some significance perhaps is that it is the children in professional families who overwhelmingly regard their father as a 'distant' figure.

PARENTING STYLES

Data presented by Youniss and Smollar (1985) challenge, it is claimed, the views of people who express concern that contemporary parents are no longer involved in the socialisation process. They found that fathers and mothers are perceived as having standards and expectations that they want their sons and daughters to meet. Sons and daughters in turn articulate a clear sense of wanting to live up to their parents' expectations.

Certainly the data from the YPLL study confirm this. Evidence from the 1987 survey shows a high proportion of young people affirming the strong views of parents on appearance and their control over children's evening activities for instance. For girls in particular, the need to account for their movements in the evening remains strong until the very oldest cohorts.

A number of theorists have explored the *way* in which parents exercise control over their children's behaviour and choices, and this has resulted in a number of different models of family functioning. The majority of them aim to describe the most important dimensions of family functioning, and, by way of useful extension, to identify those dimensions which most effectively discriminate between 'healthy' and poorly functioning families.

Beavers and his colleagues (Beavers, 1981; Beavers and Voeller, 1983), for example, concentrated on two dimensions characterised as competence and family style. 'Competence' in this context is a multi-faceted variable comprising measures of power structure within the family, degree of negotiation and encouragement of autonomy. The style dimension is one where families are characterised on a continuum from centripetal (inward-focused) to centrifugal (outward-focused).

Thus, as Figure 6.1 attempts to show, 'healthy' families are balanced in style, with activities and loyalties focused sometimes on the family and at other times on friends and others in the community. 'Unhealthy' families, according to this model, are always low in competence and tend to extremes, being 'either strongly centripetal with intense family loyalties and activities generally centred in the family, or strongly centrifugal with weak family bonds and activities centred outside the family' (Noller and Callan, 1991: 3).

Associated with these extreme family styles are different psycho-pathologies. In centripetal families adolescents may be more likely to develop internally focused symptoms such as depression and schizophrenia. Those in centrifugal families may manifest externally focused symptoms such as general 'acting out' and delinquency.

A further model is that developed by Baumrind (1968, 1971), in which two major dimensions have been suggested as underlying parent–child relationships – parental acceptance and parental control. Baumrind uses these dimensions to identify four parenting styles; authoritarian, authoritative, neglectful and permissive, as illustrated in Figure 6.2.

The authoritarian style involves rigidly enforced rules with low acceptance. The authoritative style combines reasoned control with love and affection; i.e. it involves setting firm limits but demonstrating acceptance by explaining the reasons behind policies and by encouraging verbal give-

Figure 6.1 Family functioning characterised in terms of level of competence and family 'style'

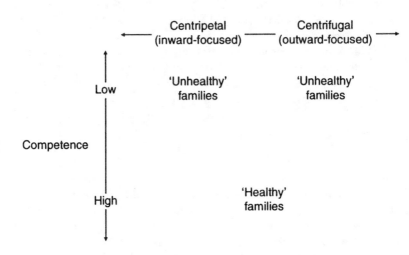

Source: Adapted from Beavers 1981

Figure 6.2 Parenting styles as interactions of parental acceptance and control

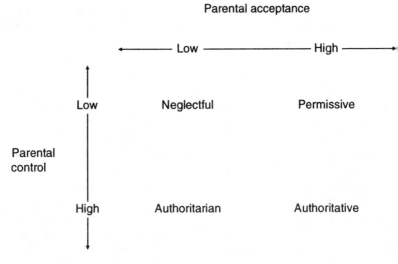

Source: Adapted from Baumrind 1971

and-take with the child. In studying the effects of three of these styles, Baumrind found that children reared with the authoritative style were the most autonomous and content with themselves, while those reared with the permissive style were judged to be the least well developed in these areas. The level of the development of the children reared by authoritarian parents was in between the first two groups.

Noller and Callan's summary of the various models of family functioning pulls these threads together:

> In general theorists agree that families should provide members with moderate levels of cohesion as well as moderate levels of flexibility about rules and roles. In addition, autonomy should be encouraged and communication clear and direct.
>
> (Noller and Callan, 1991: 3)

The internal dynamics of family functioning are fascinating, of course, not only because of what they tell us about what goes on behind closed doors in communities throughout the land, but also because the healthiness or otherwise of family relations tends to be reflected in dealings beyond the boundaries of the family.

Family function can tell us much about the ease with which individuals cope with pressure from friends and peers for instance. 'Neglectful' parents or those encouraging autonomy at too early an age, for instance, put adolescents at risk from peer pressure (Steinberg and Silverberg, 1986). But, equally, too-controlling families also put children at risk from peers (Burt *et al.*, 1988).

The key to this transfer of patterning from family to the external world lies in the extent to which families shape adolescent identities. Identity, in Newman and Murray's words, is

> like a blueprint for future commitments and life choices. It is a set of beliefs and goals about one's relationships with family members, lovers and friends, one's role as worker, citizen and religious believer and one's aspirations for achievement.
>
> (B.A. Newman and Murray, 1983: 294)

Newman and Murray see the parent's use of power in the family as critical in influencing the willingness of adolescents to be involved in identity exploration. Coercion rather than inductive methods of upbringing, combined with low levels of support, are seen to produce problems in identity formation, externalised moral standards, a susceptibility to peer pressure and low self-confidence and self-esteem, a formulation akin to the one postulated in Baumrind's model. Coercive methods are associated with working class parents.

Berg (1985) extended the modelling of family functioning to look beyond the family and take into account its interactions with the world beyond. He introduced the notion of 'themes', stating that each family has its own unique view of the world. Family themes act as filters through which the world is viewed and which affect the child's interpretation of other people, events and ideas. Berg selected three broad types of families in terms of their attitudes to the outside world. 'Opaque' (or closed) families are those which have an impermeable boundary. Information and ideas from outside are excluded or heavily censored, thus polarising the world into an 'inside' and 'outside', a 'we' and 'they' situation. Those who lay beyond this pale are unacceptable or undesirable because of their class, race, ethnic or subcultural origins, their level of education (higher or lower) and so on.

'Transparent' families demonstrate a very realistic view of the world. Values are absent, inconsistent or poorly expressed and there are few if any filters on inputs to the family from the outer world. Thus there is no interpretation for the adolescent of behaviours and ideas. Any behaviour may be seen as appropriate, depending on the circumstances.

'Translucent' families sit somewhere between these two extreme positions. Such families seek to filter and pass external views and observations on to their offspring. This is accomplished by upholding the reasonableness of their views and assessing the compatibility of those views with those of others. Not all views are accepted or acceptable, but those behaviours or ideas which are rejected are excluded for given reasons.

The majority of commentators view the latter family type as the 'healthiest' or most likely to prepare the young person to be a satisfactory and successful member of society.

AN EMPIRICAL STUDY OF FAMILY STYLES

A detailed examination can be made of different types of family styles in mid-adolescence using data drawn from the middle two cohorts of the first large-scale YPLL survey in 1987. Young people in these two cohorts ($n = 4,384$) were 13–14 years of age and 15–16 years of age at this stage of the study. Over thirty 'family' items were selected for analysis from the 1987 questionnaire. These related to: socioeconomic position of the household, the perceived importance of the family, the quality of relationships with parents, parental support and concern, parental expectations, attitudes to parental authority, behaviours leading to conflict with parents and to problems for parents, parental approval of appearance and of friends, parental influences on appearance and health behaviours, the amount of spare time spent with the family and the frequency of contact with relatives. It is important to remember that these items represent young people's self-assessments of their families. Further, the items are of two types: they either reflect broad background influences on the family (i.e. mother's education) or are related to the ways in which a family functions (i.e. parents supportive of interests and activities).

Our first task was to derive a small number of meaningful 'family' dimensions from the large and varied collection of questionnaire items selected. In order to achieve this the data were subjected to a principal components analysis. Seven factors were identified. A brief description of each of these factors is given below.

1 Relationships with parents were good and the family was supportive and concerned.
2 Behaviour was a problem to parents and resulted in conflict, parents were disappointed and parental expectations were too high.
3 Parents were critical of friends, parents were critical of appearance and parental expectations were too high.
4 Parents continued education beyond school and the head of the household was employed in a middle class occupation.
5 Parents were the most important influence in matters relating to alcohol, drugs, sex and general health.
6 Parents were the most important influence in choosing what to wear, parents ought to be stricter with young people who 'get into trouble' and parents were critical of dress and appearance.
7 Visits to relatives were frequent and a lot of spare time was spent with the family.

How do these factors relate to the dimensions of family functioning identified in the models proposed by Beavers (1981) and Beavers and Voeller (1983) and by Baumrind (1968, 1971)? Factor 1 appears to relate to the notion of the 'healthy' family which was regarded in both models as an outcome of family functioning. By contrast, factors 2 and 3 can be viewed as reflecting what Baumrind described as 'low parental acceptance', whilst factor 6 appears to relate to 'high parental control' in the Baumrind model and to what Beavers and Voeller identify as a failure to develop 'competence' (i.e. dominating parents, who perceive little need for negotiation or autonomy). Factor 5 can also be regarded as reflecting the development of competence (i.e. independence or autonomy from parental influences). Factors 4 and 7 are not directly related to the models. Nevertheless these two factors relate to other important dimensions of family life. Factor 4 serves as a reminder that broader socioeconomic factors exert important influences on the family, whilst factor 7 indicates that the wider family network can also play a significant role.

In what ways do experiences of family life in mid-adolescence differ for young men and young women in adolescence? Are there differences associated with age or social class? In order to answer these questions six of the seven family factors were analysed for gender, age and social-class-based differences. Rather than describe the results of this more general analysis, the findings are illustrated by using 'sampler' variables which are representative of the six family factors. The questionnaire items selected to represent the factors were as follows:

1 'I get on well with my parent(s)';
2 'I cause trouble to my family';
3 'My parent(s) disapprove of some of my friends';
4 this factor was excluded from the analysis;
5 'I pay most attention to my parent(s) when sorting out problems with alcohol or drugs';
6 'My parent(s) have strong views about my appearance';
7 'I spend a lot of spare time with my family'.

These representative variables were then analysed for gender, age and social class differences. Figure 6.3 shows how causing problems for the family, parental criticism of friends and parental criticism of appearance vary across the middle years of adolescence for young men and young women. Looking at the results of the analysis, it is clear that there are gender differences. Parents are more likely to be critical of a daughter's male friends than they are of a son's female friends. By contrast, parents are more likely to be critical of a son's male friends than they are of a daughter's female friends. Further, young men were more likely than young women to regard their parents as holding strong views about their appearance. Interestingly, young men are no more likely than young women to perceive themselves as 'causing problems' to their family, and young men and young women are equally likely to regard themselves as 'getting on well' with their parents. Finally, young women spend more of their 'spare' time with their family, and parental influences on problems relating to alcohol and drugs are felt more strongly by young women than by young men.

Turning to age-related differences across the mid-adolescent years, there is a significant decrease in parental disapproval of same-sex friends between 13–14 years of age and 15–16 years of age. Parental attitudes on appearance also soften. Parental influences weaken and the amount of spare time spent with the family diminishes. Nevertheless, the perceived quality of relationships with parents remains good. There were also class-based differences. In general, young people from working class backgrounds are less likely to regard themselves as getting on well with their parents and

Figure 6.3 Variables relating to family functioning: (a) I cause trouble to my family; (b) parents critical of (same-sex) friends; (c) parents have strong views about my appearance

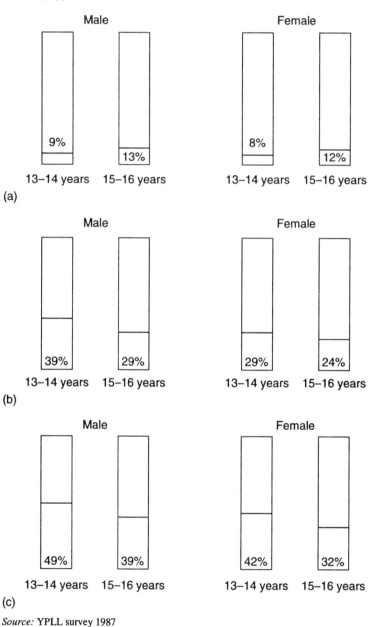

Source: YPLL survey 1987

they are also more likely to view their parents as critical of both their male and female friends.

In summary, the degree of acceptance and control within the family differs for young men and young women. Nevertheless, for both sexes, the results suggest that parental acceptance increases and parental control decreases as young people mature. There is also a corresponding weakening of parental influences on young people's attitudes and behaviours. Despite this movement towards independence from parental authority, relationships with parents in general remain good. However, we know from separate analyses of the 1987 survey data that compared with young people in early or late adolescence, young people in middle adolescence are more likely to report family conflict and problems. Returning to the present results, there is a clear class-based component to family life. Middle class parents are more likely to be perceived as 'accepting' and young people from middle class families are more likely to view themselves as getting on well with their parents.

These findings appear to reinforce the conventional stereotype of the middle class family as a model of 'healthy' family functioning, but there are inherent dangers in establishing criteria which are then used to label families as 'good'. Therefore, in order to examine family functioning more fully, the analysis was extended to develop a typology of family styles.

Twenty-five of the 'family' items from the 1987 questionnaire were selected as the basis for a cluster analysis. The aim of the analysis was to identify distinct family styles in mid-adolescence. The selected items either related to general socioeconomic background factors (e.g. parental occupation, parental education) or they related to young people's interactions with their family (e.g. relationships, support and concern, expectations, attitudes to authority, conflict and problems, acceptance and control, influences on attitudes and behaviours). Separate analyses were conducted for young men and young women. The solution obtained for mid-adolescent males is described in Table 6.2.

Thumbnail descriptions of the clusters are as follows.

Cluster 1: (middle class permissive)   Middle class family. Don't cause problems for the family. Parental expectations aren't too high. Parents aren't disappointed. Get on well with both parents. Parents are supportive. Don't see a need for parents to be stricter. Parents aren't disapproving of friends or appearance. Pay less attention to parents in relation to appearance, use of spare time and health behaviours.

Cluster 2: (middle class authoritative)   Middle class family. Don't cause problems for the family. Get on well with both parents. Parents are

Table 6.2 Family styles of young men in mid-adolescence

	Cluster	n	%
1	Middle class permissive	218	10
2	Middle class authoritative	373	17
3	Working class permissive	489	22
4	Working class authoritative	354	16
5	Authoritarian	234	12
6	Neglectful	299	13
	Unclassified	225	10

Source: YPLL panel 1987

supportive. Think parents ought to be stricter with children who cause trouble. Parents are critical of appearance. Pay more attention to parents in relation to use of spare time and health behaviours.

Cluster 3: (working class permissive) Working class family. Don't cause problems for the family. Parental expectations aren't too high. Parents aren't disappointed. Get on well with both parents. Parents are supportive. Don't see a need for parents to be stricter. Parents aren't disapproving of friends or appearance. Pay less attention to parents in relation to use of spare time and keeping healthy.

Cluster 4: (working class authoritative) Working class family. Get on well with mother. Parents are supportive. Think parents ought to be stricter with children who cause trouble. Parents are critical of friends and appearance. Pay more attention to parents in relation to appearance, use of spare time and health behaviours.

Cluster 5: (authoritarian) Mix of backgrounds, but more likely to come from a working class family. Don't cause problems for the family. Parents expect too much. Parents are disappointed. Get on well with parents. Parents want to know where I go to in the evenings. Parents are critical of friends and appearance. Pay little attention to parents in relation to health behaviours.

Cluster 6: (neglectful) Mix of backgrounds, but less likely to come from a middle class family. Cause problems for the family. Parents expect too much. Parents are disappointed. Don't get on well with parents, and in particular with father. Parents are seen as unsupportive and uninterested.

Pay little attention to parents in relation to use of spare time and health behaviours.

These six 'family' clusters can be readily identified with the four parenting styles described in Baumrind's (1971) model of family functioning. Clusters 1 and 3 can be identified with a 'permissive' style of parenting. Although there are some differences between the two clusters, clusters 2 and 4 can be similarly identified with an 'authoritative' style of parenting. Cluster 5 can be associated with an 'authoritarian' style of parenting. Finally, cluster 6 can be associated with 'neglectful' parenting. It is also important to note that authoritative parenting is not exclusive to middle class families (compare clusters 2 and 4) and permissive parenting is not exclusive to working class families (compare clusters 1 and 3).

Looking more closely at the relationship between parenting styles and social class, the relative sizes of the first four clusters suggest that authoritative parents are more likely to be middle class and permissive parents are more likely to be working class. As can be seen from the descriptions of clusters 5 and 6, authoritarian and neglectful parents are also more likely to be working class, although there is a much broader mix of social class backgrounds within cluster 6.

Turning to the relationship between young people's age and family styles, it was found that in general parents employed styles which were age appropriate. For example, authoritative parenting was associated with younger adolescent males and permissive parenting was associated with older adolescent males. Neglectful parenting was also associated with older adolescent males. However, authoritarian parenting was unrelated to the young person's age, perhaps reflecting the inflexibility common to this style of parenting.

Next, differences amongst the six family clusters were examined in terms of a variety of other variables drawn from the 1987 questionnaire. It was found that young men from cluster 6 – neglectful families – spent less 'spare' time with their family, probably as a consequence of poor relationships with parents. With regard to family type, again cluster 6 stood out. Amongst the young men in cluster 6, only 69 per cent were living within an intact nuclear family, whilst 19 per cent were living with a single parent and 11 per cent were living with a step-parent. In fact, cluster 6 stood out as markedly different from the other clusters in a number of ways.

Looking at educational attitudes, for example, young men from the 'middle class' clusters 1 and 2 (permissive and authoritative family styles) were more likely to be positive about school. But young males from cluster 6 – despite the broad mix of social class backgrounds – held distinctly negative attitudes towards school. These negative attitudes towards school mirrored their negative attitudes towards the family. With regard to relationships with peers, young men in cluster 6 were more likely than other adolescents to spend a lot of 'spare' time with groups of males and, in particular, to 'hang around in the street with their friends'. They were less likely to describe themselves as 'easy to get along with' and they were less likely to view 'being friendly' as relevant to 'being liked'. They were also more likely to regard 'drinking and smoking' as necessary to acceptance by the peer group and to feel that 'some people deserve to have their belongings stolen or vandalised'. Finally, they were more likely to report symptoms of psychological stress.

Moving on two years to 1989 survey data, we looked for longer-term differences amongst the family clusters in relation to leaving home, general health and health behaviours. Young men from cluster 6 were more likely than other males to have left home by 1989, possibly as a reflection of family problems. Levels of psychological stress remained higher and they were also less likely to assess their general health as good. With regard to cigarette smoking, young men from cluster 6 were much more likely to have tried smoking at some time and they were also much more likely to smoke cigarettes at present. Interestingly, two years on, young men from cluster 5 – authoritarian families – were the most likely to claim 'I have never smoked a cigarette'.

To sum up the results reported in this section, using principal components analysis, it is possible to identify several dimensions of family functioning in mid-adolescence: quality of relationships with parents, parental support and concern; problems and conflict within the family; criticism and lack of acceptance; influences on attitudes and values; levels of control; and the family network. The relative importance of these family dimensions differs for young men and young women, but for both sexes levels of criticism, influence and control diminish as young people mature. Also, in general, adolescents from middle class families have 'better' relationships with their parents and middle class parents are also more 'accepting' of their children. These findings can be seen as reinforcing the conventional stereotype of the 'healthy' middle class family.

Next, using cluster analysis, a detailed investigation was undertaken of how socioeconomic factors, relationships, support, concern, problems, conflict, acceptance, influence and control interact within different types of families. The results are described for adolescent males. Six clusters are obtained from the cluster analysis and from these clusters four distinct family styles are identified. These family styles correspond closely to the four parenting styles derived by Baumrind from a consideration of parental acceptance and control.

For young men in mid-adolescence, the predominating family styles are apparently 'authoritative' and 'permissive'. An authoritative style is associated with younger males and a permissive style is associated with older males. Further, an authoritative style tends to be associated with middle class families, whilst a permissive style tends to be associated with working class families. However, it is important to note that there is a substantial cluster of 'authoritative working class families' and there is a substantial cluster of 'permissive middle class families'. There are two other family styles: 'authoritarian' and 'neglectful'. The authoritarian style is unrelated to age, but tends to be associated with working class families. Finally, the neglectful style is associated with older males and is also more likely to be associated with working class families, although it is important to note that there is a broad mix of social class backgrounds within this cluster.

When the six clusters are analysed in terms of other variables from the 1987 survey – which were not included in the cluster analysis – we find that the cluster reflecting a neglectful family style stands out as quite distinct from the others. Young males in this cluster are more likely to come from single-parent families or from families with a step-parent. These young men spend more time with the peer group than other adolescents and they have very negative attitudes towards school as well as to the family. They are also more likely to feel peer pressure to 'drink and smoke' and to regard 'theft and vandalism' as justified in some circumstances. Although they 'hang around' with friends, they do not regard themselves as 'easy to get along with' and they are more likely to report psychological stress. This picture of adolescent 'storm and stress' appears to have a long-term impact. For example, two years later in 1989, levels of psychological stress are still raised amongst this group and general health is more likely to be assessed as not good.

Returning to the middle class family as a model of 'healthy' functioning, the results of the cluster analysis can be seen as a qualified confirmation of this stereotypical view, but only in so far as 'authoritative' can be regarded as reflecting a 'healthy' family style and 'permissive', 'authoritarian' and 'neglectful' can be regarded as reflecting 'unhealthy' family styles. What the cluster analysis does demonstrate very clearly is that the lives of adolescent males from 'neglectful' families are markedly different. They are characterised by problems, conflict and stress. In consequence, it is perhaps more appropriate to focus on the neglectful family as a model of 'unhealthy' family functioning. Finally, it is important to note that although the evidence indicates that a neglectful family style is linked to poorer socioeconomic circumstances, such 'problem' families are to be found across a broad range of social classes.

SUMMARY

In this chapter an attempt has been made to look at the importance of the family in influencing the development of young people's lifestyles and, indirectly, their leisure. An acknowledgement of the diversity of family types (extended, nuclear, step-parent, single parent) is made at the start of the chapter. Some thoughts on the impact of these differing types of families on young people's well-being are included, but the research evidence is contradictory. The amount of time spent with the family is examined through both survey and panel data from the YPLL study. Not surprisingly, activities shared within the family setting change with age and vary by gender and social class.

Evidence on the quality of family relationships is also discussed. Minor squabbles seem to characterise family life for the majority of young people, but relationships on the whole are good and this does not appear to be (from the young person's perspective at least) a time of dreadful turmoil within the family.

Some theoretical models of family functioning are discussed. Elements of these models are examined in the light of YPLL survey data. The analysis is strongly supportive of Baumrind's model which characterises family dynamics in terms of 'acceptance' and 'control'. Whilst crude social class differences do exist in patterns of parenting, a finer grain analysis reveals considerable variety within social classes. Of particular interest is the clear identification of an 'unhealthy' family style which is associated with multiple problems for the young person.

7 Young people, peers and friends

INTRODUCTION

Adolescence differs in essence from earlier years in the nature of the challenges encountered and in the capacity of the individual to respond effectively to these challenges. Adolescence is the first phase of life requiring, and presumably stimulating, mature patterns of functioning, relating to others, and the development of a clear-cut personal and social identity. Conversely, failure to cope effectively with the challenges of adolescence may have negative consequences for subsequent development.

We saw in Chapter 3 that across the adolescent years the majority of young people make the transition from adult-led leisure groups and organisations through casual peer-oriented groups to commercial leisure contexts where entry may often be dependent on their economic circumstances. Commercial contexts allow small networks of older adolescents of both sexes to interact socially. Such settings also confer adult status.

In connection with the development of social competency, Hendry (1983) has drawn attention to these three broad leisure phases as allowing young people *in sequence*: to observe their peers; to rehearse personal and social skills and strategies; and then to 'try out' these roles and behaviour patterns for their acceptance in adult society. This suggests that in general the use of peer groups (to rehearse skills, social strategies and behaviours, to observe others' strategies and to confirm tentative views about appropriate behaviour in various contexts) is central to social development in adolescence. Hence, although it is relationships with parents that determine in large measure our longer-term preferences, attitudes and values, during adolescence (in the shorter term at least) it is relationships with friends that cause most concern and which most preoccupy the consciousness of young people as they grow up.

Friendships, as Youniss and Smollar (1985) pointed out, are based on a completely different set of structural relationships to those with parents. They are more symmetrical, involve reciprocity and are evolutionary through adolescence. Whilst friendships are also important to younger children, there is a change at the beginning of adolescence – a move to intimacy that includes the development of a more exclusive focus, openness to self-disclosure and the sharing of problems and advice. Youniss and Smollar (1985) commented that the central notion is that friends tell one another, and get to know, just about everything that is going on in one another's lives. Friends literally reason together in order to organise experience and to define themselves as persons.

FROM FAMILY SETTINGS TO PEER GROUPS AND FRIENDSHIPS

Adolescence as a transitional period from childhood to adulthood requires changes from child–parent relationships to young adult–parent relationships. This may not necessarily be an easy change for either young people or their parents. Family settings may magnify, diminish or transform individual development depending on the degree of self-agency the adolescent possesses and the life events parents are facing. As we saw in Chapter 6, the structure of the family can be important to the development of young people's life skills and competency. Noller and Callan stated:

> There is quite a bit of evidence that the support of the family is crucial to adolescents, and that those who do not have strong support from parents are more likely to become involved in undesirable behaviours.
>
> (Noller and Callan, 1991: 123)

They go on to argue that parental support and effective communication lessen the adolescent's reliance on the peer group and decrease the likelihood of substance abuse and sexual involvement at a young age.

Ochiltree (1990) suggested that adolescents take their major values in life from parents. Nevertheless the general trend across adolescence is towards the increasing importance of peer relationships. These provide vital intimate feedback to adolescents at times of rapid personal and social change and enable them to communicate with others as equal partners. The major function of friends and of the peer group generally then is to provide a base of security outside the family. Lloyd argued that:

> This allows the young person to begin the process of emotional detachment from parents. The separation process takes place over a period of years and doesn't usually mean that adolescents suddenly reject their parents or their parents' values. Instead, they gradually 'let go' in order to learn how to be emotionally self-supporting adults.
>
> (Lloyd, 1985: 195)

In addition, the peer group provides opportunities for practising new behaviours and developing the necessary social skills for interactions with the same sex and with opposite-sex friends. Adams (1983) pointed out three areas of growth in social competencies which can be gained from peer group participation. First, a growth in social knowledge through learning the appropriate emotional status to adopt in varying social contexts. Second, a growth in the ability to express empathy with others. Third, a growing belief in the power of self-initiation (i.e. a state of self-confidence in presenting and carrying out plans within one's group). However, the price for all this is conformity to the peer group in such matters as dress, personal appearance, musical tastes and leisure activities.

The values of parents and peers may overlap during the adolescent's emergence from the family towards independence (Offer and Offer, 1975), but where there is less parental interest or in areas of parental uncertainty the adolescent is likely to turn to his or her peer group for help and advice with decisions, or to discuss current events and activities (Hunter, 1985). Thus, simultaneous parent and peer influences are not necessarily contradictory (Kandel and Lesser, 1972) and parents' counsel is more often preferred to that of peers in important situations involving values and future decision making (Smith, 1976). In addition, Rosenberg (1979) reported that parents ranked higher than peers in interpersonal significance throughout adolescence. However, adolescents are more likely to seek help from peers when they perceive their parents as rejecting or indifferent (Larson, 1972; Smith, 1976).

Several developmental changes serve to alter the manner in which adolescents interact with family and peers. These include more advanced cognitive, verbal and reasoning abilities and the changes associated with puberty. In addition, many of the developmental tasks of adolescence involve relationships and require new, and more complex, interpersonal skills (Hartup, 1982). The transition from concrete to abstract generalised thinking allows the adolescent to understand better friends' thoughts and feelings. They become more aware of the importance of mutuality and reciprocity, which can foster stable and meaningful friendships (Berndt, 1982). A study by Leyva and Furth (1986) confirmed that compromises were more likely to be formulated in peer relations than in authority relations. In fact many adolescents, in describing conflicts in authority contexts, explicitly stated that the adults would win the conflict merely because they were in a power position. The peer context seemed more favourable to an equal exchange of ideas and a situation where one's view would be heard and respected. The development of a mature approach to conflict resolution by mutual agreement and respect is an important function of peer relations.

FRIENDSHIP GROUPS IN ADOLESCENCE

In adolescence friendships normally exist within the larger social structure of peer relationships. In this larger social setting each adolescent has a more or less well-defined peer status. Close friendships are not independent of such status. Friends tend to be similar in their positions within the larger group. The quality of a friendship is of particular importance. Popularity is usually measured in research studies by an index of the number of friends children have and not by an examination of the quality of these relationships (Buhrmester and Furman, 1986). Yet it may be possible for a single high-quality friendship to make up for a lack of sociometric status (Mannarino, 1978). As Solano (1986) pointed out, having a friend *per se* is a form of social status, and Csikszentmihalyi and Larson (1984) defined an ideal friendship as one that contributed to security and order at both the personal and social levels in the shorter term, and at the same time helped the individual to find a meaningful place in the world over the years. Thus peers are not the same as friends. Whereas peer group norms can set highly influential markers around acceptable and unacceptable behaviours for young people, it is in individual friendships that young people find support and security, negotiate their emotional independence, exchange information, verbalise beliefs and feelings and develop a new and different perspective of themselves.

There is a wealth of evidence that young men and young women use and view friendships in quite different ways. For example, Douvan and Adelson's (1966) study examined the development of friendships in young women and traced it through an early adolescent period when emotional commitments are minimal and the focus of friendship is common activities to a period in mid-adolescence when young women become most anxious about being rejected or excluded from a same-sex friendship. There is strong emphasis on loyalty and support at this stage.

> People should remember that you need attention too, and not ignore you and sneak away from you. People who sneak away from you cannot really be your friends in the first place. Sometimes friends gang up on you. So you have to make another friend in another class. That is not pleasant. I should know . . .
>
> (Adolescent girl, Aberdeen, YPLL study)

Friendships become easier for young women in later adolescence as they develop a clearer sense of self-identity and become more familiar with their sexuality. Young women of this age showed a high regard for each other's individuality and a greater ability to tolerate differences. Young men's friendships rarely achieve the depth of intimacy of young women's. Larger peer groups often appear more important than individual friendships. Young men in middle adolescence describe their friends in terms similar to those used by pre-adolescent girls – failing to see emotional support, closeness or security as important qualities of a friendship.

Special importance is attributed to friendships during adolescence, and by early adolescence friendship is already characterised by a sense of reciprocity and equality. Peer conversations involve more sharing, explaining and mutual understanding, whereas adolescent–parent conversations can often involve parents explaining their ideas even at the expense of not understanding their children's alternative views of events and life situations (Hunter, 1985). Friendships are transformed between childhood and adolescence into more complex, psychologically fuller and more adult-like relationships.

Coffield *et al.* (1986) examined friendships in late adolescence/early adulthood by studying a small number of young people over a period of two years in the north-east of England. They identified five types of friendship groups: all female; all male; mixed sex groups (including both couples and single people); best friend same sex; and relationship with a partner. Coffield *et al.* found that young adults could in fact be a member of several friendship groups at any one stage. They also noted that affiliation to the peer group did not tail off after 'couples' formed. On the contrary, young women maintained contact with 'the lasses' and typically went out with this exclusively female group once a week. Men, even after marriage, generally kept in contact with their male friendship group. Coffield *et al.* noted that this social pattern was influenced by 'north-east' culture and they emphasised the importance of social class and gender and their effects on peer group involvement.

FRIENDSHIPS IN THE YOUNG PEOPLE'S LEISURE AND LIFESTYLES STUDY

Given findings such as those of Coffield *et al.*, what does the YPLL Project tell us about friendship groups in adolescence? Young people in our study were asked how much 'spare time' they spent with particular individuals and groups. If we focus attention on the amount of time spent either alone, with a best friend of the same sex, with groups of peers of the same sex, with a boy-friend/girl-friend and with mixed sex groups, we gain some understanding of various social groupings across adolescence. Levels of involvement with these various friendship groupings were analysed for gender, age and social class differences. Data on how involvement with a best friend, with a boy-friend/girl-friend and with same-sex groups varied across the adolescent years are presented in Figure 7.1.

Figure 7.1 Associations with a best friend, a same-sex peer group and a girl-friend/boy-friend: (a) percentage spending a lot of spare time with a same-sex best friend; (b) percentage spending a lot of spare time with a same-sex peer group; (c) percentage spending a lot of spare time with a girl-friend/boy-friend

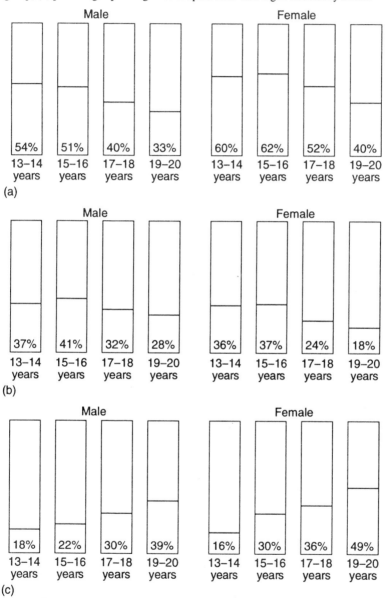

Source: YPLL survey 1987

Looking at the results in detail, it was found that the amount of spare time young people spent *alone* is unrelated to gender, age and social class. Younger women are more likely than young men to spend a lot of time with a best friend of the same sex at all stages of adolescence, and overall for young people of both sexes. The peak period for association with best friends is early to mid-adolescence (13–16 years of age). Associations with same-sex groups are also more likely in early to mid-adolescence and diminish thereafter. Young women in particular have left behind friendships with groups of their own sex by late adolescence.

By contrast, young women are more likely than young men to spend time with groups of young men and women throughout adolescence. Both sexes spend less time with mixed groups in late adolescence (19–20 years). In later adolescence there are also interesting class-based differences. Beyond 16 years of age, for instance, young people from working class backgrounds show a gradual decline in the amount of spare time spent with mixed sex groups, whereas young people from middle class backgrounds show a corresponding increase.

Looking at the formation of partnerships, there is, not surprisingly, a marked increase in time spent with a boy-friend/girl-friend across the adolescent years. In early adolescence both boys and girls indulge to an equal extent in friendships with a partner of the opposite sex, but by mid-adolescence such relationships with the opposite sex are more likely amongst young women. This trend persists into late adolescence. Finally, although the differences are less marked, working class young men and women are more likely than those from middle class backgrounds to spend time with a boy-friend/girl-friend.

The general trend, in summary, is for relations with friends of the same sex to decline after early adolescence whilst involvement with boy-friends/girl-friends shows a corresponding increase. Young women form longer and stronger attachments to a best friend and are more heavily involved with boy-friends and with mixed sex groups throughout adolescence. Boys' friendships are characterised, particularly in later adolescence, by association with groups of their own sex. Lastly, young people from working class backgrounds are more likely to spend time with a boy-friend/girl-friend whereas young people from middle class backgrounds are more likely to associate with mixed sex groups.

PARTNERS AND FRIENDS

Analysis of the YPLL data was then extended by examining whether the pattern of other friendships is related to partnership formation for young men and young women at the different stages of adolescence. Overall it was found that involvement with a particular best friend is strongly related to a broader involvement with friends of the same sex. These associations are, however, unrelated to partnership formation (Table 7.1). Such findings are reminiscent of those reported by Coffield *et al.* (1986) for young adults. In sum it would appear that in adolescence same-sex friendships typically function within the context of same-sex friendship *groups* and that such close friendships are independent of the presence of a boy-friend/girl-friend except where young people have formed a 'courting couple' at the expense of same-sex friendships.

There were clear gender and age differences in the relationship between time spent with a friend of the same sex and time spent with a partner. In

Table 7.1 Interrelationships among the amount of leisure time young people spend with a (same-sex) best friend, with an (opposite-sex) boy-friend/girl-friend and with a (same-sex) peer group

Percentage of respondents who spend a lot of their leisure time with a (same-sex) peer group (13–20 years)

A lot of time with a best friend and a lot of time with a boy-/girl-friend (%)	*A lot of time with a best friend but little time with a boy-/girl-friend (%)*	*Little time with a best friend but a lot of time with a boy-/girl-friend (%)*	*Little time with a best friend and little time with a boy-/girl-friend (%)*
46	45	16	25

Percentage of respondents who spend a lot of their leisure time with an (opposite-sex) boy-friend/girl-friend (13–20 years)

	Amount of leisure time spent with a best friend						
	13–14 years		*15–16 years*		*17–18 years*		*19–20 years*
	Little time (%)	*A lot of time (%)*	*Little time (%)*	*A lot of time (%)*	*Little time (%)*	*A lot of time (%)*	*Little time (%)*	*A lot of time (%)*
Male	13	21	18	26	29	30	39	39
Females	13	19	27	32	40	32	56	39

Source: YPLL survey 1987

early adolescence to mid-adolescence (for both sexes) those who spent little time with a particular friend of the same sex were less likely to be involved with a partner. However, in later adolescence there were marked changes in this pattern. Amongst young men, time spent with a best friend was un-related to time spent with a partner, whereas for young women spending a lot of time with a partner was associated with less involvement with a best friend (see Table 7.1). It would appear, therefore, that across adolescence there is a transition towards forming partnerships and this is a move that young women are more likely to make. In later adolescence young women may be more inclined to sacrifice close female friendships for the sake of boy-friends.

How do these findings equate with other key studies? The develop-mental pattern of peer conformity, shifting across adolescence in conjunction with the intensity of the adolescent's allegiance to the crowd reported by J.C. Coleman (1974), is consistent with Dunphy's (1972) contention that peer groups serve primarily to socialise adolescents into appropriate heterosexual interests and behaviour. Dunphy claimed that crowds evolved through several stages during adolescence. In early ado-lescence (stage 1), in the pre-crowd stage, children are usually limited to small same-sex cliques. Usually the clique is dominated by an obvious 'leader' who possesses all the traits admired by its members. Then some of the small cliques begin to join together to form small crowds, often of mixed sex, usually involving members of cliques living close to one another or from adjacent residential areas. Any actual heterosexual inter-action at this stage in the form of 'going out' or 'dating' is seen as very daring – most boy–girl interactions take place in the safe presence of other clique members.

In stage 3 the heterosexual clique begins to form. Often it is the 'leaders' of the pre-adolescent same-sex cliques who are the first to begin going out with the opposite sex and other clique members soon follow. Stage 4 is characterised by the fully developed crowd comprised of well-established heterosexual cliques which closely interact. In stage 5, by the end of adolescence, the crowd slowly disintegrates and is replaced by loosely associated groups of couples who are 'going steady'.

Additionally, Newman and Newman (1976) have argued that one major task of early adolescence is to affiliate with a peer group that can accept the individual's budding sense of identity and provide supportive social rela-tionships to offset the teenager's withdrawal from emotional dependence on parents. As a more autonomous sense of identity emerges in later adolescence, the need for strong peer group identification diminishes. The study by Brown *et al.* (1986) involving 1,300 adolescents also showed that the importance of crowd affiliation declined across the teenage years.

Younger adolescents generally favoured group membership, emphasising the crowd's ability to provide emotional or instrumental support, foster friendships and facilitate social interaction, whereas older adolescents expressed dissatisfactions with the conformity demands of crowds and felt their smaller and more intimate established friendship networks obviated the need for peer group ties.

These models of the peer group as a vehicle for developing heterosexual relations were tested to some extent with the YPLL findings. In addition to confirming the model the YPLL results point to (additional) gender and social class influences. While the importance of peer groupings reaches a peak in mid-adolescence according to quoted studies the YPLL data has indicated that there are important subcultural differences. Partnerships are seen to be more significant to working class young people, and this preoccupation is seen to be accompanied by a decline in involvement in groups of young men and women. In contrast, mixed sex groups become more important to middle class adolescents perhaps as a feature of their move towards higher education.

With regard to gender differences, young women are more likely than young men to be involved in courting or romantic dyads, (same-sex) best friends *and* groups of young men and women. Young men were more likely to spend their leisure with their 'mates' but, unlike young women, continued these social leisure meetings even when 'going steady' and 'courting'. Young women are more likely to sacrifice same-sex friendships when going out with a boy-friend. The latter finding is more supportive of Dunphy's (1972) claims than those of Coffield *et al.* (1986), though we would agree with Coffield *et al.* that young people inhabit a network of different peer groupings across adolescence.

THE ROLE OF THE PEER GROUP

Thus, peers and friends serve multiple functions in the lives of adolescents. Rather than serving as a constant in the lives of teenagers, peer groups appear to have a dynamic role, the function and influence of which shifts across adolescence and varies according to the characteristics of the adolescents' neighbourhood. By experiencing the values and norms of the peer group, the adolescent is able to evaluate the perspectives of others, while developing his or her own values and attitudes. Because all groups are oriented towards fostering identity development, certain developmental trends in peer pressures can be expected to supersede group differences.

Style of dress, hairstyles, musical interests, speech and language use, leisure activities and values are among the socially relevant characteristics that teenagers appear to learn, in part, by exposure to peer models. Further, teenagers learn methods of handling social relationships by observing and imitating peers. Thus peer groups act as a source of behavioural standards in some contexts, and particularly where parental influence is not strong. Peer groups offer adolescents opportunities both for role-taking and for role-modelling.

Being liked, accepted and defining one's role within a social group are important features of life at any age, but can be of particular importance in adolescence. Because peers play such an important role in the lives of adolescents, social acceptance is an urgent concern for most young people (Berscheid and Walster, 1972). Cavior and Dokecki (1973) suggested that acceptance and popularity in the peer group was related to perceived similarity of attitudes and to perceived attractiveness. In interpersonal relations the effect of personal appearance seems crucial. A physically attractive individual is generally believed to possess more favourable personal qualities (Miller, 1970) and such individuals are viewed as having greater social power (Sigall and Aronson, 1969).

A study by Hendry and Jamie (1978) showed that in terms of peer group popularity adolescents tended to emphasise physical characteristics and abilities (such as 'handsome' and 'sporting' for young men and 'pretty' and 'nice figure' for young women). Young women also considered attributes related to social relations (such as 'considerate' and 'has personality') to be of importance. There are links here to an earlier American study by J.S. Coleman (1961) which showed that similar qualities (such as athleticism for young men and sexual attractiveness for young women) were related to peer group popularity. The physical attributes referred to by young men in their descriptions of the most popular young women were much more overtly sexual ones than were the young women's descriptions of popular young men. Perhaps gender role stereotypes play a part in such evaluations. Further, in Hendry and Jamie's study, a number of adolescents used 'negative' qualities to describe peer popularity. Young men were more likely than young women to be described in this way. The use of qualities such as 'hard' and 'show off' as criteria for peer group popularity may reflect an identification with what Hargreaves (1967) much earlier referred to as 'delinquescent' subcultures.

Young people in the YPLL study were asked to rate the importance of being liked and accepted by peers and also to identify from a list which items they felt were of relevance to popularity and unpopularity amongst friends. First, looking at acceptance by the peer group, it was found that young women and young men attached similar levels of importance to acceptance by peers and, although this was still viewed by the majority as important in later adolescence, there was a significant decline in concern beyond 16 years of age (Figure 7.2). There were no class-based differences.

Figure 7.2 Peer acceptance and popularity: (a) percentage perceiving peer group acceptance as important; (b) percentage perceiving smoking and drinking as important to peer group popularity; (c) percentage perceiving conformity in appearance as important to peer group popularity

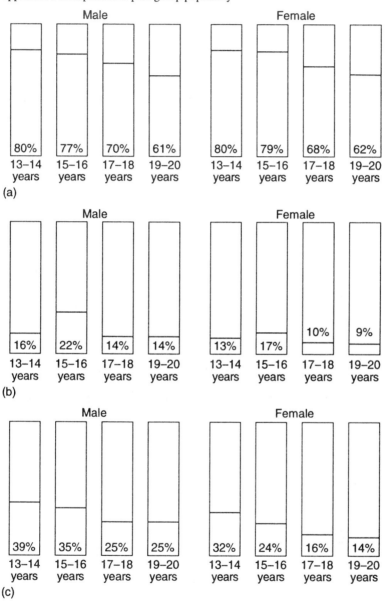

Source: YPLL survey 1987

In order to identify the major components underlying YPLL data on peer popularity, eleven items relating to popularity and thirteen items relating to unpopularity were subjected to a principal components analysis. Six factors relating to popularity/unpopularity are identified in Table 7.2.

As can be seen from the table there were factors relating to social relations, peer pressure to conform to 'proscribed' behaviours, peer pressure to conform in appearance and fashion, physical attributes, sport and education and overly confident and exaggerated behaviour. These factors were then analysed for gender, age and social class differences.

Throughout adolescence, attributes associated with social relations such as 'has personality' are perceived to be more relevant to peer popularity amongst young women and amongst young people from middle class backgrounds. By contrast, young men are more likely to view peer pressure to participate in more adult-oriented behaviours such as 'smoking and drinking' as important. For both sexes such pressures peak at 15–16 years of age and decline in importance thereafter. Peer pressure to conform in appearance and fashion are, somewhat surprisingly, felt more strongly by young men but this concern declines in importance beyond age 16. Young people from working class backgrounds are more likely to feel it is important to be like their friends in appearance. Turning to physical attributes, again young men are more likely to perceive these as important to peer popularity but their importance declines throughout adolescence. Involvement in sport and education is also viewed as more important by the young males in the survey. Young women lose their concern with this as a factor in earning popularity at an earlier age. Interestingly, sport and education are seen as less relevant to peer popularity amongst young people from the middle classes. Finally, 'over-doing it' and 'being full of oneself' are seen

Table 7.2 Factors relating to perceived popularity/unpopularity with peers

	Popular if		*Unpopular if*
1	sense of humour, cheerful helpful, get along with others good personality honest, trustworthy willing to join in	1	doesn't drink, smoke etc. studies too much too straight too shy or quiet doesn't go out with opposite sex
2	like friends in dress, speech etc. fashionable not individual	2	no interest in sport doesn't study at all unfit and not good at sport
3	good-looking/attractive good physique/figure	3	arrogant or full of themselves always overdoes it at parties etc.

Source: YPLL survey 1987

as far less desirable characteristics by young women. Some of these general findings are illustrated in Figure 7.2 for the questionnaire items relating to 'smoking and drinking' and 'conformity in appearance'.

In summary, young men are more likely to regard conformity in behaviour and appearance and physical attributes as important, whereas young women are more likely to value social relations. The importance attached to attractiveness and peer pressures declines throughout the adolescent years. Lastly, there are class-based differences. For example, more importance is attached to qualities such as 'a good personality' and 'being oneself' by young people from middle class backgrounds.

These findings highlight the importance of peer pressures in adolescence. Peer pressures transmit group norms and maintain loyalties amongst group members. However, conformity to the group is the price that has to be paid for approval and acceptance by peers. As can be seen from the social class differences noted above, the content of peer pressures can vary amongst different groups. For example 'being an individual' was regarded by young people from working class backgrounds as of less importance to peer popularity. Yet, YPLL results also indicate that developmental trends typically supersede group differences. For instance, it was found that *in general* conformity to peer group norms diminished in importance beyond 16 years of age. However, in one important respect group differences do predominate: clear gender differences were found which were related to development. Hence, acceptance by peers was as important to young women as it was to young men at all stages of adolescence, but the criteria regarded as necessary for peer popularity were different for males and females. Further, the ways in which the relative importance attached to these criteria varied across the adolescent years were also different for young men and young women. By way of example, 'being oneself' was viewed as more important by young women and the general increase in the perceived importance of individuality across adolescence was also more marked amongst young women.

Earlier it was noted that a component of perceived peer popularity involved conformity to the peer group with respect to behaviours such as 'drinking and smoking', 'studying too much', 'being straight' and 'going out with the opposite sex'. Adopting a similar strategy of asking adolescents to report on the expectations of friends, Brown (1982) discovered that in general adolescents reported significantly stronger peer pressure to spend time with peers (and conform to peer norms) than to spend time in extracurricular school activities. In particular, he found that peer pressure to drink alcohol shifted from relative disapproval of drinking in early adolescence towards a raised pressure to drink in mid-adolescence, whereas pressures to use drugs and have sexual intercourse were strongest in later adolescence. However, Brown also noted that adolescents often actively discouraged such activities. The results of the present study agree with these findings. For instance, peer pressure to 'drink and smoke' was greatest at 15–16 years of age in mid-adolescence but at the same time many adolescents did not perceive such behaviours as particularly relevant to acceptance by the peer group.

Young people in the YPLL study were also asked to describe themselves in relation to friends and peers (Table 7.3). These self-perceptions were found to centre around three main themes: friendship formation; self-confidence; and rejection. Perceived ability to form friendships was unrelated to gender, age and social class but (although the differences were small) young people were more likely to claim to 'have many friends' in mid-adolescence. These results complement YPLL findings on the amount of time spent alone and with same-sex groups across adolescence. Turning to self-confidence, young people of both sexes generally regarded themselves as 'relaxed', 'easy to get along with' and 'thought well of' by peers. These self-perceptions steadily increased with age. Finally, although only a minority of young people regarded themselves as being 'picked on' and being 'made fun of', young men were more likely to perceive themselves as victimised or ridiculed. These feelings diminished for both sexes across adolescence. Interestingly, young men were more defensive against (or less sensitised to) being 'thought badly of by others'. They were much more likely than young women to claim that 'it didn't bother them'. This was also true of young people from working class backgrounds.

ALONE AND LONELY

One set of findings by J.C. Coleman (1974) included evidence of a concern with personal loneliness and the absence of confidants among a substantial

Table 7.3 Self-concept and self-esteem in relation to the peer group

Self-perceptions	13–14 years (%)	15–16 years (%)	17–18 years (%)	19–20 years (%)	All (%)
Hard to make friends	9	9	10	9	9
I have many friends	62	65	59	58	62
Easy to get along with	57	66	72	75	65
Made fun of by peers	17	12	7	4	12

Source: YPLL survey 1987

number of adolescents. Mussen *et al.* (1974) stated that though adolescence is generally a time of intense sociability, it can also often be a time of intense loneliness. Being with peers and friends does not necessarily solve this feeling of inner loneliness. Csikszentmihalyi and Larson (1984) also found that adolescents recorded frequent shifts in mood and frequent periods of rumination over relationships and identity, and often spent time alone.

The prevalence of reported loneliness, shyness and social anxiety among adolescents is significant. In the YPLL study a sixth of adolescents reported spending a lot of spare time on their own. Zimbardo (1977) stated that more than half of a sample of younger adolescents labelled themselves as overly shy, whereas Arkowitz *et al.* (1978) reported that a third of older adolescents in a survey sample indicated social interactions with members of the opposite sex as problematic. Other investigators have suggested that social anxiety, shyness and social inhibition affect anything from an eighth to one-half of adolescents (Borkovec *et al.*, 1974; Bryant and Trower, 1974). Little is known about the severity of these social difficulties, the frequency with which relationship problems are a transient concern and the degree to which young people are able to overcome social anxiety or inhibition on their own or through increased exposure to naturally occurring social interactions throughout adolescence. Frydenberg and Lewis (1991) have studied the ways in which early adolescents cope with the main concerns in their lives. They found clear differences between the ways in which boys and girls cope. Girls sought more social support and generally were more likely than boys to focus on relationships. They also employed more strategies associated with 'hoping for the best' and wishful thinking. The panel members in the YPLL study were asked to respond to a number of statements about what they would do if they had a problem. Confiding in a friend when unhappy or worried tended to be something which young women rather than young men were inclined to do.

The more negative and distressing aspects of friendship are rarely examined in the literature on adolescence. By way of exploring this neglected area members of the YPLL panel group were invited to talk about problems with friends. Such discussions with panel members highlighted the significance of arguments and broken friendships. Asked about what might spoil a friendship, the breaking of a confidence and (for boys) 'stealing' another person's girl-friend were considered particularly disloyal. Young people are not alone in having problems with friendships, but the psycho-social issues that confront adolescents make it more certain that such difficulties are likely to be of concern to them. Adolescents can be highly egocentric. They sometimes find it difficult to see other people's point of view and to interpret other people's behaviour. They can be touchy and hypersensitive to rejection and their social skills are, as yet, underdeveloped.

Equally, at times, adolescents feel the need to 'escape' and to be on their own. The YPLL panel study asked young people: 'Where do you go and what do you do if you just want to be alone to think?' The answers highlighted young people's desire for a private place of their own. The overwhelming response was to escape to the bedroom:

> In my room – close the door, ask not to be disturbed, and put on some soothing music, sit on my bed, relaxed, and think . . .

Another young person disclosed:

> I stay in my room and if I'm feeling troubled about something I write it out on paper and that helps me to work things out.

Others went out:

> I go down to the swing park and swing slowly on a swing.

Other places frequently mentioned were walks in parks or woods. A number of young men mentioned going off on their bikes to get away from it all, and amongst older adolescents driving around or driving out of town and parking to view the scenery were popular 'escape' mechanisms.

Brennan (1982) has indicated that adolescents reporting themselves to be lonely, shy or socially anxious appeared to participate less often than their more sociable counterparts in peer activities. For example, lonely adolescents reported dating less often and participating in fewer extra-curricular activities than other young people. On the other hand, Jones (1981) wrote that lonely and more sociable adolescents do not necessarily differ in the *frequency* of their social interactions, but instead they differed in the reported *quality* of the interactions. Lonely young people reported less warmth and intimacy in their social relationships.

SUMMARY

This chapter has introduced the notion that, as the individual adolescent seeks to grow more independent of the family, peer groups and friendship groups become important points of reference in social development. Peer groups and friendships provide social contexts for shaping the day-to-day behaviour of adolescents, and encourage conformity to standard norms and values, even though these may be similar to parental values in some instances. Such groupings have a developmental potential in enabling young people to learn certain social adjustments which may be useful to their acceptance in adult society.

YPLL data were used to show that patterns of friendships change across adolescence, with same-sex friendships occurring within a context of same-sex peer groupings. Such close friendships are mainly independent of relationships with boy-friends/girl-friends. Further, in the transition towards the formation of partnerships in later adolescence, young women are more likely to be in advance of young men, even if it occurs at the expense of best (same-sex) friendships. This move towards 'serious' heterosexual partnerships may emphasise the earlier social sophistication of young women at all stages of adolescence.

Turning to peer acceptance and popularity, young men are more likely to emphasise the importance of factors like appearance and social behaviour, whereas young women stress the importance of social relations as the necessary qualities for integration into the peer group.

Social class differences are apparent in the perceived values of individuality in relation to popularity with friends and peers, with middle class adolescents being more likely to subscribe to this as a worthwhile characteristic. Peer pressure is seen to lessen across adolescence, perhaps as a manifestation of growing confidence and independence. This can be linked to YPLL findings that self-perceptions associated with friends and peers show that 'having many friends' is most important in mid-adolescence.

Finally, the positive and negative influences of being on one's own were briefly explored showing something of the coping strategies employed by adolescents in the face of social or personal concerns in their day-to-day lives.

8   Young people and health

INTRODUCTION

This chapter looks at the issue of young people's health. The physical growth and change that young women and men experience during adolescence is fundamental to their image of self and the development of self-identity. This is reviewed briefly in the first section. Previous chapters, notably Chapter 2, have looked at the social and psychological transitions that young people also experience, and this is a theme which has been explored using empirical data from the YPLL project. One of the topics which was touched on and which has particular resonance in relation to young people's health is that of risk taking. To what extent do adolescents have a particular affinity for risk-taking behaviour, and what are the consequences in terms of the choices they make in health issues? Young people often use risk-taking behaviours to identify with adult patterns of behaviour. Subsequent sections of this chapter look at particular forms of health behaviour of most concern in adolescence – smoking, drinking, drug taking and sexual behaviour.

Finally, the chapter looks at class-based health inequalities and whether or not it is possible to identify healthy and unhealthy lifestyles amongst young people.

YOUNG PEOPLE'S PHYSICAL TRANSITIONS

There seems little doubt that some of the most important changes to which young people must adjust are the multitude of physiological and bodily alterations which occur during early adolescence and which are associated with puberty.

Sexual maturation is closely linked to physical changes. Such changes inevitably exercise a profound effect upon the individual. The body alters radically in size and shape, and it is not surprising that many adolescents experience a period of clumsiness as they attempt to adapt to these changes. Perhaps most important of all, however, is the effect that such physical changes have upon identity. The development of the individual's identity requires not only the notion of being separate and different from others, but also a sense of self-consistency and a firm knowledge of how one appears to the rest of the world. Needless to say dramatic bodily changes seriously affect these aspects of identity, and represent a considerable challenge in adaptation for even the most well-adjusted young person.

Experimental evidence has clearly shown that the average adolescent is not only sensitive to, but often critical of, his or her changing physical self (Clausen, 1975; Davies and Furnham, 1986). Teenagers, like the rest of us, tend to have idealised norms for physical attractiveness, and to feel inadequate if they do not match these unrealistic criteria. Lerner and Karabenick (1974) showed that adolescents who perceived themselves as deviating physically from cultural stereotypes were likely to have impaired self-concepts, and many other studies have pointed out the important role that physical characteristics play in determining self-esteem, especially in the younger adolescent. Thus, for example, both Rosen and Ross (1968) and Simmons and Rosenberg (1975) have reported studies in which adolescents were asked what they did and did not like about themselves. Results showed that those in early adolescence used primarily physical characteristics to describe themselves, and it was these characteristics which were most often disliked. It was not until later adolescence that intellectual or social aspects of personality were widely used in self-description. It is therefore just at the time of most rapid physical change that appearance is of critical importance for the individual, both for his or her self-esteem as well as for popularity. Because of the complexities of modern society young people now approach physical maturity before many of them are capable of functioning well in adult social roles. The disjunction between physical capabilities, socially approved independence and power and the ambiguities in their current status can be stressful for young people.

YOUNG PEOPLE AND RISK-TAKING BEHAVIOURS

Young people are particularly associated with risk-taking behaviours. Those who work closely with young people may wonder whether this is a gross calumny resting on a well-established caricature of youth. Some young people, in some areas of their lives at least, seem very little inclined to take risks. Some of the foundation for the caricature may rest in the fact that despite their physical ability to start acting as free agents and the pressure from society to start operating independently as they move into adulthood, adolescents have little ability to foresee consequences and insufficient opportunities to have learned from experience. This is not to deny, however, that for many young people in their teenage years the desire to seek out thrills will be as real as it was in childhood. As a young child the individual may legitimately seek out physical thrills in the adventure playground or on a funfair ride. Once a start is made on the journey into adulthood there are fewer and fewer legitimate venues for such thrill-seeking outside the world of organised or commercial leisure and the ones left open to us as adults often bear more serious consequences. Those who see in the current fad among young people for stealing cars and 'joyriding' only a protest of the underprivileged against those who 'have', deny the very real thrill that such delinquent activities can inspire.

Over the past decade or so, Csikszentmihalyi and his colleagues at the University of Chicago have developed a model of optimal experience. It has also been called the flow model, 'flow' being the word used by interview subjects themselves to describe the experience of intense involvement in some activity – whether it be chess, rock climbing, dancing or performing heart surgery – where there is total concentration, little or no self-consciousness and a sense of self-transcendence resulting from a merging of consciousness with action (Csikszentmihalyi, 1975). The activities which afford such experience must be sufficiently challenging to engage a full measure of the individual's skill, but not so demanding as to be anxiety provoking. Activities which provide clear feedback, such as those just mentioned, are most likely to be flow producing. But the matching of challenges and skills is critical. If challenges are greater than skills, anxiety results, while a lack of challenge in relation to available skills is likely to be experienced as boredom. What is certain is that 'flow' in leisure provides a highly vivid climactic set of experiences.

What the 'flow' model does seem to suggest is that certain qualities intrinsic to a variety of leisure pursuits are conducive to mental well-being. Sport, for example, offers advantages in terms of structural conditions, but it appears to fall short with respect to such things as self-expression (Kleiber and Rickards, 1985). Sport in general can be a positive experience for certain adolescents, but as Csikszentmihalyi and Larson (1984) have pointed out, so too can general socialising, eating and travelling in a car. So too, we could add, can stealing and driving away someone else's car. The possibility that illegal or deviant activities (for example, drug use) may be among the more attractive alternatives for youth must be considered.

Some indication of the links between activity type and well-being can be gauged from YPLL data. In the YPLL study psychological well-being was assessed using a measure developed by Goldberg and Williams (1988) based on twelve questionnaire items (GHQ12). Using the leisure dimensions from the questionnaire (relating to sport and organised activities, meeting friends and commercial entertainment) it is clear that there were indeed links between leisure involvement and psychological well-being. Organised leisure activities such as attending youth clubs, attending sports clubs and playing sport were related positively to psychological well-being and (although less marked) frequent pub attendance was associated with poorer psychological health. These associations between leisure and psychological health persisted across the adolescent years and were similar for young women and young men. Turning to general attitudes to leisure some interesting differences emerged. Those young people who claimed to be 'often bored' in their 'spare time' and those who claimed to be 'too busy doing jobs at home to have spare time' both reported poorer psychological well-being.

It appears that the quest for excitement and violence is often symbolic in the sense that young people 'use' such behaviours to identify, however misguidedly, with adult patterns of behaviour. Research has focused especially on drug and alcohol use, cigarette smoking, sexual behaviour and delinquency (Jessor and Jessor, 1977). Most of these behaviours would not be alarming if seen in adults but are perceived as being inappropriate for young people in the process of growing up. Silbereisen *et al.* (1987) have proposed that a number of so-called anti-social activities are, in fact, purposive, self-regulating and aimed at coping with aspects of adolescent development. They can play a constructive developmental role at least over a short term. Early sexual activity and early child-bearing may serve similar functions (Petersen *et al.*, 1987).

While such behaviour is symbolic (i.e. these activities are usually engaged in because of a desire to create a self-image of toughness and maturity or as a perceived means of attaining attractiveness and sociability) they nevertheless often put adolescents at risk in terms of their current and future health.

YOUNG PEOPLE AND SMOKING

Golding (1987) notes that the decrease in smoking in industrialised countries has been dramatic. In three decades, smoking prevalence amongst adult United Kingdom males has fallen from 70 per cent to 40 per cent, for example. However, within this general trend a number of themes in relation to gender, social class and age gradients in smoking prevalence can be noted. Amongst Golding's adult population, 'current regular cigarette smoking' rates (a respondent currently smoking more than one cigarette per day) were at 35 per cent of men and 31 per cent of women. However, 44 per cent of the youngest male cohort (18–20 years) had 'never smoked'.

Strong socioeconomic group gradients are noted in the adult population, the prevalence of smoking being highest in the 'unskilled manual' and lowest in the 'professional' groups. Regional differences also exist, with smoking prevalence being higher in Northern England and Scotland. How far are these characteristics replicated in the adolescent population?

The Social Survey Division of the Office of Population, Censuses and Survey (OPCS) carried out a series of studies of smoking amongst secondary school children in the 1980s. A number of problems emerge in looking at this data. First, at a definitional level, 'regular' smoking is defined as smoking at least one cigarette a week, a category threshold so low as to be intuitively rather worrying. Second, no analysis by social class is available. Third, the coverage of Scotland is variable, and missing entirely in the 1988 survey. From these figures, however, it appears that amongst the adolescent population the prevalence of 'regular' smoking has indeed declined. The 1986 OPCS figures show rates in Scotland being higher and a bigger difference appearing between the rates for boys and girls. Among those who do smoke, however, boys continue to be heavier smokers than girls. A study of school pupils aged 14–15 carried out in the 1980s on a non-representative sample, for instance, found that the average daily consumption of girl smokers was six cigarettes, compared with eight cigarettes for boys (Balding, 1986). Balding speculates, however, that at least part of the explanation for this discrepancy might lie in the earlier social maturity of girls. In other words, the fact that girls tend to socialise with boys who are older than themselves might make it more logical to compare the smoking of 15-year-old girls with that of 17-year-old boys, for example.

In 1988, about one-fifth of regular smokers – 2 per cent of all pupils covered by the OPCS survey – had smoked an average of at least ten cigarettes a day during the preceding week. Children were much more likely to be smokers if other people at home smoked. Brothers and sisters appeared to have more influence in this respect than did parents.

Coggans *et al.* (1990) undertook a large-scale prevalence study in Scotland as part of a national evaluation of drug education. The young people in this study were all in the second, third or fourth year of their secondary school careers and were identified as representative of the range both of social class and drug education experience typifying Scottish school pupils in these age groups. It is worth pointing out, however, that though statistically representative along the dimensions of gender, age, social class and experience of drug education, the pupil sample was drawn entirely from the Central Belt of Scotland.

Something like 15 per cent of the Coggans sample smoked at the 'regular' level defined by OPCS as at least one cigarette a week. Such a figure may seem to reverse the trend of decline in smoking in this age group, but the rise is likely to be a consequence of differences in sampling procedure. Davis and Coggans (1991: 23) note the strangely bimodal distribution of smoking in the adolescent population, one sizable group smoking very infrequently (19 per cent) and the other group (14 per cent) being frequent smokers. Trends within this dataset replicate those in the OPCs studies. In other words, older adolescents are more likely to smoke than younger ones, females are more likely to smoke than males and young people from lower socioeconomic groups are more likely to smoke than their counterparts in higher socioeconomic groups.

Data collected in 1987 on a 15 year old cohort as part of the MRC Medical Sociology Unit's study known as 'The West of Scotland Twenty-07 Study', confirm the trends noted above. This study is a longitudinal design looking at the social patterning of health in the Central Clydeside conurbation. The sample, then, is not nationally representative but has interesting features. As well as a regional sample, two further 'locality samples' were drawn, one from an area in the north-west of the region with a predominantly middle class population and one in the south-west with a predominantly working class population (for further details, see Macintyre *et al.*, 1989). Just over 12 per cent of 15 year olds in this regional sample claimed to smoke regularly (quantities are not defined), but the rate varies from 10 per cent in the north-west to 19 per cent in the south-west locality samples, highlighting the social class differences noted above.

The most recent Scottish data on adolescents comes from the YPLL study. The data presented here relate to a 'core' sample of 1,666 longitudinal cases from the third survey sweep in 1991. 19 per cent of 13–24 year olds considered themselves to be smokers. A clear trend with age is discernible, with the proportion of smokers rising to a peak in the early twenties and then falling slightly. Table 8.1 shows the proportions of young people smoking regularly (i.e. more than ten cigarettes per week).

Table 8.1 Smoking prevalence by age group

Smoking status	13–14 years (%)	15–16 years (%)	17–18 years (%)	19–20 years (%)	21–2 years (%)	23–4 years (%)
Non-smoker/ infrequent	99	84	85	83	82	80
Regular smoker, > 10 per week	1	16	15	17	18	20

Source: YPLL survey 1991

Contrary to the findings in some other studies of young people no gender effects were discernible. Similar trends were visible to those noted in the OPCS data, with slightly greater proportions of girls than boys smoking at each age stage, but these differences were statistically not significant for the YPLL sample. Males were, however, more likely never to have tried smoking. Looking at the relative influences of family and peers, having a father that smoked was more influential in determining the adolescent's smoking status than having a mother who smoked, but peers and contemporaries had the strongest impact on smoking behaviour, especially at age 15–16.

Social class differences, when measured in the traditional way by social class of head of household, in this case parent/father, were non-significant though the trend was in the same direction noted in other studies (non-manual giving 11 per cent regular smokers, manual giving 14 per cent regular smokers). However, for the oldest four cohorts it was possible to measure current social class rather than class of origin. In other words, the current socioeconomic position occupied by young people themselves at the time of the survey was measured (e.g. in full-time education, employed in semi-skilled occupation etc.). Using this measure, significant differences do emerge in smoking status between groups of young people engaged in different types of economic activity. As Table 8.2 shows, only 11–13 per cent of young people in further education or professional and intermediate categories are 'regular' smokers, compared with 28 per cent of the unemployed, for example.

For the four older cohorts an analysis was made of smoking status by a variable known as ACORN. ACORN is an index derived from census variables and characterised by housing settings related to social class. A fuller account of the index can be found in Shaw (1984). The results are summarised below in Table 8.3 and demonstrate raised levels of smoking in the older groups in rural areas, with the lowest prevalence in areas of modern family housing with higher incomes.

Since the YPLL sample was clustered (using thirty school catchments) an analysis was done of smoking prevalence by school for the two youngest age groups still at secondary school. Differences emerged, with rates varying from 5 per cent to 16 per cent, but they were not statistically significant and it is difficult to characterise the patterns that emerge, reflecting as they do, a complex mix of social class, local economic and subcultural variables.

YOUNG PEOPLE AND CONSUMPTION OF ALCOHOL

Measuring the consumption of alcohol poses as many problems as measuring smoking prevalence. Studies requiring respondents to classify

Table 8.2 Smoking prevalence by current socioeconomic status (17–24 years)

Smoking status	Full-time education (%)	Employed 1/2 (%)	Employed 3 (%)	Employed 4/5 (%)	Unemployed (%)	Non-employed (%)
Non-smoker/infrequent	87	89	85	81	72	79
Regular smoker, > 10 per week	13	11	15	20	28	21

Source: YPLL survey 1991

Notes: 1/2, Registrar General's professional and intermediate classes; 3, Registrar General's skilled non-manual and manual classes; 4/5, Registrar General's semi-skilled and unskilled classes.

Table 8.3 Percentages of self-reported smoking in ACORN areas (17–24 years)

Smoking status	Rural/agricultural areas (%)	Modern family housing, Higher incomes (%)	Older housing, Intermediate/poor (%)	Better-off council estates (%)	Less well-off council estates (%)	Affluent suburban housing (%)
Current smoker	34	14	27	26	28	27

Source: YPLL survey 1991

themselves as 'light' or 'heavy' drinkers can produce very variable results – one person's 'light' may be another person's 'heavy'. One of the best methods of validating the data is by comparison of diaries of drinking. Specific information on what has been drunk as well as the quantity can enable the researcher to convert the declared consumption into units of pure alcohol and apply definitions of light, moderate and heavy with more precision. These definitions also apply different standards to men and women, a customary practice justified not only by typical differences in body weight and in social norms but also by the evidence that the threshold where consumption becomes damaging in women may be lower than in men. Overall there is a problem of under-reportage of drinking levels, though the reverse may be true in adolescent populations, and this is particularly likely in surveys of a more general kind. In surveys focused specifically on alcohol consumption interviewers may be more skilled at eliciting reliable information.

Amongst the adult population (Blaxter, 1987) there are big regional differences, with the heaviest consumers amongst men being in the north of England, Scotland and Wales, and the heaviest consumers amongst females being in Yorkshire, Greater London and the West Midlands. Blaxter comments that the social characteristic most regularly associated with greater consumption is income. This results in a pattern of heavier drinking among men in managerial, self-employed manual and skilled manual occupational classes at younger ages, and in the professional, employers and managers classes in middle age. The retired and the unemployed drink less. Women who work outside the house drink more than housewives. Divorced/ separated men and women are particularly likely to be moderate or heavy drinkers. Amongst adults the pattern of their own parents' drinking is a powerful determinant of their own drinking status. Women's drinking is particularly clearly associated with that of their mothers.

Are these patterns reproduced in the adolescent population? The literature on young people drinking describes such behaviour as part of the socialisation process from child to adult (Stacey and Davies, 1970; Barnes, 1977; Sharp and Lowe, 1989). In England and Wales, the majority of adolescents have had their first 'proper' drink by the age of 13 (82 per cent of boys and 77 per cent of girls). In Scotland, schoolchildren are introduced to alcohol a little later (71 per cent of 12-year-old boys and 57 per cent of girls) but catch up with their English and Welsh peers by the age of 15 (Marsh *et al.*, 1986). Lest these young drinkers cause great concern, it needs to be pointed out that most only drank alcohol a few times a year. Most adolescents' early drinking is done at home with parents. Only as they grow older does the context for their drinking spread to parties, then clubs and discos and lastly to pubs. Scottish adolescents are much less likely than their English and Welsh counterparts to drink in pubs. Marsh *et al.* (1986) comment:

Among the younger Scottish adolescents, particularly the 14 and 15 year olds, the proportion who claim usually to drink in pubs is small, less than half the values claimed in England and Wales. Scottish adolescents are far more likely to say they drink 'elsewhere'. Since this is not at home, nor on licensed premises, 'elsewhere' must be mostly outside on the streets, or wherever else Scottish adolescents may drink unobserved by parents or authorities.

(Marsh *et al.*, 1986: 19)

Most young people's drinking is done at weekends, as diary evidence shows. In relation to quantities, girls in every age group drank less than boys in the OPCS survey. Boys' consumption grows annually, with some very high levels being reached by age 17, whereas girls' consumption peaks in the last year of schooling. In Scotland, boys on average drink three times more than girls.

Whilst the long-term health consequences of regularly drinking large amounts of alcohol are well understood, there are also short-term health and social consequences of infrequent but very heavy drinking. Consequently, some of the data on 'drunkenness' is actually of more interest. In the OPCS survey (Marsh *et al.*, 1986) about 30 per cent of the youngest boys and 23 per cent of the youngest girls who drank in Scotland admitted to being 'very drunk' once or more than once. Note that these figures do not include young people who were not drinkers. Bearing in mind the caveat that such measurements are very subjective, it would seem that such behaviour peaks for both boys and girls at age 15, but declines more rapidly for girls thereafter.

The majority of adolescents associate drinking with positive reactions, but Marsh *et al.* (1986) note that associated with such specific bouts of drunkenness were not only the inevitable physical symptoms but also drinking-related problems such as vandalism, attracting the attention of the police and so on.

More recent data from the YPLL survey confirm the trends noted above, with 5 per cent of 13–14 year olds being 'frequent' drinkers (once a week or more often), rising to 48 per cent of 17–18 year olds and 66 per cent of 23–4 year olds. In this sample 65 per cent of 17–18 year olds went to a pub once a month or more. Pub-going seemed to peak in the late teens and thereafter tail off.

No significant differences emerged in drinking behaviour over the whole sample in terms of gender although in the youngest two cohorts boys were more likely to be frequent drinkers and to be buying alcohol from supermarkets. Across the whole sample there were no significant differences in drinking prevalence by social class of head of household. An analysis of the drinking data for the oldest four cohorts by the ACORN variable showed raised levels of frequent drinking in the most affluent areas, but this was not statistically significant.

Analysis by school catchment of the youngest groups of children did, however, show significant variability. The Highlands and Islands catchments showed the smallest proportion of youngsters who never drank. Two of these three catchments also held the highest proportions of frequent drinkers (approximately 16 per cent of those who drank). The proportion of frequent drinkers ranged between 2 per cent and 18 per cent, indicating the variety of local 'cultures' within which young people drink.

A discussion of local cultures brings us to look at some of the admirable anthropological type research done on young peoples' culture. The emergence of the 'lager lout' in recent years has generated considerable media attention. Young drinkers are blamed for innumerable instances of disorderliness in county towns or on football terraces. Tragedies such as those at the Hysel stadium or Hillsborough are blamed on drunkenness. What seems to generate most distress in the tabloid newspapers is that these are patently not young people without hope, drinking to relieve their sorrows. Many of the young people involved have good jobs and reasonable incomes. A study undertaken by Gofton (1990) sheds some light on the phenomenon.

Dorn (1983) has documented ambivalence towards drink. The market for alcohol is immensely profitable, and there has been a huge expansion in city centre drink retailing and leisure provision specifically targeted at younger consumers with high disposable incomes. Market forces are freely allowed to exploit this market, aided by central government's relaxation of licensing laws. But drink has always been seen as the vice of the working classes, unable to control their appetites and regulate their lives. Social order is maintained by the dominant class policing and controlling the activity.

Gofton took the view that drinkers do, in fact, police themselves, and that the *internal* set of rules and constraints that operate within a drinking group is far more important in determining behaviour than any externally applied restraint.

Gofton's empirical data is supplied by young drinkers in the north-east of England and a contrast is made between old-style drinkers and the young. Although traditional drinking in the area involved heavy consumption, it was also invested with meaning. Drinkers in pubs were almost exclusively male, pubs were local and customers were loyal, drinking was social and value was placed on 'holding your drink'.

Young drinkers cause concern to the older generation in the area more because of the way they drink rather than the fact that they drink too much. Leisure drinking for the young involves women too, at least until they marry and have children. Indeed women are central to the rituals that have evolved, rather than simply being tolerated within it. Pub forms have changed dramatically, neighbourhood loyalties have disintegrated, the young are mobile.

A typical drinking bout takes place at weekends only and starts with a group of between three and twenty gathering from the outskirts of the city where they live. They then move systematically around a circuit of pubs and clubs. Each visit may only last about twenty minutes, each place is over-crowded and noisy. The atmosphere and style of each venue is very important to its customers. This is reflected both in the designer drinks consumed by young men and young women and by the fact that the whole circuit is dominated by courtship. Both men and women are on the lookout for 'talent' in the spots they visit.

These trappings are all-important, but what distances young drinkers too from their older counterparts is their attitudes to drunkenness. Younger drinkers seem less concerned with staying in control; many deliberately drink to get drunk.

> Many see alcohol as a major mood-altering drug, and both seek and expect to get drunk in the course of a weekend session. The range of drink consumed, and their manner of consumption indicates clearly that young drinkers see it this way. Many said they drank 'for strong effect' and that they would choose a drink because of its potency.
>
> (Gofton, 1990: 37)

Gofton looks at the function of drinking in the leisure lives of these two age groups. For the traditional drinkers, leisure time drinking is almost a celebration of the old working class values of community, masculinity, social order. For the young drinkers leisure is seen as transformative and magical rather than reinforcing an existing lifestyle. Drink for the young is a means of making a shift into a world of heightened sensations.

The present moral panic over lager louts is essentially about control and lawlessness, 'the latest version of a perennial problem' (Gofton, 1990: 38), rather than about health. What is clear is that health education aimed at young people on the subject of alcohol consumption has to attack the very fundamental changes identified both in patterns of drinking and reasons for drunkenness.

YOUNG PEOPLE AND DRUG MISUSE

One of the forms of drug misuse associated with the youngest adolescent is solvent misuse. Solvent misuse is not illegal, of course, but it is discouraged both because of the short-term and long-term dangers to health and safety that it presents. One of the characteristic features of solvent misuse is that it is often very localised and very transitory, becoming wildly popular with a cohort of young people on a particular estate or in a school, for instance, then quickly disappearing. So, in some places at some times, large numbers of children will be experimenting, but only a few of these young people will carry on misusing solvents after the 'fad' has passed.

Recent British studies (Ives, 1990a) suggest that between 4 per cent and 8 per cent of secondary school pupils have tried solvents, and that sniffing peaks around ages 13–15 (third and fourth year of secondary schooling in England, second and third year of schooling in Scotland). In Coggan's sample, nearly 11 per cent of the sample had used solvents at least once although less than 1 per cent reported using solvents once a month or more frequently. Most of those who had used solvents had used them only once or a few times (Davis and Coggans, 1991).

However, despite the low incidence of continued misuse, it is clear that the fashion for solvent misuse has not gone away despite attracting less media attention in recent years. Numbers of solvent-related deaths give some indication of the problem's continuation. In 1983, when concern was at its highest, deaths totalled eighty-two. In 1988 there were 134 deaths, more deaths per annum than are attributed to the misuse of any other illegal drug (Wright, 1991). Part of the concern rests in the fact that published guidelines to retailers on the sale of glues – the most well-known solvent – have led to a trend towards misuse of more dangerous products such as aerosols (Ives, 1990b; Ramsey, 1990).

More common in usage amongst adolescents is cannabis, ranking third behind alcohol and cigarettes as a preferred drug. Davis and Coggans (1991) note that although 15 per cent of their sample of school-age children had tried cannabis at least once, only 2 per cent carried on using it about once a month or more frequently.

Cannabis is not in itself addictive and is not associated with any significant long-term damage to health. It is, however, an illegal substance, and thus most of the problems associated with its use stem from social rather than medical causes. There is some evidence that young people view cannabis in quite a different light from those offering health education on the topic (Hendry *et al.*, 1991a). Those concerned with health promotion for young people are often bound by professional guidelines to group cannabis with other illegal drugs and must effectively prohibit its use. Young people's own culture, however, denies that cannabis is harmful – it is often seen as less dangerous than alcohol, both in terms of the quantities consumed and the fact that it is less likely than drink to provoke violent behaviour. The association of cannabis with other illegal substances diminishes the validity of the message that health educators promote.

The study reported by Davis and Coggans (1991) demonstrates how low is the incidence of other illegal drugs in school-age populations. 6 per cent reported having used LSD at least once. Figures for heroin and cocaine were 1 per cent. Ecstasy was recorded at below 1 per cent of young people having used it, although more recent surveys might highlight the fashion in use of such designer drugs in dance settings.

However, Davis and Coggans comment:

> Data of this sort are reassuring for parents worried about the probability of their children taking drugs, but it should be said that this low level of probability is not evenly spread throughout society.
>
> (Davis and Coggans, 1991: 36)

No direct question was asked about personal drug taking behaviours in the YPLL study but young people were asked both about their attitudes to drug taking and about the proportions of young people in their peer group who used drugs. Boys were more likely than girls to state that some of their close friends used drugs. Age 17–18 was the peak period for drug use with 41 per cent of this age group claiming that some of their close friends used drugs. The details are shown in Table 8.4.

There was a significant link between those claiming a close friend as a drug user and social class, with 32 per cent of young people from professional or intermediate social classes making this claim compared with 23 per cent of those from semi-skilled or unskilled social classes. One could postulate that this puts the lie to theories about use of drugs in general and social deprivation and highlights the advent of expensive designer drugs or the predominance of cannabis. This was reinforced by analysing those claiming to have close friends who used drugs by the ACORN variable – the measure of residential neighbourhood type. Significant differences emerged, with the lowest declarations of drug use amongst peers in

Table 8.4 Percentages of young people claiming drug users for 'close' friends by age

Level of drug use amongst 'close' friends	13–14 years (%)	15–16 years (%)	17–18 years (%)	19–20 years (%)	21–2 years (%)	23–4 years (%)
Some use drugs	14	35	41	39	32	28

Source: YPLL survey 1991

agricultural areas (16 per cent) and the highest (48 per cent) in affluent areas of private housing.

Again, there was significant variability amongst the school catchments for the youngest two cohorts of the survey sample. The lowest claims for drug use amongst peers were in the rural areas of the Highlands and Islands (10 per cent), the highest were in some of the catchments in the Central Belt (40 per cent).

Of particular interest are the data on this topic for the oldest cohorts analysed by the current social class of the respondents themselves. The results demonstrate a distinctly bimodal distribution in which the highest claims for drug use amongst friends are in the groups currently engaged in higher education and those who are unemployed.

A recent article by Fraser *et al.* (1991) reporting on a small section of Brighton's population, highlights another aspect of drug use in youth culture, namely attitudes to recreational drug use. Most young people would be highly disapproving of the type of activity described in this study, but again it is worth focusing on because of the way in which it demonstrates how health issues are embedded in lifestyle choices.

The 'Pleasuredome' was the researchers' nickname for the entertainment centre of Brighton, part of a town centre location turned over at night to leisure consumption with boutiques, style pubs, wine bars, live music venues, fast food outlets and amusement arcades, targeted specifically at young people.

Use of drugs was considered by the young people who frequented this area to be as valid a component of their leisure as drink, choice of friends or music and dress style.

Workers at a drug advisory and information service working nearby (DAIS) shed some light on the phenomenon as they pick up the casualties. Most young people who referred themselves to the service were suffering from the side effects of stimulant or hallucinogenic drugs, rather than being the traditional 'junkie'. One DAIS worker described them as 'a different and nicer type of drug user'.

An examination of the DAIS records showed that most of the casualties fell within a very narrow age bracket (18–22). Men's use of the drugs clearly proved more problematic, even though equal numbers of women frequented the area. Almost all of the casualties were in employment or in further education and lived at home with parents. The concomitant of this was that, though their actual incomes were not necessarily very high, their living expenses were small, and so they had relatively large disposable incomes for leisure.

Most thus lived quiet 'normal' lives at home for the rest of the week, bingeing at weekends only in association with peer group leisure activities.

They were 'dedicated polyabusers', using not one drug but a whole range of different drugs concurrently. Cannabis, ecstasy, amphetamine sulphate and LSD form a potent cocktail. The reasons for taking such a mixture are to get high as quickly as possible in order to separate a magic world of leisure from the humdrum lives of mid-week.

Characteristically, they saw themselves and their drug use as unproblematic, believing that the problem drug takers were heroin users: '(Heroin) isn't a fun drug and it's not lively enough to be appealing . . . It's a drug that's popular among young people in high unemployment areas.'

However, a quarter of those reporting to DAIS had injected amphetamine and of these nearly half admitted sharing syringes. Such drug use is also clearly associated with unsafe and unprotected sex.

Fraser *et al.* point to the fact that such a group of young people clearly see traditional anti-drugs campaigns as irrelevant. The interventions planned in the local area take account of the leisure context of such drug use by advertising the information and counselling service in local entertainment magazines, listings and even on club coasters. The chief message of the intervention revolves around harm reduction. Users are advised to take one drug at a time, monitor their own symptoms and avoid sexual intercourse when 'stoned'.

The peer group is obviously an extremely important factor in this whole equation, encouraging individuals into 'a kind of stylised recklessness' (Fraser *et al.*, 1991: 13). Infiltration of the peer group may thus be a key in any health intervention strategy.

Klee reinforces this message in comparing young amphetamine users with heroin users:

> For example, the extent of sharing needles and syringes was greater. Motivations were different too. Sharing was not a consequence of desperation for an injection when experiencing withdrawal symptoms. The sharing of amphetamine users tended to relate to group involvement and the norms associated with it, in a much more pronounced way than was the case with heroin users. They were not only a more sociable group, they were also considerably more sexually active.
>
> (Klee, 1991: 3)

SOLVENT USE ON A COUNCIL ESTATE

This account of a gang of 'sniffers' comes from a study carried out in north London in the mid-1980s (O'Bryan, 1989). Those who work on these problems with young people will recognise the account as fairly typical of what is happening in many city areas. Again, it identifies health concerns

within lifestyle issues and makes the point that health education interventions have to tackle the issue – in this case, solvent abuse – according to
the meaning and role it has for participants.

At the time of the study local residents, youth workers and so on had
become alarmed at the 'wave' of glue-sniffing that had washed in on the estate,
though it was known that neighbouring estates had been affected earlier.

All the solvent users were boys of around 14. Little sniffing was done in
female company; in fact, these seemed to be boys who were particularly
awkward with girls. Girls anyway were not part of the culture of hanging
about on the streets in which sniffing flourishes.

The 'gang' was only loosely constituted, though they identified themselves by their smart 'casual' sportswear, by particular types of music (rap
and beatbox). There were clear leaders amongst the group.

When the 'wave' hit the estate large numbers of boys experimented with
sniffing. Debate exists over the usual proportion of regular to experimental
users. The ratio of one to five proposed by Cohen (1973) is probably closest
to the truth. Cohen had suggested that experimenters tried sniffing anything
from one to ten times before deciding to abstain. O'Bryan noticed, instead,
a seasonal element defining the degree of use. Summer holidays, for
instance, provided the perfect opportunity for experimentation, with time
on the hands of the young people concerned and no weather restrictions on
outdoor activities. Almost all experimental sniffing took place in groups.

For the majority the end of the school holidays signalled the end of the
practice. For a core group, however, even the cold weather did not deter
them and use moved from group to individual settings. The core users soon
switched from glue to butane gas canisters, partly because it was less easy
for parents and teachers to detect and partly because local shopkeepers had
acted to limit glue sales.

YOUNG PEOPLE, SEXUALITY AND RELATIONSHIPS

Adolescent sexual behaviour has always been a cause of concern to adults
in society. Fears about sexual activity leading to unwanted pregnancy are
coupled with a desire to protect the younger adolescent from exploitation
and pressure to become sexually active before they have the emotional or
social maturity to cope. Apart from risks to mental and social well-being,
there are risks to health both in the short term and long term. Early
pregnancies are associated with increased risk for both mother and baby,
early onset of sexual behaviour has been statistically linked in females with
cancers of the reproductive organs appearing in later life, and sexually
transmitted diseases pose threats to the health and well-being of young
people of both sexes.

In recent years, of course, the spread of HIV through sexual activity has caused increased focus to be put on young people's activities. Bury comments:

> Teenagers are often regarded as key factors in the future of the heterosexual epidemic. Unfortunately this is sometimes due to myths about their sexual behaviour, as they are often seen as promiscuous and irresponsible in their attitude to protection. Although there is much evidence to suggest that this image misrepresents the vast majority of teenagers in Britain, teenagers do remain a key factor in the heterosexual epidemic for other reasons. Adolescence is a time of experimentation; young people tend to see themselves as invulnerable, yet they are particularly vulnerable when they are at the stage of seeking a sexual partner.
>
> (Bury, 1991: 43)

The difficulties in obtaining accurate information either on sexual behaviours or on HIV status are almost too well known to need rehearsing. Recent figures for Scotland attesting to the fact that 9 per cent of those infected with HIV (i.e. 8 per cent of infected men and 12 per cent of infected women) are aged between 15 and 19, highlight, however, the need to know about the reality of young people's sexual behaviour and attitudes so that appropriately targeted health interventions can be made. There have been two main studies of young people's sexual behaviour in Britain, one in the mid-1960s (Schofield, 1965) and the other ten years later (Farrell, 1978). Since then all other studies have been localised and small scale.

Ford (1987) has identified the important indicators of patterns of heterosexual activity as age at first intercourse, the level of pre-marital sex, the number of sex partners and the proportion using the condom.

With regard to the first of these, the trend has been for teenagers to begin sexual intercourse at a younger age than in the past. In a sample of 1,500 16–19 year olds in England and Wales in 1975, 51 per cent said they were sexually experienced (Farrell, 1978). Differences between boys and girls were evident (32 per cent of 16-year-old males and 21 per cent of 16-year-old females claimed to be sexually experienced) but the gap between the genders was seen to be closing.

Social class differences in early sexual experience were significant in the 1970s, with young working class men significantly more likely than their middle class counterparts to be sexually experienced, but these differences appear to be insignificant in more recent data collections (MORI, 1990). Again, this may be a misleading artefact of the way data have been collected. As reported in previous sections, 'current' social class (based on the young person's current level of economic activity) may be of more import than 'ascribed' social class (based on the occupation of father). Bowie and Ford's (1989) work, for instance, suggests that those in full-time education are twice as likely not to have had sexual intercourse as those in full-time employment, housewives or the unemployed.

It is important to mention again the vast diversity in the individual experiences of young people. Conger and Petersen (1984) make a particular point of emphasising the importance of looking at individual differences when considering figures such as these. Apart from age, sex and nationality, variables such as social class, ethnic origin and cultural background will obviously play their part in determining sexual behaviour. The broad social trends described above also need to be considered in the light of other studies which have highlighted the different experience of young people in urban and rural settings. Ford and Bowie (1989) found only 56 per cent of youngsters in rural areas were sexually experienced compared with 70 per cent of their counterparts in urban and semi-urban areas.

Although teenagers are more likely to be sexually experienced than they have been in the past, there is no evidence that they are more likely to have casual sex relationships. Ford and Morgan (1989) claim that over 70 per cent of teenagers have intercourse only within a committed, loyal relationship. Such a claim would seem to be borne out by Stegen's (1983) and Tobin's (1985) studies of female teenage family planning clinic attenders. This evidence, now nearly 10 years old, showed that approximately 90 per cent of those attending had had only one or two sexual partners.

Bury (1984) has characterised adolescent sexual relationships as being 'serial monogamy'. More recent data seem to confirm this pattern too (RUHBC, 1989; Abrams *et al.*, 1990). What evidence there is suggests that roughly the same proportion of young men and women have had only one sexual partner, though there are great differences between genders in the numbers of men claiming multiple sexual partners. Urban–rural differences are also significant with young people in rural areas having fewer sexual partners (Ford and Bowie, 1989).

A small proportion of young people have multiple sexual partners, and it is a behaviour often associated with emotional deprivation or serious psychological problems (Hein *et al.*, 1978). Studies which have focused on 'sexually delinquent' youth (those who have committed sexual offences against other persons) and runaways emphasise the very high-risk pattern of sexual activity common in some groups which require very targeted and specific health education interventions (Rotheram-Borus *et al.*, 1991). Again there is a boundary problem here as to how significant a problem this is seen to be. MORI (1990) reports that 11 per cent of 16–19 year olds had four or more sexual partners in the previous year. Although some of these sexual encounters may have been monogamous and not undertaken in a promiscuous fashion at the time, there is clearly room for debate about the impact of such activities in increasing the risk factor for young people.

Contraceptive use amongst teenagers has risen in line with the rise in those claiming sexual experience in the teenage years, but such use has been shown in numerous studies to be inconsistent.

The condom is the only contraceptive which assists in the prevention of sexually transmitted diseases and the HIV virus. The most recent data (Bowie and Ford, 1989; RUHBC, 1989) seem to suggest that about a third of sexually active young people use condoms, but almost all use them for contraceptive rather than disease prevention purposes (Hendry *et al.*, 1991a). Despite the recent campaigning for condom use, a complex web of cultural and social factors conspire to make them unappealing and unusable for many young people (Wight, 1990).

Despite the fact that contraception is still difficult for many young people to access or negotiate with a partner, the evidence of data relating to teenage pregnancies attests to the fact that young women are no more likely now than in the past to conceive children at this early stage in their lives. J.C. Coleman and Hendry (1990) summarise thus:

> Figures published by he Office of Population Censuses and Surveys in the UK show that in the period 1969–84 the numbers of pregnancies for both 13 to 15 year olds and 15 to 19 year olds have remained relatively steady. If anything, the figures show a declining level of teenage pregnancy since the early 1970s.
>
> (J.C. Coleman and Hendry, 1990: 147)

All of the foregoing relates to heterosexual activity. Very little is known about rates of homosexual activity amongst adolescents. Kent-Baguley (1990) notes that 'not surprisingly, the majority of young lesbians and gays feel marginalised, isolated and unhappy at school, often feeling obliged to participate in queer-bashing talk to avoid self-revelation'. Little wonder then that the extent of the phenomenon is so unclear. A MORI poll carried out for the Health Education Authority (MORI, 1990) asked 16–19-year-old respondents to place themselves on a scale indicating their sexual orientation. MORI concluded that 88 per cent in this age group were clearly heterosexual and only 1 per cent clearly homosexual. A further 6 per cent, however, were bisexual or had a bisexual orientation.

Also in question is the extent to which homosexual practices place young people at risk. Blanket assumptions about the nature of sexual acts or the levels of promiscuity in this subgroup too often reflect simple stereotypes and prejudices. Young people themselves are particularly confused about the nature of the AIDS danger in relation to homosexuality since there is almost no discussion within health education about sexuality *per se* and homosexuality in particular.

HEALTH AND CLASS GRADIENTS

A number of measures of general physical and mental health were included in the YPLL surveys. All of them, however, relied on the young person's self-assessment of their own condition. Three such subjective measures of health were used. First, a measure of self-assessed general health was based on the General Household Survey (OPCS, 1989) question 'Over the last 12 months how has your health been?' Second, a question was included to identify those with a disability or long-standing illness. Third, a measure of psychological well-being was derived from the General Health Questionnaire (GHQ12) (Goldberg and Williams, 1988).

The data in Table 8.5 provide a general picture of the self-assessed health of the older four YPLL cohorts in 1989. These young people ranged between 15 and 22 years of age at this stage of the study. From the table it can be seen that, overall, young people's self-assessment of their general physical and mental health was independent of age. However, irrespective of age, young men were more likely than young women to report good

Table 8.5 Self-assessed health status by gender and age

	General health (good) (%)	Mental health (GHQ12 score > 2) (%)	Disability or long- standing illness (%)
Males			
13–14 years	82	18	13
15–16 years	84	22	13
17–18 years	84	22	10
19–20 years	83	22	9
All	83	20	11
Females			
13–14 years	70	29	13
15–16 years	68	30	10
17–18 years	68	29	12
19–20 years	67	26	8
All	69	29	11

Source: YPLL survey 1989

general health and they were less likely to report symptoms of psychological distress. There were no gender differences for disability or long-standing illness.

It might be expected intuitively that social class background (measured by parents' occupation) would have a strong impact on the general health and well-being of young people. Surprisingly, contemporary studies have found little evidence for such class-based health inequalities during the school years, though differentiation occurs both in infancy and in adulthood (West, 1988).

One explanation for this is that the relative absence of class-based inequalities in health amongst young people is an artefact of the measure of class used (West *et al.*, 1990). YPLL empirical data was used to test this supposition (see Glendinning *et al.*, 1992). Social class in adolescence is usually derived from parental socioeconomic characteristics.

None of the measures of social class origin (including parental education) produced evidence of health inequalities in the adolescent sample. An attempt was then made to characterise social class in a different way, using two ecological variables deriving from respondents postcodes and describing separate characterisation of residential neighbourhood.

The first of these, ACORN, identifies neighbourhood types based on forty separate census variables which take account of demographic, housing and employment characteristics. The second characterisation of residential neighbourhood employed an index of neighbourhood deprivation developed by Duguid and Grant (1984) to identify areas of special need in Scotland. Social class differences were not apparent using these indices either.

These findings confirm and extend the work of Macintyre and West (1991) using self-assessed measures of health. The foregoing characterisations of social class used to describe young people, though more extensive than usual, were fairly classical in being based upon the social circumstances of the parents. The analysis then turned to a consideration of the impact of current socioeconomic status, circumstances and educational attainment of young people themselves. This analysis was carried out for three older age groups of 17–18 year olds, 19–20 year olds and 21–2 year olds. These characterisations of socioeconomic position did produce substantial differences or health inequalities across the cohorts. For instance, young men currently in full-time education were more likely to report 'good' general health, whilst those on youth training schemes or currently seeking employment were less likely to do so (Table 8.6). The data for young women suggest that those on training schemes and full-time housewives were also less likely to report 'good' general health. Further analysis showed there was no evidence to suggest that these variations in self-evaluated general health can be explained by raised numbers of young people reporting disability or long-standing illness amongst those on training schemes, the unemployed or full-time housewives.

Looking at data for self-assessed mental health young women on training schemes, those seeking employment and non-employed housewives were more likely to report symptoms of psychological stress. Amongst young men, those on training schemes and the unemployed were more likely to report stress.

Further evidence of social class inequalities in health amongst adolescents can be seen if we look more closely at those young people in paid employment or on youth training schemes. Adopting a threefold job classification the results showed that, while there was no clear evidence for class-based differentials in either self-assessed general health or mental health, disability or long-standing illness was more likely to be associated with those young people in semi-skilled or unskilled jobs and was less likely to be found amongst those in professional or intermediate occupations.

Table 8.6   Self-assessed health status by social class of head of household

	General health (good)	Mental health (GHQ12 score > 2)	Disability or long-standing illness
	(%)	(%)	(%)
Males			
Professional/intermediate classes	85	22	8
Non-manual/manual skilled classes	86	18	9
Semi-skilled/unskilled classes	82	20	14
All	85	19	9
Females			
Professional/intermediate classes	68	31	8
Non-manual/manual skilled classes	71	28	10
Semi-skilled/unskilled classes	74	22	9
All	71	29	10

Source: YPLL survey 1989

Next, educational qualifications were examined in relation to health status, and health inequalities were again evident. The results showed that 'good' self-evaluated general health was associated with better qualifications (three or more 'higher' grades) while disability or long-standing illness was associated with poorer qualifications. Psychological well-being was found to be independent of educational attainment.

Thus in essence the YPLL data provide evidence of health inequalities for attributes reflecting the respondent's current social position but not for attributes based on parental characteristics.

The analysis then considered the connection between social class of origin and current socioeconomic circumstances. Inter-generational occupational mobility was investigated by comparing 'ascribed' and current positions, accepting the fact that such transitions are not yet complete.

The movement of young people from social class of origin to current social class was associated with differential health outcomes. Two types of young people stood out in terms of health inequalities. First, those young men who remain at the lowest end of the social class scale in semi-skilled or unskilled jobs (i.e. those presently in classes 4 and 5 with fathers similarly positioned) were less likely to report 'good' general health. Second, those young women who move downwards into semi-skilled and unskilled occupations from a skilled home background (i.e. those presently in classes 4 and 5 with fathers in social class 3) were more likely to report disability or long-standing illness. These findings are illustrative of the complex underlying processes at work in the production of health inequalities (West, 1991).

In summary, young people's social class of origin is not directly related to their present health status. Instead, the focus of the analysis needs to be shifted to the current socioeconomic circumstances of young people themselves (and also to the relationship between their current circumstances and their class of origin) because these already have a significant impact on young people's health in adolescence. An analysis based solely on measures of social class of origin or upbringing fails to recognise the diversity of attitudes, behaviours, activities, employment, education and training that exist amongst young people.

YOUNG PEOPLE AND HEALTHY LIFESTYLES

Overall then, by recognising the importance and diversity of young people's current social circumstances, we are able to identify class-based inequalities in health status at this stage of the life cycle. This, however, is only a first step in establishing what processes are important at what ages and for what types of inequalities in health. It is likely that further evidence of class-based health inequalities will be found by considering the inter-vening effects of behaviours and attitudes on the health status of the young people in our sample.

Are there, for instance, particular types of 'working class' and 'middle class' lifestyles in early adolescence to mid-adolescence which impact on the later health and physical activity of young people? To answer this question we first need to specify what we mean by lifestyle and then to identify different types of adolescent lifestyles.

A fuller discussion of the concept of lifestyle is currently being developed within the project. Some discussion of this forms the basis for Chapter 9. For the purposes of the present analyses, the concept of lifestyle was characterised in terms of the following variables: residential neigh-bourhood; social class background; family structure; living arrangements; educational qualifications and attitudes; economic activity status; dis-posable income and consumer spending; organised, casual and commercial leisure, including sports involvement and attitudes; self-assessed physical and mental health, health behaviours and attitudes and the health be-haviours of family and peers; self-concept and self-esteem; life priorities; views on 'getting into trouble' and perceptions of authority figures; and finally relationships with family and peers.

The interrelationships among these lifestyle variables were investigated using the statistical techniques of factor and cluster analysis. There were two main aims to these analyses: (1) to establish what the major dimensions (factors) underlying our data on young peoples' lifestyles were; (2) to identify different types (clusters) of adolescent lifestyle.

Turning to the factor analyses and the dimensions underlying the data on young people aged 15–16 years in 1987, there are a number of sport and health factors behind the variables used to characterise lifestyle. Looking at factors relating to sports involvement, factor 3 is associated with young women who spend money on sports goods, view themselves as athletic and play competitive sport frequently. Interestingly, the analysis for young men identifies two distinct sports factors. Involvement in competitive sport and sports clubs (factor 6) is distinguished from an athletic self-concept and positive attitudes towards health and sport (factor 3). There are also factors relating to health behaviours. For young women, factor 8 relates to dis-approval of drinking alcohol and the use of drugs, while for young men, factor 2 relates to disapproval of smoking cigarettes and the use of drugs (Table 8.7).

Table 8.8 provides a brief description of the types of adolescent lifestyle derived from the cluster analyses. First, different lifestyles (clusters) are associated with different social class backgrounds. In fact, using parents' occupation, parents' level of education and the young person's local

Table 8.7 Factors underlying the data used to characterise mid-adolescent lifestyles (15–16 years)

Factors for young women		*Factors for young men*
1	Visit friends and visited by friends often	1	Intend to go to college or university before seeking employment
	Spend a lot of time with a same-sex best friend		View this as a priority
	Go to dancing and discos regularly		Positive attitude towards school
	Hang about in the street with groups of friends		From professional/intermediate classes
2	Earning money, having a job you like, having friends, having a good time and family are important	2	Don't spend money on cigarettes
			Disapprove of drugs
			Have a hobby
3	Spend most money on sports goods	3	Positive attitude towards sport
	A leader in sports and games		Health conscious
	View self as athletic and competitive		View self as athletic and competitive
	Play competitive sport often		
4	Intend to go to college or university before seeking employment	4	Get on well with father
	View this as a priority		No family conflict
5	Get on well with mother	5	Out-going and content
	Confident about finding a job		
	Unstressed		
	Spend little time alone		
6	Spend most money on entertainments and in particular go to cinema regularly	6	Play competitive sport often
	Spend a lot of time with a boy-friend		Member of a sports club
7	Family conflict	7	Hang about in street with friends
	Bored in free time		Go dancing and to discos regularly
	Vandalism and theft can be justified		Don't disapprove of young people drinking alcohol
	Don't avoid getting into trouble		
8	Disapprove of alcohol and drug use		
	Spend little spare time with opposite sex		

Source: YPLL survey 1987

residential neighbourhood, it is possible to describe the clusters (lifestyles) nearer to the top of Table 8.8 as 'working class' and those nearer to the bottom as 'middle class'. These class labels are also consistent with the intended educational and employment trajectories of young people within the different clusters. For instance, among both young women and men, the middle class clusters 4 and 5 are associated with the intention to go on to college or university before seeking employment.

Focusing on the results of the cluster analysis for young women and looking at the connections between health, sport and lifestyle, cluster 2 can be identified with an unhealthy lifestyle and cluster 4 with a healthy lifestyle. Young women in cluster 2 view themselves as less healthy and as

Table 8.8　A typology of mid-adolescent lifestyles (15–16 years)

Clusters for young women	Clusters for young men
1 (36%) From skilled, semi-skilled or unskilled classes; part-time job; health conscious; no stress; visited by and visit female friends often; gregarious; spend a lot of spare time with family; organised and casual leisure; play sport for recreation and go to sports fixtures	1 (7%) From semi-skilled or unskilled classes; part-time job; won't continue education; view getting a job as a priority; content; hang about in street, but avoid trouble; disapprove of alcohol; feel parents are unsupportive; organised and casual leisure; think local sports facilities are poor; positive about sport, go to sports fixtures and play sport competitively
2 (6%) From skilled classes; dislike school; get a job rather than continue education, but not confident about finding one; less healthy and more stressed; not content; hang about in street; casual leisure only; bored; lots of spare time alone or with a best friend; little involvement in sport	2 (18%) From skilled, semi-skilled or unskilled classes; intend to get a job as soon as possible; feel stressed and view self as unfit; not out-going; don't get on with father and parents unsupportive; little leisure; bored; little involvement in sport
3 (18%) From a mix of social backgrounds, but few from semi-skilled or unskilled classes; visited by and visit female friends often; more time with peers and a boy-friend and less time with family; family conflict; spend money on cigarettes; hang about in street; casual and commercial leisure; play sport for recreation	3 (16%) From skilled classes; part-time job; won't continue education; intend to enter manual employment and train on the job; not health conscious; out-going; spend money on clothes; time with a girl-friend; don't disapprove of young people drinking; organised, casual and commercial leisure; hang about in street; play sport for recreation and go to sports fixtures
4 (7%) Professional, intermediate, skilled classes; intend to continue with education; confident about finding employment; healthy and content; disapprove of alcohol; spend a lot of spare time with family; get on with parents; organised leisure; spend money on sports goods, member of a sports club and play competitive sport	4 (38%) Professional, intermediate, skilled classes; intend to continue with education and then enter non-manual employment; gregarious; health conscious; disapprove of alcohol; parents supportive and get on with them; organised leisure; buy sports goods, member of sports club and play competitive sport
5 (19%) Professional, intermediate, skilled classes; intend to continue with education; confident about finding employment; view self as healthy, but feel stressed; not content; little time with a close friend; little interest or involvement in sport	5 (9%) Professional, intermediate, skilled classes; intend to continue with education and then enter non-manual employment; not content; disapprove of alcohol; spend much time alone; little organised or casual leisure; negative about sport, don't go to sports fixtures; little involvement in sport
(12%) Unclassified	(9%) Unclassified

Source: YPLL survey 1987

more stressed and have little interest or involvement in sport, while young women in cluster 4 assess themselves as healthy and are involved in competitive sport and sports clubs. It would be a mistake to think of these two clusters as typical of the differences between a working class lifestyle (cluster 2) and a middle class lifestyle (cluster 4). If anything, young women in cluster 1 can be viewed as representative of a typically working class lifestyle. They are health conscious, not subject to stress, have a network of female friends, get on well with their parents and regularly participate in sport, but for recreation only. The results also show there are distinctly different types of middle class lifestyle. As has been shown, young women in cluster 4 can be regarded as having a healthy middle class lifestyle. By contrast, although young women in cluster 5 are equally middle class and also assess themselves as healthy, they report significantly more stress and have little interest or involvement in sport.

Looking at the results for young men, broadly similar types of lifestyles are apparent and once again it is possible to connect these to health and sport. For example, young men in clusters 4 and 5 come from equally middle class backgrounds, but males in the smaller cluster 5 tend to be unhappy, socially isolated and negative about sport, while those in the larger cluster 4 are gregarious, health conscious and much involved in sport. Among working class males, young men in the smaller cluster 1 are more involved in sport, while those in the larger cluster 2 have little interest in sport.

Thus, although analysis of YPLL data for young people in early adolescence to mid-adolescence suggests that there is no direct link between physical health, mental health or sports involvement and social class background, an analysis of health inequalities in terms of parental occupation alone ignores important variations within and between working class youth and middle class youth. The YPLL data suggest that such variations are in fact reflected in the lifestyles young people lead.

In fact, once a typology of adolescent lifestyles has been constructed, these different types of lifestyle can be identified with young people's social background and their local neighbourhood. In other words, it is possible to label most adolescent lifestyles as 'working class' or 'middle class'. It is also clear that there are identifiably healthy and unhealthy lifestyles in mid-adolescence. For example, looking at the lifestyles of young women, there is a small working class group who lead an inactive and unhealthy life and there is a small middle class group who have an active and healthy lifestyle. But this is not true of working class or middle class young women in general. The majority of working class women lead a relatively healthy and active life and there are a significant number of middle class women who have a relatively stressed and inactive lifestyle. Broadly similar remarks can be made about the lifestyles of young men at this stage of adolescence.

SUMMARY

In summary, physical changes in body shape and functioning provide a backdrop for a concern about the transitions in young people's health status and the risks to which they become exposed in their adolescent years. Whilst risk taking is a feature of society throughout the lifespan, adolescents may be particularly prone to take health risks through a variety of social and situational factors.

A range of health-related behaviours have been reviewed to assess the extent to which young people's health may be jeopardised. It is a minority of young people whose smoking habits give cause for concern. Though large numbers of young people may experiment, only something in the region of 14 per cent of schoolchildren are smoking with any regularity. Despite an overall reduction in the numbers of young people smoking there is cause for concern because the disaggregated figures show particular groups putting their health at risk through heavy smoking. Social disadvantage is a clear marker for increased rates of smoking prevalence, an issue poorly addressed by intervention strategies which instead concentrate on a broad attack on young people's attitudes and behaviours through media campaigns and school work.

The consumption of alcohol is clearly much more widespread than that of tobacco. Alcohol is seen to be a social drug (Special Committee of the Royal College of Psychiatrists, 1986) whose use is both open and condoned by the parents of growing children. Hawker (1978) found that only 14 per cent of parents actually disapproved of their offspring drinking alcohol while under age, and since most alcohol consumption in early adolescence takes place at home under parental supervision if not encouragement, we must conclude that the sensible use of alcohol is indeed one of the social elements that parents try to inculcate in their young.

In the latter stages of secondary school drinking moves out of the home. A large amount of alcohol consumed with friends is purchased illegally from licensed premises, supermarkets and friends. At this age, too, the incidence of drunkenness increases rapidly and is associated with a range of physically and socially negative consequences.

National statistics perhaps offer false reassurance about the levels of drug misuse amongst young people. Flattened out as national averages, the figures for almost every illegal drug except cannabis seem minute, particularly in the school-age population. What has to be accepted is that great local variations can exist in the prevalence of misuse, so that local epidemics can appear very serious to those working in the field with young people.

Drug misuse has social consequences which are often of far more concern in the short term than the physical consequences, but some drugs do pose hazards to the lives and well-being of young people even when taken irregularly or over a short period of their lives.

It is clearly inappropriate to treat drug misuse as a unitary problem. Drug misuse and attitudes to drug misuse are differentiated by age, gender, social class and locality. Different problems require different treatments. Davis and Coggans (1991) are probably right in stating that we need to stop thinking of drug misuse as a problem of personal inadequacy, of social deprivation or of peer group pressure. All of these may be instrumental in forcing young people's choices, but people also take drugs for positive reasons (as they perceive them) and this fact is most difficult for traditional models of education to take on board.

The paltry statistics that we have indicate that sexual activity is admitted to by a greater proportion of young people in mid-adolescence now than in previous generations. There seems to be a natural lower age limit to such activity. Individual differences in such behaviours must be emphasised, but more general variables like social class seem to be having less impact as such behaviour becomes 'normalised'. Despite the prevalence of early sexual intercourse there has been no increase in the number of teenage pregnancies nationally, though young people clearly express problems about getting access to and successfully negotiating the use of contraceptives. Young people tend to limit their sexual activity within monogamous relationships, but these are often short-lived, and a significant proportion of young people have four or more partners in sequence in any one year. Contraceptives, where they are used, are seen as useful for preventing unwanted pregnancy; prevention of sexually transmitted disease is a very secondary concern. Little is known about the degree of risk associated with the sexual practices of heterosexual couples or homosexual young people in relation to the transmission of HIV.

Finally an opportunity is taken to examine the extent to which these individual facets of health behaviours build up into a picture of general health. The question of health inequalities related to social class is addressed using evidence from YPLL data. The inequalities found in young children's health associated with social class differences apparently disappear in adolescence, only to reappear in adulthood. Evidence is presented to sustain the claim that the absence of discernible health inequalities in adolescence simply reflects the complexity of the processes at work. When social class in older adolescents is measured using the young person's current social position rather than class of origin, then significant differences between groups emerge. The question of which variables actually promote healthy or unhealthy lifestyles has begun to be explored within the YPLL work and a brief discussion of this is included. Lifestyles are associated with social class groupings, but both healthy and unhealthy patterns of behaviour are found within working class and middle class settings.

9   Developing lifestyles in adolescence

INTRODUCTION

In the preceding chapters an attempt was made to understand the lives of adolescents in terms of J.C. Coleman's focal theory of adolescent development. According to this theory adolescents reach maturity by addressing a variety of challenges including gender identity, peers and parental authority. Each of these 'focal concerns' is tackled and resolved in sequence, although the patterning of the actions necessary is recognised as being variable among adolescents. Next a link was made with adolescent leisure transitions. Thus, issues concerning sexual identity are experienced at a time of interest in organised leisure, concerns over peer relationships are played out in the domain of casual leisure and finally parental authority is confronted around the time that commercial leisure interests come to the fore. The resulting matrix of relationships, interests and domains may well imply a diversity of ways of life for adolescents at different stages of development. If this is the case, can such ways of life be identified with distinctive adolescent lifestyles?

The concept of lifestyle is poorly defined within social scientific discourse, despite antecedents in the writings of Weber (1966) and Veblen (1966), both of whom developed theories of lifestyle as a way of explaining social status and patterns of consumption. Contemporary usage has often bordered on the tautological or the universal: lifestyle is thus a 'way of life'; or lifestyle 'incorporates . . . not only consumption . . . (but) also values and attitudes, demographics, gender differences, economic status, occupation and social class, and leisure participation (sic)' (Veal, 1989: 215). In short, it has come to mean nothing and everything and its explanatory force has been weakened accordingly. However, the concept remains valuable in so far as it can be shown to relate to (and to explicate) a phenomenon which would otherwise be subsumed erroneously under broader headings such as class and culture. Lifestyle is related to both but resides in neither.

A useful starting point in examining lifestyle is to consider the analogous concept of style. Style might be regarded both as an evaluation and as a description. In relation to architecture, for example, the art historian might refer to a building as belonging either to the neoclassical or to the vernacular style. Each label provides a description of the building, but also implies a distinct cultural tradition: during the Victorian era neo-classicism was seen as providing a direct link to the 'Golden Age' of classical antiquity, whereas the vernacular style was seen as a celebration of indigenous British culture.

In the present context, however, both the evaluative and the descriptive use of style refer primarily to expressive phenomena. Style is something visible residing in the world of symbols which others are invited to read (e.g. Goffman, 1971). A life style then, is, at the very least, a *recognisable* mode of living. Lifestyles are not simply a means of classification, but as the evaluative use of the word 'style' implies, denote a hierarchical order or set of preferences. They differentiate between more or less valued and distinctive ways of life. Lifestyles, in short, are rooted in what Brake calls the 'symbolism of appearance' (Brake, 1980: 14), through which individuals assert their identity and make statements about their social and cultural environment.

If lifestyles are about expressions of identity, what elements serve to constrain such behaviour? According to Weber, society is stratified across three principal axes: class, status and party. It is in the interplay of each of these sets of relationships that one's life chances are determined. Put simply, class differentiation is based on (and objectively measured by) productive relations and market position or potential. Status, however, differentiates between people on patterns of consumption and is subjectively recognised by people themselves. Finally, political action influences both our work situation and social status by defining the 'legal privileges' underpinning society. Overall, Weber assigns priority to the legal order as the primary source of social division. However, membership of (influential) political parties is the prerogative of those of high standing or status in society which in turn is derived, in part, from one's economic or market situation. Lifestyle – the 'styles of life' associated with patterns of consumption in the Weberian analysis – becomes the means through which honour, prestige and social standing can be perceived and affirmed. Conspicuous lifestyles legitimise the divisions within the social order. Hence, the 'plot' or rationale for a particular lifestyle relates to the need for a group in society to confirm, both to themselves and to others, the validity of their (separate) existence.

The need to assert and confirm a separate identity is clearly evident amongst young people. Here the peer group often acts to regulate expressive behaviour. Accordingly, it becomes difficult for adolescents to resist what Brake (1980) calls the 'quasi-delinquent style' in the hiatus between childhood and adulthood, given the absence of clear social roles for them to perform. For example, the machismo associated with male working class youth subculture (e.g. 'joy-riding', aggressive behaviour) represents a group response to the objective realities facing young people in a world of unemployment, low pay and low self-esteem (see Murdock and Phelps, 1973; Willis, 1977). To be 16, out of work and living in an inner city area invites a particular lifestyle.

Hence, lifestyles express a collective identity for the group members and lifestyles differentiate the group from some wider audience. Such audiences may be real or imagined, as in the pursuit of a 'healthy lifestyle' measured against an abstract notion of wholesomeness and good living which need never be 'personified' in any particular group. The important point, however, is that lifestyle sets a particular group apart. An echo of this is to be found in Bourdieu's description of cultural dominance and the relation of other groups to it.

Bourdieu attempted in *Distinction* (1984) to reconceptualise Weber's model of social stratification, in particular the relation between 'class' and 'status'. In doing so he began to map out the beginnings of a model of class lifestyles, distinguishing and commenting on the bourgeoisie (the dominant class), the petite bourgeoisie and the working class.

It is within the dominant class, the bourgeoisie, that symbolic struggles are most severe as the definition of cultural legitimacy is fought over (Jenkins, 1992: 142). There is also a struggle to define the relative importance of economic, educational and social capitals held in different quantities by different class fractions with different lifestyles. The outcome of this struggle is 'legitimate culture'.

The social standing of individuals in the petite bourgeoisie is either rising or falling, and in this area of uncertainty the key to the game is 'cultural goodwill', manifested as a 'reverence' for Culture – an 'avidity combined with anxiety' (Bourdieu, 1984: 327). Such a combination may lead individuals in the petite bourgeoisie into stylistic mistakes or transformations – everything they touch is transformed into 'middle-brow' culture. They are, however, also very internally differentiated as a group.

Amongst the working classes, 'realistic hedonism' and 'sceptical materialism' are seen to rule. Economic constraints and working class practices and perceptions result in a culture which is simply dismissive of the dominant class. Again, class fractions within the group differentiate between, for instance, the skilled workers (who remain typical of their class) and office workers already in the race for social mobility.

Despite describing *Distinction* as 'truly impressive', Jenkins notes that

Bourdieu's analysis is flawed in terms of its analysis of the relationship between lifestyles and class fractions (Jenkins, 1992: 148). Bourdieu defines class fractions empirically in terms of occupation and employment status. Lifestyles, however, are not so easily identified given that their constituent parts are scattered across a variety of fields. Jenkins identifies a circularity in the way Bourdieu has operationalised his variables, so that it is little surprise that different class fractions exhibit distinct lifestyles. He suggests instead that lifestyle identities should perhaps have been allocated on the basis of either patterns of social interaction or self-identification (Jenkins, 1992: 148).

In contemporary society dominant ideas about work, health and leisure are the backdrop against which many lifestyles are enacted. For example, there has been much recent interest in lifestyles in relation to health and in particular health promotion (Aaro *et al.*, 1986). In the context of health Wenzel (1982) defined the lifestyle of an individual as 'the entirety of normative orientation and behaviour patterns which are developed through the processes of socialisation'. Abel and McQueen (1992) comment that such characterisations of lifestyle have great theoretical and methodological appeal but that a fully developed conceptual approach still appears to be lacking. Also starting from a Weberian frame of reference they operationalise lifestyle in terms of a complex patterning of three basic elements: behaviours, orientations and resources. The first two of these are elements of choice or conduct. The third is related to the structural factor of 'life chances'. These basic dimensions interact to form an individual's way of life. Structural constraints at a societal level (e.g. Giddens, 1984) affect these interactions amongst behaviours, orientations and resources. Hence the interplay of structurally rooted 'life chances' and individual 'life conduct' results in the emergence of lifestyles as collective phenomena which allow for social differentiation both within and between groups.

To conclude this introductory section, lifestyles can be regarded as the product of interactions amongst a complex network of interdependent factors. They are the means through which individuals assert and confirm their position within society. Understanding adolescent lifestyles consists not only of gauging young people's behaviour but also includes understanding their attitudes, values and orientations in relation to the material and cultural resources available to them.

ADOLESCENT LIFESTYLES

Previous chapters of the book have adopted a thematic approach to the study of adolescents' lives. Elements such as health, leisure and family relations have been considered very much in isolation from each other.

Here we prefer to focus attention on the interrelationships among different elements of young people's lives. In doing so our intention is to identify some of the major factors underlying adolescent socialisation and leisure transitions and also to identify differing types of adolescent lifestyle. Basic elements in young people's lives were established using principal components analysis and differing types of adolescent lifestyles were identified using cluster analysis. This approach is guided by the conceptions of adolescent lifestyles introduced in the previous section.

Questionnaire items drawn from the 1987 and 1989 YPLL surveys were used to provide a basis for our characterisation of adolescent lifestyles. These items included: locality; socioeconomic background; family structure; living arrangements; educational qualifications and attitudes; economic activity status; disposable income and consumer spending; organised, casual and commercial leisure activities, including sports involvement and attitudes; self-assessed physical and mental health, health behaviours and attitudes, and health behaviours of family and peers; self-concept and self-esteem; life priorities; views on 'getting into trouble' and perceptions of authority figures; and finally relationships with family and peers. Data relating to these questionnaire items were analysed for one cohort of young people from the YPLL sample. The young people in this cohort were 15–16 years of age in 1987 and 17–18 years of age in 1989. Separate analyses were conducted for young women and young men using 1987 YPLL data and corresponding analyses were conducted using 1989 YPLL data.

Before discussing the results of the principal components and cluster analyses in detail, it is important to note that any consideration of young people's lives within modern Britain must first acknowledge the structure of society itself. Despite dramatic structural shifts in British society in recent years, there is still a profound linkage between social class background and the life chances (and so lifestyles) of young people. Figure 9.1 reports the results of a log-linear analysis of the social class background and current socioeconomic status of the 17–20 age group in the YPLL survey of 1989. The findings graphically illustrate the connections between social class of origin and the employment–educational trajectories of British youth. It is hardly the 'classless society' for the 1990s envisaged by some commentators and politicians. These findings point to clear subcultural differences in lifestyle between middle class and working class youth. Nevertheless we may still find equally distinct differences in lifestyle within middle class and within working class youth.

We turn now to the results of the lifestyle analysis. In order to focus in some detail on aspects of the adolescent transition, we discuss the findings for young women of 15–16 years of age in 1987. These young women were

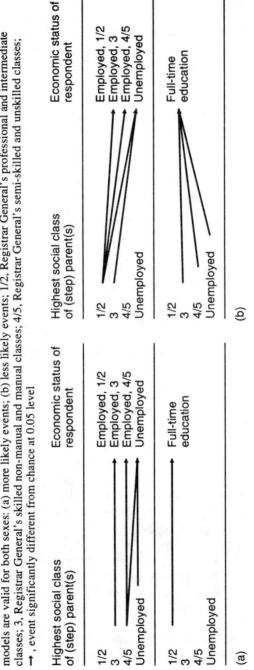

Figure 9.1 'The classless society': intergenerational class mobility for young people of 17–22 years of age (*n* = 989). The statistical models are valid for both sexes: (a) more likely events; (b) less likely events; 1/2, Registrar General's professional and intermediate classes; 3, Registrar General's skilled non-manual and manual classes; 4/5, Registrar General's semi-skilled and unskilled classes; →, event significantly different from chance at 0.05 level

Source: YPLL survey 1989

still within the statutory education system in 1987, but by 1989 were beyond secondary school age and had entered adult society. First we examine the results of the principal components analysis for this group. The factors identified by the analysis comprise the basic elements which underlie our 'description' of young women's lives at this stage of adolescence. They were:

1 'close' relationships with female friends;
2 life values and priorities;
3 involvement in sport;
4 intended educational–employment trajectories;
5 psychological well-being and adjustment;
6 commercial leisure and boy-friends;
7 family conflict and 'trouble'; and
8 disapproval of drugs and alcohol.

Essentially these are the elements which interrelate to produce the clusters which form the basis for our identification of mid-adolescent female lifestyles.

The results of the cluster analyses for young women are presented in Figure 9.2. If we look at the clusters for young women at 15–16 years of age it is clear that adolescent lifestyles are in general characterised in terms of social class differences. These differences are an amalgam of social class of origin (i.e. parental occupation), parents' experience of education beyond school (i.e. parental education) and type of residential neighbourhood or locality as characterised by the ACORN classification (i.e. parental residence) (Shaw, 1984). These interrelated social and ecological aspects of living conditions produce a clear class-based differentiation of lifestyles for most young women in mid-adolescence. As can be seen from Figure 9.2, clusters 1 and 3 could be labelled as 'working class' while clusters 4 and 5 could be labelled as 'middle class'. Cluster 2 is more varied and appears to represent a lifestyle associated with young women from a mix of social backgrounds. Brake (1985) has argued that we are born into particular social settings possessing distinct ways of life. Thus young people influence and are influenced by the perceptions, values and behaviours of these social groups. Within this complex pattern of social relations and meanings, individual adolescents begin to form a personal identity and a lifestyle.

But considerations of social class alone do not account for the five clusters obtained. Differences in lifestyles also emerge within social class boundaries. For example, if we were to examine mid-adolescent women's involvement in sport for class-based variations – whilst ignoring all the other elements which we have used to characterise mid-adolescent lifestyles – we would find no clear differences between classes. Yet it is

Figure 9.2   Young women's developing lifestyles (cluster analyses – abridged from)

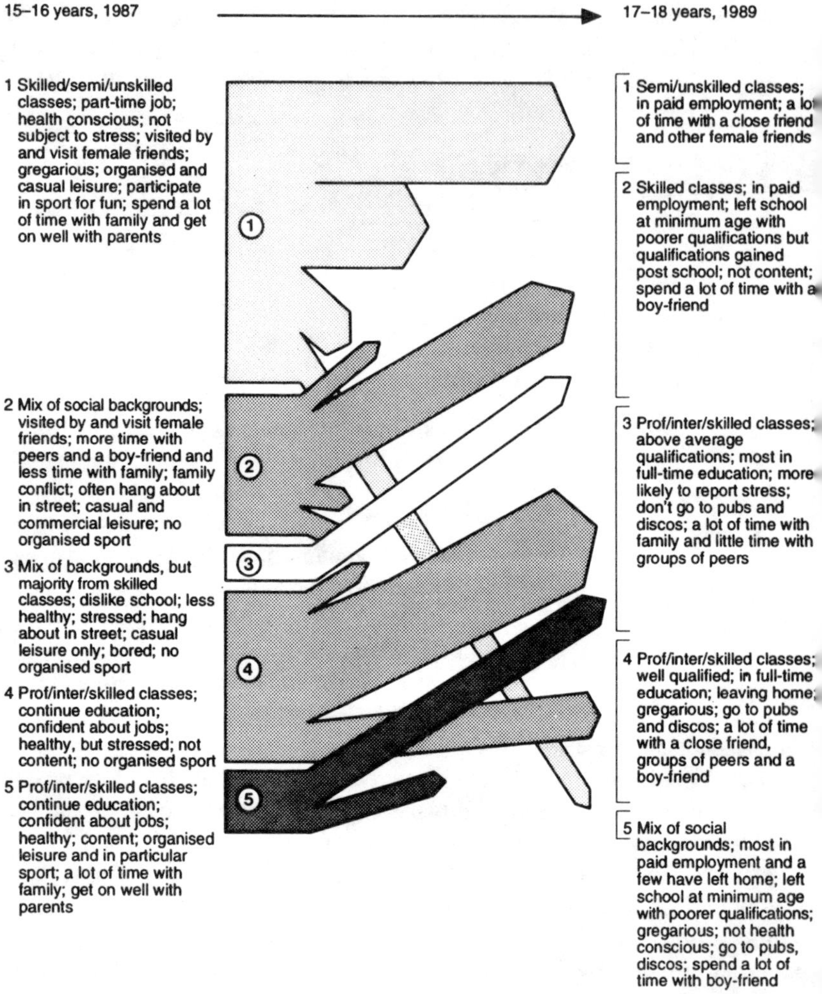

15–16 years, 1987 ———————————————————▶ 17–18 years, 1989

1 Skilled/semi/unskilled classes; part-time job; health conscious; not subject to stress; visited by and visit female friends; gregarious; organised and casual leisure; participate in sport for fun; spend a lot of time with family and get on well with parents

2 Mix of social backgrounds; visited by and visit female friends; more time with peers and a boy-friend and less time with family; family conflict; often hang about in street; casual and commercial leisure; no organised sport

3 Mix of backgrounds, but majority from skilled classes; dislike school; less healthy; stressed; hang about in street; casual leisure only; bored; no organised sport

4 Prof/inter/skilled classes; continue education; confident about jobs; healthy, but stressed; not content; no organised sport

5 Prof/inter/skilled classes; continue education; confident about jobs; healthy; content; organised leisure and in particular sport; a lot of time with family; get on well with parents

1 Semi/unskilled classes; in paid employment; a lot of time with a close friend and other female friends

2 Skilled classes; in paid employment; left school at minimum age with poorer qualifications but qualifications gained post school; not content; spend a lot of time with a boy-friend

3 Prof/inter/skilled classes; above average qualifications; most in full-time education; more likely to report stress; don't go to pubs and discos; a lot of time with family and little time with groups of peers

4 Prof/inter/skilled classes; well qualified; in full-time education; leaving home; gregarious; go to pubs and discos; a lot of time with a close friend, groups of peers and a boy-friend

5 Mix of social backgrounds; most in paid employment and a few have left home; left school at minimum age with poorer qualifications; gregarious; not health conscious; go to pubs, discos; spend a lot of time with boy-friend

Sources: YPLL surveys 1987 and 1989

clear from Figure 9.2 that variations in levels of sports participation with respect to social class do exist among the five lifestyles identified. These variations only become apparent once we begin to distinguish between different working class lifestyles and different middle class lifestyles. For the two middle class clusters in particular, individuals in cluster 5 are highly involved in sport – they spend money on sports goods, they are members of sports clubs, attend sports fixtures and play sport competitively – whereas those in cluster 4 have little interest or involvement in sport. If we had not differentiated between those two groups we would have been in danger of concluding that middle class young women are not particularly involved in sport, and certainly no more so than working class women. Thus there are also clear 'within social class' differences in lifestyle development.

Additionally, it is important to note that some lifestyles cut across class boundaries: they are common to both middle and working class young women. For example, cluster 2 seems to fit one stereotypical view of adolescent young women as spending a lot of time with a close female friend, hanging about the neighbourhood in groups, being interested in boy-friends, being in conflict with the family, going to discos and pubs and spending money on entertainments and fashion. This lifestyle pattern appears to cut across class boundaries in its adherence to 'youth culture' values (e.g. Brake, 1985).

When we examine the longitudinal transitions made by young women between the period when they are still at school (i.e. 15–16 years of age) and when they have left school and moved into adult society (i.e. 17–18 years of age) we begin to note identifiable lifestyles emerging. For young women aged 17–18 years in 1989 there are once again clear-cut middle class and working class clusters, with one small cluster from a mix of social backgrounds (see Figure 9.2). Additionally, between 1987 and 1989 the class basis of these clusterings of young women appears to be relatively stable. Thus the migration of individuals from one type of lifestyle to another is predominantly within social class boundaries. For example, young women from clusters 4 and 5 in 1987 move into clusters 3 and 4 in 1989. Hence these different groupings of young women are differentiated by their own occupational status and educational attainments as much as by their social class origins. It would appear that social context and occupational–educational trajectories have a powerful impact on lifestyle development – as was indicated previously by our analysis of the connections between social class of origin and current labour market position (see Figure 9.1).

Turning to a consideration of the results for mid-adolescent males in 1987, and two years on in 1989, there were broad similarities with young women's lifestyles, but equally differences emerged (Figure 9.3). Some-

Figure 9.3   Young men's developing lifestyles (cluster analyses – abridged form)

15–16 years, 1987 ────────────────────────────▶ 17–18 years, 1989

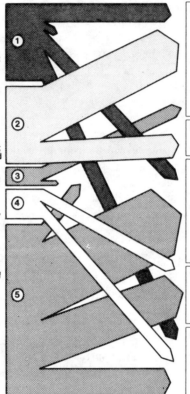

1 Skilled/semi/unskilled classes; won't continue with education; getting job important; little leisure and bored; no sports involvement; feel parents are unsupportive and don't get on with father

2 Skilled classes; part-time job; won't continue with education; enter manual employment and train on the job; gregarious; not health conscious; organised, casual and commercial leisure but little sport; hang about in street; a lot of time with a girl-friend

3 Semi/unskilled classes; part-time job; won't continue with education; content; organised and casual leisure; positive about sport; hang about in street, but avoid trouble; feel parents are unsupportive

4 Prof/inter/skilled classes; academic; not content; little leisure time and don't hang about in street; no sports involvement; a lot of time alone and little free time with peers

5 Prof/inter/skilled classes; academic; gregarious; health conscious; involved in sport and organised leisure in general; don't hang about in street; get on well with parents and feel they are supportive

2 Skilled/semi/unskilled classes; in paid employment; left school at minimum age with average qualifications; trained post school; assess health as good; gregarious; involved in competitive sport; a lot of time with a close friend or a girl-friend

3 Skilled/semi/unskilled classes; left school at minimum age with poorer qualifications; employed; visit friends less; bored; no sports involvement; a lot of time with a close friend or a girl-friend but little time with mixed groups

4 Mix of classes; in full-time education; good qualifications; some have left home; healthy; gregarious; content; visit friends often; spend a lot of time studying and with colleagues

5 Prof/inter classes; in education; good qualifications; some have left home; healthy; don't make friends easily but visit a few friends often; involved in sport; no girl-friend

6 Prof/inter/skilled classes; in employment or full-time education; good qualifications; live with parents; healthy; not gregarious; not content; not involved in sport; spend little time with mixed groups

Sources: YPLL surveys 1987 and 1989·

what similar factors to those identified for young women lay behind our description of male lifestyle and in mid-adolescence broadly comparable male and female lifestyles were found. By late adolescence, however, our results suggest a much greater differentiation of lifestyle patterns between the sexes.

Looking beyond an examination of lifestyle patterns from the perspective of gender and class, it is clear that particular clusters could be regarded as representative of 'health' lifestyles for example (see Figure 9.3). Among young men at 15–16 years of age, cluster 5 is reminiscent of a stereotypically healthy middle class lifestyle. By contrast cluster 4 represents a much less active middle class lifestyle, whereas cluster 2 has the all the elements of an unhealthy working class lifestyle. Thus health-related behaviours such as smoking, drug usage and drinking, together with involvement in sport and physical activity and attitudes to sport and health generally were seen to act as important differentiators among adolescent lifestyles. These elements were in turn linked to perceived physical and mental health status.

In relation to the psycho-social and leisure transitions between mid-adolescence and late adolescence proposed by focal theory (J.C. Coleman and Hendry, 1990), the results of the principal components analysis do indeed highlight peer and parental relations and casual and commercial leisure as important underlying elements of the adolescent transition. The results of the cluster analyses provide further support for the claim that relational issues and leisure interests are important factors in the development of adolescent lifestyles. However, the results also indicate that these factors alone are not sufficient to characterise young people's lives: they function in combination with elements such as the individual's current socioeconomic circumstances to produce the diversity of lifestyle patterns observed.

SUMMARY

The results of the analyses point to clear class-based differences in young people's developing lifestyles. Hence in general adolescent lifestyles do seem to have a class basis. Within the empirical framework used in our examination of mid-adolescent lifestyles, class comprised of a number of elements relating to: parents' occupation; parents' residential neighbourhood; parents' education; and young people's educational and occupational aspirations. By late-adolescence our characterisation of class was further supplemented by young people's educational attainment and their labour market position or participation in post-compulsory education. Thus, lifestyle development between mid-adolescence and late adolescence would appear to be strongly linked to young people's educational–occupational trajectories and to their 'life chances'. However, it is important to note: that there were a variety of working class lifestyles; that there were a variety of middle class lifestyles; and that a few adolescent lifestyles cut across class boundaries and these were typically associated with youth-oriented culture.

In conclusion, to answer the question raised at the beginning of this chapter, there *are* a variety of distinctive adolescent lifestyles. Within these differing lifestyles, adolescent psycho-social and leisure transitions appear to be predicated by elements of social position and material resource. The result is the generation of a system of behaviours and values which may have important implications for young people – in relation to their future health, for example.

10 Some concluding thoughts

INTRODUCTION

This chapter sets out to fulfil two purposes: first, to provide an overview of the key findings from the YPLL Project which may offer insights into the adolescent transition in British society; and second, in relation to these findings, to propose a number of emergent themes concerning theoretical interpretations and future research issues.

In recent years social conventions have given adolescents greater self-determination at steadily younger ages and current social expectations for youth are remarkably problematic. The transition to adulthood is complicated by the fact that there are no symbolic rites of passage. The adolescent's route towards adulthood is not marked out by clearly defined signposts. For example, at 16 an adolescent can marry or join a trade union yet cannot be tattooed or own a house or flat. At 17 the adolescent can drive most vehicles, buy a firearm, hold a pilot's licence, join the military, yet cannot vote, serve on a jury or make a will.

As adolescents grow up they are exposed to a larger number and variety of adult role models, both in school and elsewhere and as our society has become more diverse the number of social roles and choices available to most teenagers increases dramatically. Yet the ways in which young people select among these roles is harder to predict because political and moral values have become more diffuse as we have moved to a pluralistic society. The greater freedom for adolescents carries with it more risks and costs of errors in judgement: 'dropping out' of school, being out of work, teenage pregnancy, sexually transmitted diseases, being homeless, drug addiction and suicide are powerful examples of the price that some young people pay for their extended freedom. The impact of making 'wrong' choices on individuals, families and wider society underscores the need for a better understanding of normal adolescent development and the transition to adulthood.

Young people enter adolescence having been shaped by their biological and psychological characteristics and their earlier social experiences. Taken together, the experience of the younger child and of the adolescent are the mould from which the adult emerges. From a research perspective therefore, adolescence needs to be considered both as a distinct experience in the lifespan and also as an integral element of it.

Social shifts have created new constraints, experiences and opportunities for adolescents, in a context where even well-established social institutions can be subject to change. The family unit is one example of how a social institution has developed a variety of models in recent times. The nuclear family is now juxtaposed with 'reconstituted' families, shared custody arrangements and single-parent homes. Additionally, changes in social attitudes towards, and expectations for, adolescents have occurred in many spheres of life. To cite two examples: access to illicit drugs is now a common feature of growing up for many young people; and the transition from school to full-time employment is highly problematic at the present time.

REVIEWING THE FINDINGS

This book represents a line of enquiry which has attempted to allow young people to express their perceptions of, and reactions to, the world around them as they progress through adolescence. In this way we hoped to enable young people to indicate how they felt and to outline the concerns that they may have about their immediate circumstances and their long-term plans and goals. In the book we have preferred to view adolescence as a transitional process rather than as a stage or a series of stages of growth. To conceptualise the period in this way implies that adolescence needs to be understood as a time during which the individual passes from one state (i.e. childhood) to another (i.e. adult maturity) and indicates that the issues and problems faced by individuals during adolescence are predominantly the result of this transitional process together with young peoples' attempts to develop adult lifestyles. They do not imply any pathological condition attendant upon young people in the midst of the transition.

In Chapter 1, after a brief historical overview of adolescence in the United Kingdom, J.C. Coleman's (1979) focal theory, the ecological model of Coffield *et al.* (1986) and Lerner's (1985) lifespan framework were considered in order to look at the interactions between the psychological dynamics of growing up and the social constraints and opportunities offered to young people. From Lerner's paper on lifespan development the importance of the young person as a self-agent in his or her own transitional development was emphasised.

In Chapter 2 we stated that the YPLL Project was designed to identify and capitalise on this process of transition. A series of large-scale survey sweeps combined with a smaller qualitative panel study of young people growing up in different ecological settings enabled us to examine adolescent development from both a cross-sectional and longitudinal perspective.

The study was built around a series of initial research questions. What are young people like? What do they do in their leisure time at different ages through the adolescent period? What differences can be attributed to gender and social class effects? Can we offer plausible explanations for these findings and offer some interpretations of the main determining factors? Can we offer descriptive pathways of developing lifestyles and leisure styles amongst Scottish adolescents across the teenage years?

Three large-scale questionnaire survey sweeps in 1987, 1989 and 1991 were conducted in order to build up a picture of developing lifestyle. The array of data generated has helped us to construct and operationalise our interests. Throughout, the quantitative work has been illuminated by interview work carried out with adolescents from eleven different socio-geographic areas. The data base is a unique and rich one in several respects: the sampling frame ensures a geographical representation not found in many Scottish data sets and the data base contains not only information on leisure interests and attitudes but also detailed records of physical and mental health, family relationships and background, friendship patterns, educational attainments, career trajectories, living conditions and young people's attitudes and views on many aspects of society. All this information was set against a backcloth of details on social settings, geographic areas and the housing and living conditions of these young people. We believe that our perspective has enabled us to examine trends from the data that cut across usual notions of gender and class categories to enable a clearer examination of the nature and function of the developing adolescent.

The book then attempted to provide some understanding of adolescents and their leisure interests by considering a number of themes and contexts (Chapter 3). It was noted that there is a changing focus of emphasis in adolescents' leisure pursuits. The interplay of factors from within the individual and from the social environment which directs young people towards particular pursuits in their leisure is important to understand. These shifts involve a whole range of psycho-social factors – from personal characteristics to the role of adults and peers in the formation of subcultural values, social class membership and the effects of wider society's norms and expectations including those from the mass media, all of which influence adolescents. A crucial point to stress is the way in which the interplay of factors can vary from individual to individual as the focus of social and leisure interest changes across the adolescent years. In general, however, Hendry's (1983) focal theory of leisure suggested a coincidence of leisure transitions (from organised leisure activities through casual activities to commercial leisure) with the psycho-social foci of development proposed by J.C. Coleman (1979).

One of the findings from this chapter was that the leisure patterns displayed in pre-adolescence indicated a rather similar shifting focus to those presented across the adolescent years. Thus it is possible to suggest that a small scale anticipatory socialisation process occurs in the pre-adolescent years. The chapter on leisure not only explored the various elements of focal theory (and to some extent confirmed and extended the original hypotheses) but also looked at the impact of unemployment in later adolescence showing, as other studies have done, that unemployment tends to place older adolescents in a social limbo by preventing them from experiencing and entering the normal work/leisure 'package', thus leaving them to have a leisure existence perhaps more appropriate to younger adolescents. This delayed social transition and exclusion from mainstream social roles may have important implications for future society and for the young person's entry into adulthood. With growing unemployment young people are continuing to live in the parental home and their access to independent living and lifestyles is more constrained. The impact on social development and adult maturity awaits further research. The chapter also considered ecological dimensions of leisure by showing how young people make particular and 'alternative' uses of community facilities. We found that certain leisure settings were dominated by particular subcultural groups which create territorial 'no-go' areas for other young people in the community.

The fourth chapter considered sport both within the setting of schooling and in the wider community. One significant set of results showed important gender differences in young people's attitudes and approaches to sport. In general, young women were not attracted by male formulations of sport as competitive activities and policy makers may need to take account of young women's social and recreational needs in a more positive way if they are to target continued participation by young women. Another important finding was the link between participation in sports and perceived physical and mental health. If this is linked back to our previous comments about young women's involvement, a whole area of investigation becomes apparent in looking at the motivations and contexts necessary to ensure an active lifestyle in young people. It also raises policy questions for those commissioned by society to provide sports facilities and resources for adolescents.

Chapter 5 investigated schooling and its relationship to occupational transitions into adult society. No longer is the transition from school to work a direct one. Young people can be unemployed, on a training scheme into employment and made redundant all in a short period of time. In rather similar vein to the ESRC 16–19 Initiative, our results revealed various trajectories and 'sorting' processes that occurred from the time young people leave school at 16 until they reach later adolescence. In terms of education and employment, social class remains an important factor in sifting young people into employment, further education or vocational training. Young people's expectations of future employment are largely confirmed once they enter the labour market. Although young people at the start of their careers may be difficult to categorise occupationally, class- and gender-based differences are already evident in late adolescence. When we looked at the evidence for or against mobility between the social classes we found that in general the social boundaries of British society remain firm for the present generation of young people.

In relation to families (Chapter 6) a key research finding was that teenagers and their parents have less stormy relationships than might be generally imagined. Adolescence need not – and typically does not – mark the onset of either open or covert conflict as young people seek to establish a sense of autonomy. Parents remain an important influence throughout the adolescent years helping young people mould their sense of self and shape future life choices. Although they have to adapt to the changes that accompany adolescence, parents remain actively involved with their children and most young people feel close to their parents despite a range of minor disagreements between the two generations in day-to-day domestic situations. What does change is how these interactions are structured to acknowledge and accommodate the growing independence of young people. Thus, adolescence is not necessarily a stressful period in relationships between young people and adults. Where important values, future plans and attitudes are concerned adolescents appear to be largely in agreement with their parents: a generation gap in terms of fundamental values seems to be a somewhat erroneous idea. Rather, many young people accept their parents as behavioural models and develop a lifestyle compatible with their subcultural upbringing and experiences.

Our study has extended the previous work of such researchers as Baumrind (1971). More importantly, our work has suggested links between family types and particular kinds of (reported) adolescent behaviour. Perhaps, therefore, the most significant pointer from this chapter is the apparently far reaching effect of the 'neglectful' family which appeared to be evident in all types of social class settings and revealed possible family influences on subsequent lack of adolescent adjustment, anti-social behaviour and trauma.

As was discussed in Chapter 7 youth does not seem to be as counter-cultural as it is often depicted nor does it seem to be uniformly hedonistic and self-centred. In fact, peers often support traditional parental attitudes and beliefs and often work in concert with, rather than in opposition to, adult goals and achievements. Nevertheless, peer influences may become more critically important for young people whose access to parental influences is impaired. Youth appears to reflect societal values and behaviours. For example, adolescent drug and alcohol use and sexual activity seem to be interconnected with shifts and attitudes among the adult population, yet issues of timing and modes of transition for such attitudinal shifts are not particularly well understood.

We were able to look at the important influence of friends within the wider network of peer groupings and discovered gender differences in the way elements of popularity change across the adolescent years. Young women, for instance, are more likely than young men to sacrifice same-sex friendships when moving into courting dyads in adolescence. We also claimed that peers and friends serve multiple functions in the lives of adolescents. Peer groups have a dynamic role and vary according to the characteristics of individual young people.

Too often adolescents are portrayed as passive recipients of circumstances and resources that others make available to them. In reality they play an active role in choosing and shaping the context in which they operate – their friends, their activities and their lifestyles. By experiencing the values and norms of a particular peer group the adolescent begins to evaluate the perspectives of others whilst developing his or her own values and attitudes. Dress, hairstyles, musical interests, language, leisure activities and values are among the socially relevant characteristics that teenagers appear to learn at least in part from peer models. In addition, teenagers learn methods of handling social relationships by observing and imitating peers. The emphasis between observing, imitating and trying out behaviours appears to shift across adolescence. Peer and friendship groups act as sources of behavioural standards particularly where parental influence is not strong and these groups offer young people opportunities for role taking and role modelling. One important finding from our study was the fact that acceptance by peers was important to young women just as much as it was to young men although the criteria regarded as necessary for popularity did demonstrate gender differences. Additionally, the ways in which the relative importance attached to these characteristics shifted across the adolescent years was different for young men and young women.

Peer pressures to carry out certain behaviours such as smoking and drinking reached a peak in mid-adolescence but later in the transitional stage such behaviours were not seen to be particularly relevant to acceptance and peer pressures lessened.

Because of the complexities of modern society children now approach adulthood before many of them are capable of functioning skilfully in adult social roles. The disjunction between their physical capabilities, socially approved independence and power and the ambiguities of their current status can be stressful for young people. A considerable body of empirical evidence now exists to support the idea that an active leisure life can improve overall self-esteem and mental and physical health. Put simply, leisure has a big part to play in helping young people to make healthy and successful adjustments in this phase of their life. Much of the existing evidence on the relationship between health and active lifestyles is confined to older population samples. In youthful populations good health is the norm. Even the effects of heavy smoking and drinking do not clearly emerge until early adulthood. In Chapter 8 we saw that young people appeared to perceive themselves as generally fit and healthy and while there were gender differences in physical health statuses – with young women rating themselves less healthy than young men – there were no social class differences based on parents' occupational status. Young people with organised active and/or sociable leisure interests which ensured peer interaction and those with positive attitudes towards leisure also had better mental health scores. Conversely, those adolescents with little available leisure time and those adolescents who saw themselves having too much leisure time or being bored in their leisure had poorer mental health scores.

Whilst adolescence is in general a healthy stage of the lifespan, it may nevertheless see the genesis of behaviour patterns which are carried into adulthood with associated health risks. Whilst a relatively small number of young people smoke regularly, some did appear to be putting their health at risk through heavy smoking, those in socially disadvantaged positions being more likely to be amongst the heaviest smokers.

The consumption of alcohol was far more widespread than that of tobacco. As with other studies we found that in mid-adolescence drinking occurred within community settings and with friends. Often alcohol was purchased illegally from licensed premises and supermarkets. Around this period the incidence of drunkenness increased rapidly and was associated with physically and socially negative consequences.

Drug misuse and attitudes to drugs was found to be differentiated by age, gender, social class and locality. Like Davis and Coggans (1991) we would want to argue that there is a need to stop thinking about drug misuse simply as a problem of social or personal inadequacy. From our study it seems that young people often take drugs for 'positive reasons' *as they perceive them.*

This is an important issue for formal and informal educational agencies to address in working with young people on health education issues.

Perhaps, though, our most important finding in this chapter related to the question of health inequalities. There were no social class differences in young people's health in early adolescence based on parents' occupational statuses. Nevertheless, by mid-adolescence to late adolescence the variations in occupational status of young people themselves revealed significant health gradients with those going on to further and higher education (and including those staying on at school) and those in employment having healthier profiles than young people on training schemes, the unemployed or those in non-employed statuses (e.g. housewives), and these differences were not explained by long-term illness or disabilities. Hence, the young person's current social position rather than their social class of origin anticipated the production of the class-based differences observed within the adult population.

The question of health – within the context of lifestyles more generally – was one addressed in Chapter 9 by making considerable use of the longitudinal dimension of our study. This chapter explored how factors such as personal perceptions and expectations, previous socialisation patterns, specific personality traits and the social relations with peers and adults combine and interact to form recognisable lifestyles in adolescence. Such research emphasises a more integrated appreciation of both biological and psycho-social influences. If structural and behavioural differences can alter the nature of the adolescent experience and enhance or detract from the ability of young people to make an effective transition to adulthood, we need to study more carefully the diversity in adolescents and give greater attention to processes that may be particularly influential for different groups of young people. Added to this, as children enter adolescence they increasingly interact independently with their environment, spending ever greater amounts of time with people outside the family and steadily gaining control over where, how and with whom they spend their time. Many social forces influence these changes across the adolescent years.

Hence Chapter 9 brought together a number of broad themes dealt with throughout the book and considered young people within their social class background and offered the idea of lifestyle as a framework for examining variations within and between adolescent subcultures.

Generally speaking what we found was that there was relatively little exchange across social class boundaries in terms of lifestyle development in adolescence. Nevertheless, within social class boundaries significant variations in lifestyle clearly emerged. In addition, a few lifestyle patterns were shown to 'cut across' class boundaries, revealing particularly 'youth-oriented' lifestyles. It is important to point out that groups of young people in higher education, those in employment, on training schemes and the unemployed do appear to develop different lifestyle trajectories.

EMERGENT THEMES

The erosion of the traditional roles of the family, the church and the school – institutions originally associated with socialisation of the young – has resulted in the fragmentation of the adolescent transition since various social environments function as independent, sometimes isolated and at times competitive or even contradictory settings for teenagers. It is this confusion of purpose at the community level and the disaffection which young people may develop towards it, rather than any nationwide rebelliousness towards adult society which create the possible conflicts of the adolescent identity crisis so frequently cited in the media.

If the values expressed by different community institutions are at odds, if their directions are unclear or inconsistent, the young person will be left with an uncertain set of guiding principles. Teenagers need to learn and express societal standards and expectations, not simply as sanctioned rules but as a loose collection of shared understandings which operate to limit the variability of acceptable behaviour. Paradoxically, too often adolescents are described as passive recipients of circumstances and resources that other people make available to them. In reality, however, young people play an active role in choosing and shaping the context in which they operate and develop friendships, activities and lifestyles. The desires of parents and society at large to provide environments that promote 'acceptable' development might be simplified if we could gain a clearer understanding of why and how teenagers either resist or co-operate with such efforts from adult society. For example, why do some adolescents function successfully as adults despite having grown up in poverty or in a broken home, contexts which are associated with generally negative outcomes? Conversely, why do others struggle to achieve adjustment despite coming from settings that seem to offer every advantage? Accepting that adolescence is a multi-faceted transitional period of the life span, what are the possible themes which emerge from this book which can inform policy and future research?

SOME CONSIDERATIONS AND ISSUES

In our study of adolescents and family our analyses were strongly supportive of Baumrind's model which characterises family dynamics in terms of acceptance and control. We found crude social class differences in patterns of parenting, but our finer grain analysis revealed considerable variety *within* social classes and of particular interest was the clear identification of a family style associated with multiple problems for the young person. Although the evidence indicated that a 'neglectful' family style was linked to poorer socioeconomic circumstances, such problem families were found across a broad range of social classes. Further research needs to focus in a more detailed fashion on family interactions to examine the ways in which families influence young people and young people influence the family as they negotiate and gain independence and autonomy. Our findings regarding parenting styles and behavioural outcomes also raise questions about the influence of family styles on young women as they grow up.

Differences between the two dominant worlds of the adolescent, the family and the peer group can be a source of potential tension as the teenager becomes increasingly dependent on peers for social approval and companionship. Whilst we have suggested that peers are more supportive of parental roles than is often acknowledged, our examination of different family and parenting styles suggests the need for further study to examine the interconnections between the adolescent *in the family* and the adolescent *within the peer group*. It is important to learn how different interpersonal contexts complement or interfere with one another.

Like adults, teenagers typically adopt behaviours in the belief that they will help achieve some desired end such as peer acceptance. In doing so they are likely to ignore or discount evidence that particular behaviours may pose a potential threat to them. For example, a willingness to start smoking or to have unprotected sex can be affected by beliefs adolescents hold about peer expectations and practices. In such instances a behaviour such as smoking may serve a wide range of purposes from projecting a desired image to emulating or defying an important authority figure.

The gender and social class differences found in young people's choice of peer groups emphasises the importance of gaining a greater understanding of the influence of peer groups as an aid or hindrance to integration in adult society. Our brief examination of the positive and negative influences of being on one's own in adolescence hinted at some of the coping strategies employed by young people in the face of social and personal concerns in their everyday life. Again this aspect warrants further examination and research.

In Chapter 5 we examined the multi-faceted role of school in the lives of young people and discovered that whilst the majority of young people enjoyed school life and saw it as the road to occupational opportunities in post-school life, there were nevertheless a number of dissatisfactions with the experience of schooling. Our findings raise questions about the functions of schooling in present-day society and emphasise the need for those within the educational system to have a clearer understanding of young people's perceptions of post-school life. A better knowledge of how family and school influences interact might be helpful in informing the necessary non-academic functions of schools in fostering young people's development.

For many teenagers adult-led organisations are major sources of structured leisure time activities, creating contexts for meeting friends and observing adult role models. There is a need for a more systematic assessment of organised youth activities such as sport groups, music groups, formal youth clubs and uniformed organisations. We need to know more about adolescent–adult interactions (and mentoring roles) within such contexts. We lament the lack of an ethnography of adolescent life which would explore the ways in which young people use and perceive their leisure environments. There is a need to take an anthropological perspective to study the use young people make of leisure contexts in greater detail than previously.

Our study of leisure supported and extended the focal theories of J.C. Coleman and Hendry (1990) but further questions need to be pursued regarding the personal and social factors which initiate – or indeed fail to initiate – changes in the leisure interests of individual adolescents. For example, factors such as unemployment have a major impact on leisure activities in later adolescence which may affect the transition to adulthood. A major challenge for those studying adolescent development is to elucidate pathways or mechanisms by which contexts exert their influence on the adolescent transition.

In looking at health we found young people's social class of origin not to be directly related to their health status. Instead the focus of analysis was shifted to the current social-economic circumstances of young people themselves (and also to the relationship between their current circumstances and their class of origin because these already have a significant impact on young people's health in adolescence). By recognising the importance and diversity of young people's social circumstances we were able to identify class-based inequalities in health status at this stage of the life cycle. It is likely that further evidence of class-based health inequalities will be found by considering the intervening effects of behaviours and attitudes on the health status of young people. Are there, for instance, particular types of working class and middle class lifestyles in early adolescence to mid-adolescence which impact on the later health and physical activity of young people?

In relation to specific health behaviours we need to understand better the shifting emphasis of contexts in influencing adolescent development. For example, Brown (1982) found that peer pressure to drink alcohol shifted from relative disapproval in early adolescence towards an increased pressure to drink in mid-adolescence; whereas pressures to use drugs and have sexual intercourse were strongest in later adolescence. Brown noted that adolescents often actively discouraged such activities. Our results agree with these findings. Peer pressure to drink and smoke was greatest at 15–16 years of age but at the same time many adolescents did not perceive such behaviours as particularly relevant to acceptance by the peer group. These differences in adolescents' responses to peer pressures, their willingness to resist or succumb, the length of time and the effects of their involvement are aspects for future research to address.

Longitudinal studies can be a significant component of any research agenda on normal adolescent development. They are central to any effort to clarify how one aspect of development connects with another. Adolescents face changes in all aspects of their lives. The psycho-social models adapted at the start of this book suggest that their ability to cope with these changes depends not only on intrinsic strengths and external supports but also on the timing of particular issues. If disruptions are too numerous or require too much change and too little time to develop coping strategies, they may produce negative effects. Concurrent major changes – for instance, going through puberty while entering a new school and losing established friends – may be more than many adolescents can cope with.

An alternative sociological framework was used towards the end of the book to structure a discussion of adolescent lifestyles and to introduce an analysis which attempted to bring together the varied aspects of adolescent behaviours and attitudes. These changing patterns of lifestyle development do not necessarily relate directly to J.C. Coleman and Hendry's (1990) focal theories though it is possible to note a combination of life events, relational issues, values, attitudes, occupational trajectories and leisure interests which interact as the two focal theories suggest. The lifestyle analysis points not only to clear social class and gender differences but also to important lifestyle variations within – and across – social class boundaries as young people make the transition towards adulthood. Adolescent lifestyles appear to be clearly differentiated across a range of factors including leisure. The original theoretical models were not able to take account in any detailed way of the important influencing factors on young people which come from within the individual and from the variations of contexts that young people find themselves in. These can be a mixture of self-perceptions, motivations, meanings and saliences that individual adolescents place upon various social and leisure activities which interact with social influences such as living conditions, parenting styles and family units, school peer groups and facets of wider cultural effects such as the mass media. Further, the original models did not allow us to examine important aspects of adolescence which impinge on aspects of lifestyle such as being unemployed, moving on to higher education or being involved in risk-taking behaviours. The theoretical emphases of J.C. Coleman's (1979) and Hendry's (1983) original ideas offered a broad framework for a general understanding of the adolescent condition but we are now able to use our present findings to move to a deeper level of understanding of the variations in the adolescent experience within different social class boundaries and within the social contexts explored in this book. Hence, the idea of lifestyle as representing variations within and between adolescent subcultural 'life worlds' seems to provide a promising framework for understanding young people's transition from childhood to adulthood and is one which we hope to address in further work.

Appendix: Panel study areas – types of environment

New owner-occupied suburbs

On periphery of city; cheaply built houses for young families; single-family dwellings, linked with new schools and reasonable community-based leisure facilities, but shortage of commercial facilities within the area. Upwardly mobile population.

Rural town

Small town with agricultural base; static population; schools have very comprehensive social intake over a wide catchment; low income common; population too small and scattered to support community or commercial leisure programmes.

Special school

Boarding school environment for young people with acknowledged social/emotional problems; socially disadvantaged group with problems of integration into community. Leisure activities play dominant part both in curricular and extra-curricular life.

Private school

Fee-paying boarding/day school environment for group of young people with better than average social/leisure opportunities. Sport plays dominant part in curriculum.

Old industrial settlement

Smaller town with declining industrial fortunes; schools have more comprehensive social intake than city schools; ageing population; high rates of unemployment with closure of traditional industries; decreasing leisure opportunities as personal incomes shrink with unemployment affecting success of commercial enterprises; few new areas of public investment by local government.

New town

Separate satellite town; planned to take city overspill or to generate new industry; originally young families in preponderance; own shops, leisure facilities, schools etc. but catchment too small to support full range of commercial leisure.

New town/Catholic community

As for the new town area above, but focusing on an element of the wider community with specific religious affiliations and associated differences in family structures, patterns of control and upbringing.

Inner city

Old housing stock, tenements/flatted, in poor state of repair; juxtaposed with inner city commercial leisure facilities, but inhabitants' personal incomes often too low to take advantage of this proximity; high proportion of unemployed people, ethnic minorities, single-parent families.

Inner city/Catholic community

As for the inner city area above, but focusing specifically on the Catholic community and on young people educated in a single-sex school (girls).

Established middle-class area

Older suburbs; substantial villas, detached or terraced, many now converted to office use; older population; low rate of unemployment, little penetration by ethnic groups; leisure pursuits largely followed outside area.

Council redevelopment

Newer housing stock, but not always in good repair; large-scale schemes, often on city periphery; mixed age groups resettled from inner-city tenements; high rates of unemployment, single-parent families; poorly provided with leisure facilities.

Bibliography

Aaro, L.E., Wold, B., Kannas, L. and Rimpela, M. (1986) 'Health behaviour in schoolchildren', *Health Promotion* 1 (1): 17–33.

Abel, T. and McQueen, D. (1992) 'The formation of health lifestyles: a new empirical concept', paper presented to the BSA & ESMS Joint Conference on Health in Europe, Edinburgh, 18–21 September 1992.

Abrams, D., Abraham, C., Spears, R. and Marks, D. (1990) 'Aids invulnerability: relationships, sexual behaviour and attitudes amongst 16–19 year olds', in P. Aggleton, P. Davies and G. Hart (eds) *Aids: Individual, Cultural and Policy Dimensions*, London: Falmer Press.

Adams, G.R. (1983) 'Social competence during adolescence: social sensitivity, locus of control, empathy, and peer popularity', *Journal of Youth and Adolescence* 12 (3): 203–11.

Ahlstrom, W.M. and Havighurst, R.J. (1971) *400 Losers*, San Francisco, CA: Jossey-Bass.

Allen, S. (1968) 'Some theoretical problems in the study of youth', *The Sociological Review* 16 (3): 19–31.

Almond, L. (1983) 'Health related fitness', *British Journal of Physical Education* 14: 2.

Anthony, K.H. (1985) 'The shopping mall: a teenage hangout', *Adolescence* 20: 307–12.

Arkowitz, H., Hinton, R., Perl, J. and Himadi, W. (1978) 'Treatment strategies for dating anxiety in college men based on real-life practice', *Counselling Psychologist* 7: 41–6.

Ashton, D.N. and Maguire, M.J. (1986) 'Young adults in the labour market, UK', Research Paper No. 55, London: Department of Employment.

Astrand, P.O. (1987) *Setting the Scene in Exercise-Heart-Health*, London: Coronary Prevention Group, 10.

Balding, J. (1986) 'Mayfly, a study of 1,237 pupils aged 14–15 who completed the Health Related Behaviour Questionnaire in May 1988', unpublished report, HEC Schools Health Education Unit, School of Education, University of Exeter.

Ball, S.J. (1981) *Beachside Comprehensive: A Case Study of Secondary Schooling*, Cambridge: Cambridge University Press.

Banerjee, T. and Lynch, K. (1977) 'On people and places: a comparative study of the spatial environments of adolescence', *Town Planning Review* 48: 105–15.

Barnes, G. (1977) 'The development of adolescent drinking behaviour: an evaluative review of the impact of the socialisation process within the family', *Adolescence* 12: 571–91.

Bates, I., Clarke, J., Cohen, P., Finn, D., Moore, R. and Willis, P. (1984) *Schooling for the Dole*, London: Macmillan.

Baumrind, D. (1968) 'Authoritarian versus authoritative parents control', *Adolescence* 3: 255–72.

—— (1971) 'Current patterns of parental authority', *Developmental Psychology Monograph* 4: 1–102.

Beavers, W.R. (1981) 'A systems model of family for family therapists', *Journal of Marital and Family Therapy* 7: 299–307.

Beavers, W.R. and Voeller, M.N. (1983) 'Family models: comparing and contrasting the Olson circumplex model with the Beavers systems model', *Family Process* 22: 85–98.

Beisser, A. (1966) *The Madness in Sports*, New York: Appleton-Century-Crofts.

Berg, D. (1985) 'Reality construction at the family/society interface: the internalisation of family themes and values', *Adolescent* 16: 349–58.

Berndt, T.J. (1982) 'The features and effects of friendship in early adolescence', *Child Development* 53: 1447–60.

Berscheid, E. and Walster, E. (1972) 'Beauty and the beast', *Psychology Today* 5: 42–6.

Blaxter, M. (1987) 'Alcohol consumption', in B.D. Cox, (Director) and others, *The Health and Lifestyle Survey*, Cambridge: The Health Promotion Research Trust.

Blyth, D.A., Simmons, R.G. and Carlton-Ford, S. (1983) 'The adjustment of early adolescents to school transitions', *Journal of Early Adolescence* 3 (1–2): 105–20.

Borkovec, T.D., Stone, N.M., O'Brien, G.T. and Kaloupek, D.G. (1974) 'Evaluation of a clinically relevant target behaviour for analogue outcome research', *Behaviour Therapy* 5: 503–11.

Bourdieu, P. (1984) *Distinction; A Social Critique of the Judgement of Taste*, London: Routledge.

Bowie, C. and Ford, N. (1989) 'Sexual behaviour of young people and the risk of HIV infection', *Journal of Epidemiology and Community Health* 43: 61–5.

Brake, M. (1980) *The Sociology of Youth Culture and Youth Subcultures*, London: Routledge.

—— (1985) *Comparative Youth Culture: The Sociology of Youth Cultures and Youth Sub-cultures in America, Britain and Canada*, London: Routledge.

Brennan, T. (1982) 'Loneliness at adolescence', in L. Peplau and D. Perlman (eds) *Loneliness: A Source of Current Theory*, New York: Wiley.

Brown, B.B. (1982) 'The extent and effects of peer pressure among high school students: a retrospective analysis', *Journal of Youth and Adolescence* 11: 121–33.

Brown, B.B., Eicher, S.A. and Petrie, S. (1986) 'The importance of peer group (crowd) affiliation in adolescence', *Journal of Adolescence* 9: 73–95.

Bruner, J.S., Jolly, A. and Sylva, K. (1976) *Play: Its Role in Development and Evolution*, Harmondsworth: Penguin.

Bryant, B.M. and Trower, P.E. (1974) 'Social difficulty in a student sample', *British Journal of Educational Psychology* 44: 13–21.

Buhrmester, D. and Furman, W. (1986) 'The changing functions of friends in childhood: a Neo-Sullivanian perspective', in V.G. Derlega and B.A. Winstead (eds) *Friendship and Social Interaction*, New York: Springer.

Burt, C.E., Cohen, L.H. and Bjorck, J.P. (1988) 'Perceived family environment as a moderator of young adolescents' life stress adjustment', *American Journal of Community Psychology* 16 (1): 101–22.

Bury, J. (1984) *Teenage Pregnancy in Britain*, London: Birth Control Trust.

—— (1991) 'Teenage social behaviour and the impact of AIDS', *Health Education Journal* 50 (1): 43–8.

Butson, P. (1983) *The Financing of Sport in the United Kingdom*, Information Series No. 8, London: Sports Council.

Bynner, J.M. (1987) 'Coping with transition', *Youth and Policy* 22: 25–8.

Carter, M.P. (1972) 'The world of work and the ROSLA pupil', *Education in the North* 9: 61–4.

Cavior, N. and Dokecki, P.R. (1973) 'Physical attractiveness, perceived attitude similarity, and academic achievement as contributors to inter-personal attraction among adolescents', *Developmental Psychology* 9: 44–54.

Clarke, J., Hall, S., Jefferson, T. and Roberts, B. (1976) 'Subcultures, cultures and class: a theoretical overview', in S. Halls and T. Jefferson (eds) *Resistance thro' Rituals,* London: Hutchinson, 9–79.

Clausen, J.A. (1975) 'The social meaning of differential physical and sexual maturation', in S. Dragastin and G. Elder (eds) *Adolescence in the Life Cycle*, New York: Wiley.

Coffield, F., Borrill, C. and Marshall, S. (1986) *Growing Up at the Margins*, Milton Keynes: Open University Press.

Coggans, N., Shewan, D., Henderson, M., Davies, J.D. and O'Hagan, F.J. (1990) *National Evaluation of Drug Education in Scotland: Final Report*, Edinburgh: Scottish Education Department.

Cohen, S. (1973) 'The volatile solvents', *Public Health Review* 2 (2): 185–214.

Coleman, J.C. (1974) *Relationships in Adolescence*, London: Routledge.

—— (1979) *The School Years*, London: Methuen.

Coleman, J.C. and Hendry, L.B. (1990) *The Nature of Adolescence*, 2nd edn, London: Routledge.

Coleman, J.S. (1961) *The Adolescent Society*, New York: Free Press.

Coleman, J.S. and Husen, T. (1985) *Becoming Adult in a Changing Society*, Paris: OECD.

Conger, J.T. (1979) *Adolescence: Generation under Pressure*, London: Harper & Row.

Conger, J.T. and Petersen, A.C. (1984) *Adolescence and Youth*, New York: Harper & Row.

Corrigan, P. (1979) *Schooling the Smash Street Kids*, London: Macmillan.

Covington, L.V. and Beery, R.G. (1977) *Self-worth and School Learning*, New York: Reinhart & Winston.

Cowie, C. and Lees, S. (1981) 'Slags or drags', *Feminist Review* 9: 17–31.

Cox, B.D. (1989) 'Association of leisure and sporting activities with health in the Health and Lifestyle Survey', in R. Maughan (ed.) *Fit for Life: Proceedings of a Symposium on Fitness and Leisure*, Cambridge: The Health Promotion Research Trust.

Csikszentmihalyi, M. (1975) *Beyond Boredom and Anxiety*, San Francisco, CA: Jossey-Bass.

Csikszentmihalyi, M. and Larson, R. (1984) *Being Adolescent: Conflict and Growth in the Teenage Years*, New York: Basic Books.

Currie, C., McQueen, D.V. and Tyrrell, H. (1987) 'The First Year of the RUHBC/ SHEG/WHO Survey of the Health Behaviours of Scottish Schoolchildren', Edinburgh: RUHBC.

Damon, W. and Hart, D. (1982) 'The development of self-understanding from infancy through adolescence', *Child Development* 53: 841–64.

Davies, E. and Furnham, A. (1986) 'Body satisfaction in adolescent girls', *British Journal of Medical Psychology* 59: 279–87.

Davis, J. (1990) *Youth and the Condition of Britain: Images of Adolesent Conflict*, London: Athlone Press.

Davis, J. and Coggans, N. (1991) *The Facts About Adolescent Drug Abuse*, London: Cassell.

Delamont, S. (1984) 'Sex roles and schooling', *Journal of Adolescence* 7 (4): 329–36.

Dex, S. (1987) *Women's Occupational Mobility*, London: Macmillan.

Diener, C.J. and Dweck, C.S. (1978) 'An analysis of learned helplessness: continuous changes in performance strategy and achievement cognitions following failure', *Journal of Personality and Social Psychology* 36: 451–62.

Dorn, N. (1983) *Alcohol, Youth and the State*, Oxford: Croom Helm.

Douvan, E. (1979) 'Sex role learning', in J. C. Coleman (ed.) *The School Years*, London: Methuen.

Douvan, E. and Adelson, J. (1966) *The Adolescent Experience*, New York: Wiley.

Duguid, G. and Grant, R. (1984) 'Areas of special need in Scotland', Central Research Unit Papers, Scottish Office, Edinburgh: HMSO.

Dunphy, D.C. (1972) 'Peer group socialisation', in F.J. Hunt (ed.) *Socialisation in Australia*, Sydney: Angus & Robertson.

Dweck, C.S. and Elliott, E.S. (1984) 'Achievement motivation', in M. Hetherington (ed.) *Social Development: Carmichaels Manual of Child Psychology*, New York: Wiley.

Edwards, H. (1973) *Sociology of Sport*, Homewood, IL.: Dorsey Press.

Elkin, F. and Handel, G. (1972) *The Child and Society: The Process of Socialisation*, 2nd edn, New York: Random House.

—— and —— (1978) *The Child and Society: The Process of Socialisation*, 3rd edn, New York: Random House.

Elkind, D. (1967) 'Egocentrism in adolescence', *Child Development* 38: 1025–34.

Emmett, I. (1977) 'Decline in Sports Participation After Leaving School', unpublished draft report to the Sports Council, London.

Engstrom, L.M. (1979) 'Physical activity during leisure time: A strategy for research', *Scandinavian Journal of Sports Science* 11: 32–9.

Erikson, E. (1968) *Identity: Youth and Crisis*, New York: Norton.

European Sport Charter (1975) European 'Sport for All' Charter, European Sports Ministers' Conference, Brussels, Belgium.

Farrell, C. (1978) *My Mother Said . . . The Ways Young People Learned About Sex*, London: Routledge.

Fasting, K (1987) 'Sports and women's culture', *Women's Status (International Forum)* 10 (4): 361–8.

Fletcher, S. (1984) *Women First*, London: Athlone Press.

Ford, N. (1987) 'Research into heterosexual behaviour with implications for the spread of AIDS', *British Journal of Family Planning* 13: 50–4.

Ford, N. and Bowie, C. (1989) 'Urban–rural variations in the level of heterosexual activity of young people', *Area* 21 (3): 237–48.

Ford, N. and Morgan, K. (1989) 'Heterosexual lifestyles of young people in an English city', *Journal of Population and Social Studies* 1: 167–82.

Fraser, A., Gamble, L. and Kennett, P. (1991) 'Into the pleasuredome', *Druglink*, November/December: 12–13.

Friedenberg, E.Z. (1973) 'The Vanishing Adolescent', reprinted as 'Adolescence: self-definition and conflict', in H. Silverstein (ed.) *The Sociology of Youth: Evolution and Revolution*, New York: Macmillan.

Frith, S. (1978) *The Sociology of Rock*, London: Constable.

Frydenberg, E. and Lewis, R. (1991) 'Adolescent coping: The different ways in which boys and girls cope', *Journal of Adolescence* 14 (2): 119–33.

Gans, W.J. (1968) *People and Places: Essays on Urban Problems and Solutions*, New York: Basic Books.

General Household Survey (1987) *Participation in Sport*, London: HMSO.

—— (1991) *Participation in Sport*, London: HMSO.

Giddens, A. (1984) *The Constitution of Society*, Oxford: Polity.

Gilligan, C (1990) 'Teaching Shakespeare's sister: Notes from the underground of female adolescence', preface to C. Gilligan, N.P. Lyons and T.J. Hammer (eds) *Making Connections: The Relational Worlds of Adolescent Girls at Emma Willard School*, Cambridge, MA: Harvard University Press.

Glendinning, A., Love, J., Hendry, L.B. and Shucksmith, J. (1992) 'Adolescence and health inequalities: extensions to Mcintyre and West', *Social Science and Medicine* 35 (5): 679–87.

Goffman, E. (1971) *The Presentation of Self in Everyday Life*, Harmondsworth: Pelican.

Gofton, L. (1990) 'On the town: Drink and the "new lawlessness"', *Youth and Policy* 29: 33–9.

Goldberg, D. and Williams, P. (1988) *A User's Guide to G.H.Q.*, Windsor: NFER-Nelson.

Golding, J. (1987) 'Smoking', in B.D. Cox (ed.) *The Health and Lifestyle Survey*, Cambridge: The Health Promotion Research Trust.

Gratton, C. and Tice, A. (1989) 'Sports participation and health', *Leisure Studies* 8 (1): 77–92.

Griffin, C. (1981) 'Cultures of femininity: romance revisited', unpublished monograph, University of Birmingham, Centre for Contemporary Cultural Studies.

—— (1985) *Typical Girls?*, London: Routledge.

Hall, S. (1980) 'Cultural studies and the centre: Some problematics and perspectives', in S. Hall (ed.) *Culture, Media, Language*, London: Hutchinson.

Hargreaves, D.H. (1967) *Social Relations in a Secondary School*, London: Routledge.

—— (1982) *The Challenge for the Comprehensive School*, London: Routledge.

Hargreaves, J. (1979) 'Playing like gentlemen while behaving like ladies', in J. Evans (ed.) *Physical Education, Sport and Schooling*, London: Falmer Press.

Hartley, D. (1985) 'Social education in Scotland: some sociological considerations', *Scottish Educational Review* 17 (2): 92–8.

Hartup, W.W. (1982) 'Peer relations', in C.B. Kopp and J.B. Krakow (eds) *The Child: Development in a Social Context*, Reading, MA: Addison-Wesley.

Havighurst, R.J. (1972) *Developmental Tasks and Education*, 3rd edn, New York: McKay.

Hawker, A. (1978) *Adolescents and Alcohol*, London: Edsall.

Hein, K., Cohen, M.I. and Mark, A. (1978) 'Age at first intercourse among homeless adolescent females', *Journal of Paediatrics* 93: 147–8.

Hendry, L.B. (1971) 'Don't put your daughter in the water, Mrs. Worthington (A sociological examination of the sub-culture of competitive swimming)', *British Journal of Physical Education* 2 (3): 17–29.

—— (1976) 'Early school leavers, sport and leisure', *Scottish Education Studies* 8 (1): 48–51.

—— (1978) *School, Sport and Leisure*, London: Lepus.

—— (1981) 'Sport, leisure, the family and society – the hidden dimension', Paper given to ICSPE International 'Family, sport and leisure' Seminar, Brugge, Belgium.

—— (1983) *Growing Up and Going Out*, Aberdeen: Aberdeen University Press.

—— (1992) 'Sport and leisure: The not-so-hidden curriculum', in J.C. Coleman and C.W. Warren (eds) *Youth Policy in the 1990s: The Way Forward*, London: Routledge.

Hendry, L.B. and Jamie, D. (1978) 'Pupils' self concepts and perceptions of popular qualities', *Scottish Educational Review* 10 (2): 44–52.

Hendry, L.B. and McKenzie, H.F. (1978) 'Advantages and disadvantages of raising the school-leaving age: the pupil's viewpoint', *Scottish Educational Review* 10 (2): 53–61.

Hendry, L.B. and Percy, A. (1981) 'Pre-adolescents, television styles and leisure', unpublished memorandum, University of Aberdeen.

Hendry, L.B. and Raymond, M. (1983) 'Youth unemployment and lifestyles: some educational considerations', *Scottish Educational Review* 15 (1): 28–40.

—— and —— (1985) 'Coping with unemployment', unpublished report to the Scottish Education Department, Edinburgh.

—— and —— (1986) 'Psychological/sociological aspects of youth unemployment: An interpretative theoretical model', *Journal of Adolescence* 9: 355–66.

Hendry, L.B., Brown, L., and Hutcheon, G. (1981) 'Adolescents in community centres: some urban and rural comparisons', *Scottish Journal of Physical Education* 9 (1): 28–40.

Hendry, L.B., Raymond, M. and Stewart, C. (1984) 'Unemployment, school and leisure: An adolescent study', *Leisure Studies* 3: 175–87.

Hendry, L.B., Shucksmith, J. and Love, J. (1989) 'Young people's leisure and lifestyles project: Report of phase 1, 1985–1989,' Research Report No. 11, Edinburgh: Scottish Sports Council.

Hendry, L.B., Shucksmith, J., Philip, K. and Jones, L. (1991a) 'Working with young people on drugs and HIV in Grampian Region', report of a research project for Grampian Health Board, University of Aberdeen, Department of Education.

Hendry, L.B., Craik, I., Love, J.G. and Mack, J. (1991b) 'Measuring the benefits of youth work', report to the Scottish Office Education Department, New St Andrew's House, Edinburgh.

Hetherington, E.M. (1979) 'Divorce: A childs perspective', *American Psychologist* 34: 851–8.

Hill, J. (1978) 'The psychological impact of unemployment', *New Society* 19 (1): 118–20.

Holt, M. (1983) 'Vocationalism: the next threat to universal education', *Forum* 25: 84–6.

Hunter, F.T. (1985) 'Adolescent's perception of discussions with parents and friends', *Developmental Psychology* 21: 433–40.

Iso-Ahola, S.E. and Mannell, R.C. (1984) 'Social and psychological constraints on leisure', in M. Wade (ed.) *Constraints on Leisure*, Springfield, IL.: C.C. Thomas.

Ives, R. (1990a) 'Sniffing out the solvent users', in M. Ashton (ed.) *Drug Misuse in Britain: National Audit of Drug Misuse Statistics*, London: Institute for the Study of Drug Dependence.

—— (1990b) 'The fad that refuses to fade', *Druglink* 5 (5): 12–13.

Jenkins, R. (1983) *Lads, Citizens and Ordinary Kids*, London: Routledge.

—— (1992) *Pierre Bourdieu*, London: Routledge.

Jessor, R. and Jessor, S.L. (1977) *Problem Behaviour and Psychological Development*, New York: Academic Press.

Jones, G. (1988) 'Integrating process and structure in the concept of youth: a case for secondary analysis', *The Sociology Review* 36 (4): 706–32.

Jones, W.H. (1981) 'Loneliness and social contact', *Journal of Psychology* 113: 295–6.

Kandel, D.B. and Lesser, G.S. (1972) *Youth in Two Worlds: U.S. and Denmark*, San Francisco, CA: Jossey-Bass.

Kaplan, H.B. (1980) *Deviant Behaviour in Defense of Self*, New York: Academic Press.

Keil, I (1978) *Becoming a Worker*, Leicester: Leicester Committee for Education and Industry/Training Services Agency.

Kent-Baguley, P. (1990) 'Sexuality and youth work practice', in T. Jeffs and M. Smith (eds) *Young People, Inequality and Youth Work*, London: Macmillan.

Kenyon, G.S. (1969) 'Sport involvement: A conceptual go and some consequences thereof', in G.S. Kenyon (ed.) *Aspects of Contemporary Sport Sociology*, Chicago, IL: The Athletic Institute.

Kenyon, G.S. and McPherson, B.D. (1973) 'Becoming involved in physical activity and sport: A process of socialisation', in G.L. Rarick (ed.) *Physical Activity: Human Growth and Development*, New York: Academic Press.

Keyes, S. and Coleman, J.C. (1983) 'Sex-role conflicts and personal adjustment: a study of British adolescents', *Journal of Youth Adolescence* 12 (6): 443–57.

Klee, H. (1991) 'Sexual risk among amphetamine misusers: prospects for change', paper presented at the 5th Social Aspects of Aids Conference, London (March).

Kleiber, D.A. and Rickards W.H. (1985) 'Leisure and recreation in adolescence: limitation and potential', in M. Wade (ed.) *Constraints in Leisure*, Springfield, IL: C.C. Thomas.

Landis, J. (1970) 'A comparison of children from divorced and non-divorced unhappy marriages', *Family Life Co-ordinator* 11: 61–5.

Larson, L.E. (1972) 'The influence of parents and peers during adolescence: the situation hypothesis revisited', *Journal of Marriage and the Family* 34: 67–74.

Laufer, M. and Laufer, M.E. (1985) *Adolescence and Developmental Breakdown* Yale, IL: Yale University Press.

Lerner, R.M. (1985) 'Adolescent maturational changes and psychosocial development: a dynamic interactional perspective', *Journal of Youth and Adolescence* 14: 355–72.

Lerner, R.M. and Karabenick, S. (1974) 'Physical attractiveness, body attitudes and self-concept in late adolescents', *Journal of Youth and Adolescence* 3: 7–16.

Lewin, K. (1970) 'Field theory and experiment in social psychology', in R. Muss (ed.) *Adolescent Behaviour and Society*, New York: Random House.

Leyva, F.A. and Furth, H.G. (1986) 'Compromise formation in social conflicts: the influence of age, issue and interpersonal context', *Journal of Youth and Adolescence* 15 (5): 441–51.

Lloyd, M.A. (1985) *Adolescence*, London: Harper & Row.

Macintyre, S. and West, P. (1991) 'Lack of class variation in health in adolescence: an artefact of an occupational measure of social class', *Social Science and Medicine* 32 (4): 395–402.

Macintyre, S., Annandale, E., Ecob, N., Ford, G., Hunt, K., Jamieson, B., MacIver, S., West, P. and Wyke, S. (1989) 'West of Scotland twenty-07 study: Health in the community', in C. Martin and D. McQueen (eds) *Readings for a New Public Health*, Edinburgh: Edinburgh University Press.

Mannarino, A.P. (1978) 'Friendship patterns and self-concept development in pre-adolescent males', *Journal of Genetic Psychology* 133: 105–10.

Marsh, A., Dobbs, J. and White, A. (1986) *Adolescent Drinking*, London: HMSO.

Marsh, P., Rosser, E. and Harré, R. (1978) *The Rules of Disorder*, London: Routledge.

Mason, T. (1988) *Sport in Britain*, London: Faber and Faber.

McRobbie, A. (1978) 'Working class girls and the culture of femininity', Women's Studies Group Centre for Contemporary Cultural Studies, University of Birmingham (eds) *Women Take Issue: Aspects of Women's Subordination*, London: Hutchinson.

—— (1980) 'Settling accounts with subcultures: a feminist critique', *Screen Education* 34: 37–49.

McRobbie, A. and Garber, J. (1976) 'Girls and subcultures', in S. Hall and T. Jefferson (eds) *Resistance Through Rituals*, London: Hutchinson.

Meighan, R. (1986) *The Sociology of Educating*, 2nd edn, London: Holt, Rinehart and Winston.

Miller, A.G. (1970) 'Role of physical attractiveness in impression formation', *Psychonomic Science* 19: 241–3.

Montemayor, R. (1982) 'The relationship between parent–adolescent conflict and the amount of time adolescents spend alone and with parents and peers', *Child Development* 53: 1512–19.

Montemayor, R. and Eisen, M. (1977) 'The development of self-conceptions from childhood to adolescence', *Development Psychology* 4: 314–19.

MORI (1990) *Young Adults Health and Lifestyles*, London: Health Education Authority.

Moses, J., Steptoe, A., Mathews, A. and Edwards, S. (1989) 'The effects of exercise training on mental well-being in the normal population: a controlled trial', *Journal of Psychosomatic Research* 33: 47–61.

Muncie, J. (1984) *The Trouble With Kids Today: Youth and Crime in Post War Britain*, London: Hutchinson.

Murdock, G. and McCron, R. (1976) 'Youth and class: the career of a confusion', in G. Mungham and G. Pearson (eds) *Working Class Youth Cultures*, London: Routledge.

Murdock, G. and Phelps, G. (1973) *Mass Media and the Secondary School*, London: Macmillan.

Musgrove, F. (1964) *Youth and the Social Order*, London: Routledge.

—— (1969) 'The problems of youth and the social structure', *Youth and Society* 11: 38–58.

Mussen, P.H., Conger, J.J. and Kagan, J. (1974) *Child Development and Personality*, New York: Harper & Row.

Newman, B.A. and Murray, C. (1983) 'Identity and family relations in early adolescence', *Journal of Early Adolescence* 3: 293–303.

Newman, P.R. and Newman, B.M. (1976) 'Early adolescence and its conflict: Group identity vs. alienation', *Adolescence* 11: 261–74.

Nisbet, J.D., Hendry, L.B., Stewart, C. and Watt, J. (1984) 'Participation in community groups' *Collected Resources in Education*, Oxford: Carfax.

Noller, P. and Callan, V. (1991) *The Adolescent in the Family*, London: Routledge.

O'Bryan, L (1989) 'Young people and drugs', in S. MacGregor (ed.) *Drugs and British Society: Responses to a Social Problem in the Eighties*, London: Routledge.

Ochiltree, G. (1990) *Children in Australian Families*, Melbourne: Longman.

Offer, D. and Offer, J.B. (1975) *From Teenage to Young Manhood*, New York: Basic Books.

Offer, D., Rostov, E. and Howard, K.I. (1984) *Patterns of Adolescent Self-image*, San Francisco, CA: Jossey-Bass.

OPCS (Office of Population, Censuses and Surveys) (1989) *General Household Survey, 1987*, London: HMSO.

Orlick, T.D. (1972) 'A socio-psychological analysis of early sports participation', Ph.D. Thesis, University of Alberta.

Parish, T.S. (1981) 'The impact of divorce on the family', *Adolescence* 16 (163): 577–80.

Parish, T.S. and Dostal, J.W. (1980) 'Evaluation of self and parental figures by children from intact, divorced and reconstituted families', *Journal of Youth and Adolescence* 9: 347–51.

Parish, T.S. and Taylor, J.C. (1979) 'The impact of divorce and subsequent father absence on children's and adolescent's self-concepts', *Journal of Youth and Adolescence* 8 (4): 427–32.

Parish, T.S., Dostal, J.W. and Parish, J.G. (1981) 'Evaluations of self and parents as a function of intactness of family and family happiness', *Adolescence* 16 (60): 203–10.

Petersen, A.C., Ebatta, A.T. and Graber, J.A. (1987) 'Coping with adolescence: the functions and dysfunctions of poor achievement', paper presented at the biennial meeting of the Society of Research in Child Development, Baltimore, Maryland.

Pollock, G.J. and Nicholson, V.M. (1981) *Just the Job*, Sevenoaks: Hodder and Stoughton.

Raffe, D. and Courtenay, G. (1988) '16–18 on both sides of the border', in D. Raffe (ed.) *Education and the Youth Labour Market*, London: Falmer Press.

Ramsey, S. (1990) 'Dangerous games: UK solvent deaths 1983–1988', *Druglink* 5 (5): 8–9.

Raschke, H. and Raschke, V. (1979) 'Family conflict and children's self-concepts: A comparison of intact and single-parent families', *Journal of Marriage and the Family* 41: 367–74.

Reid, M. (1972) 'Comprehensive integration outside the classroom', *Educational Research* 14 (2): 128–34.

Roberts, A. (1980) *Out to Play: The Middle Years of Childhood*, Aberdeen: Aberdeen University Press.

Roberts, J. (1981) 'The environment of family leisure', proceedings of the 9th International Seminar on 'Sport, Leisure and the Family', ICSPE, Brugge, Belgium.

Roberts, K. (1984) *School Leavers and Their Prospects*, Milton Keynes: Open University Press.

—— (1987) 'ESRC-Young people in society', *Youth and Policy* 22: 25–8.

Roberts, K. and Parsell, G. (1988) 'Opportunity structures and career trajectories from age 16 to 19', occasional paper 1, ESRC 16–19 initiative, London: City University.

—— and —— (1990) 'Young people's routes into UK labour markets in the late 1980s', occasional paper 27, ESRC 16–19 initiative, London: City University.

Robinson, T. and Carron, A.V. (1982) 'Personal and situational factors associated with dropping out versus maintaining participation in competitive sport', *Journal of Sport Psychology* 4: 4.

Rodgers, B. (1974) 'Regional recreational contrasts', in I. Appleton (ed.) *Leisure Research and Policy*, London: Scottish Academic Press.

Rosen, G. and Ross, A. (1968) 'Relationship of body image to self concept', *Journal of Consulting and Clinical Psychology* 32: 100.

Rosenberg, M. (1979) *Conceiving the Self*, New York: Basic Books.

Rotheram-Borus, M.J., Becker, J.V., Koopman, C. and Kaplan, M. (1991) 'AIDS knowledge and beliefs, and sexual behaviour of sexually delinquent and non-delinquent (runaway) adolescents', *Journal of Adolescence* 14: 229–44.

RUHBC (Research Unit in Health and Behavioural Change) (1989) 'Report on AIDS and health-related behaviour in Scotland', unpublished report, Edinburgh: RUHBC.

Schofield, M. (1965) *The Sexual Behaviour of Young People*, London: Longman.

Scottish Sports Council (1989) *Laying the Foundations*, report on school-aged sport in Scotland, Edinburgh: Scottish Sports Council.

Scraton, S.J. (1985) 'Boys muscle in where angels fear to tread: the relationship between P.E. and young women's subcultures', *Leisure Studies Association Conference Papers No. 17.*

—— (1986) 'Images of femininity and the teaching of girls' physical education', in J. Evans (ed.) *Physical Education, Sport and Schooling*, London: Falmer Press.

Selman, R.L. (1980) *The Growth of Interpersonal Understanding: Developmental and Clinical Analyses*, New York: Academic Press.

Sharp, D. and Lowe, G. (1989) 'Adolescents and alcohol – a review of the recent British research', *Journal of Adolescence* 12: 295–307.

Shaw, M. (1984) *Sport and Leisure Participation and Lifestyles in Different Residential Neighbourhoods: An Exploration of the ACORN Classification*, London: Sports Council.

Sigall, H. and Aronson, E. (1969) 'Liking an evaluator as a function of the physical attractiveness and nature of the evaluation', *Journal of Experimental Social Psychology* 5: 93–100.

Silbereisen, R.K., Noack, P. and Eyferth, K. (1987) 'Place for development: adolescents, leisure settings and developmental tasks', in R.K. Silbereisen, K. Eyferth and G. Rudinger (eds) *Development as Action in Context: Problem Behaviour and Normal Youth Development*, New York: Springer.

Simmons, R. and Rosenberg, S. (1975) 'Sex, sex roles and self image', *Journal of Youth and Adolescence* 4: 229–56.

Simmons, R., Rosenberg, F. and Rosenberg, M. (1973) 'Disturbance in the self-image of adolescents', *American Sociological Review* 38: 553–68.

Simmons, R., Blyth, D.A., Vancleave, F.F. and Bush, D.M. (1979) 'Entry into adolescence: the impact of school structure, puberty and early dating on self-esteem', *American Sociological Review* 44: 948–67.

Smith, T.E. (1976) 'Push versus pull – intra-family versus peer group variables as possible determinants of adolescent orientation toward parents', *Youth and Society* 8: 5–26.

Snyder, E.E. and Spreitzer, E. (1976) 'Socialisation into sport: an exploratory analysis', *Research Questions* 47 (5): 238–45.

—— and —— (1978) *Social Aspects of Sport*, Englewood Cliffs, NJ: Prentice Hall.

Solano, C.H. (1986) 'People without friends: loneliness and it's alternatives', in

V.J. Derlega and B.A. Winstead (eds) *Friendship and Social Interaction,* New York: Springer.

Special Committee of the Royal College of Psychiatrists (1986) *Alcohol: Our Favourite Drug,* London: Tavistock.

Spencer, C., Blades, M. and Morsley, K. (1989) *The Child in the Physical Environment: The Development of Spatial Knowledge and Cognition,* Chichester: Wiley.

Sports Council (1982) *Sport in the Community: the Next 10 Years,* London: Sports Council.

—— (1988) *Sport and Young People (School Sport Forum),* London: Sports Council.

Stacey, B. and Davies, J. (1970) 'Drinking behaviour in childhood and adolescence: an evaluative review', *British Journal of Addiction* 65: 203–12.

Stanworth, M. (1981) *Gender and Schooling,* London: Hutchinson.

Stegen, W. (1983) 'Sexual experience and contraceptive practice of young women attending a Youth Advisory Clinic', *British Journal of Family Planning* 8: 138–9.

Steinberg, L.D. and Silverberg, S.B. (1986) 'The vicissitudes of autonomy in early adolescence', *Child Development* 57: 841–51.

Steptoe, A. (1989) 'The beneficial psychological effects of moderate aerobic exercise on adults from the general population', in R. Maughan (ed.) *Fit for Life, Proceedings of a Symposium on Fitness and Leisure,* Cambridge: The Health Promotion Research Trust.

Streitmatter, J.L. (1985) 'Cross-sectional investigation of adolescent perceptions of gender roles', *Journal of Adolescence* 8: 183–93.

Sutton-Smith, B. and Roberts, J.M. (1964) 'Rubrics of competitive behaviour', *Journal of Genetic Psychology* 105: 13–37.

Thompkins, W.G. (1973), cited in H. Edwards (ed.) *Sociology of Sports,* Illinois, IL: Dorsey Press, 233.

Tobin, J.W. (1985) 'How promiscuous are our teenagers? A survey of teenage girls attending a family planning clinic', *British Journal of Family Planning* 10: 107–112.

Van Vliet, W. (1983) 'Exploring the fourth environment. An examination of the home range of city and suburban teenagers', *Environment and Behaviour* 15 (5): 567–88.

Veal A.J. (1989) 'Lifestyle, leisure and pluralism', *Leisure Studies* 8 (3): 213–18.

Veblen, T. (1966) 'The theory of the leisure class', in R. Bendix and S.M. Lipsett (eds) *Class, Status and Power,* New York: Free Press, 36–42.

Wallace, C. (1986) 'From girls and boys to women and men: the social reproduction of gender roles in the transition from school to (un)employment', in S. Walker and L. Barton (eds) *Youth Unemployment and Schooling,* Milton Keynes: Open University Press.

Wallerstein, J.S. and Kelly, J.B. (1976) 'The effects of parental divorce: experiences of the child in later latency', *Journal of Psychiatry* 137: 153–9.

Weber, M. (1966) 'Class, status and party', in R. Bendix and S.M. Lipsett (eds) *Class, Status and Power,* New York: Free Press, 21–8.

Wells, K. (1980) 'Sexual identity: gender role identity and psychological adjustment in adolescence', *Journal of Youth and Adolescence* 9: 59–74.

Wenzel, R. (1982) 'Health promotion and lifestyles: perspectives of the WHO Regional Office for Europe, Health Education Programme', paper presented to the 11th International Conference on Health Education, Tasmania.

West, M. and Newton, P. (1983) *The Transition from School to Work*, London: Croom Helm.

West, P. (1988) 'Inequalities? Social class differentials in health in British youth', *Social Science and Medicine* 27 (4): 291–6.

—— (1991) 'Rethinking the health selection explanation for health inequalities', *Social Science and Medicine* 32 (4): 373–84.

West, P., Macintyre, S., Annandale, E. and Hunt, K. (1990) 'Social class and health in youth: findings from the West of Scotland Twenty-07 study', *Social Science and Medicine* 30 (6): 665–73.

Wight, D. (1990) 'The impact of HIV/AIDS on young people's sexual behaviour: a literature review', Working Paper No. 20, Glasgow, MRC, Medical Sociology Unit.

Willis, P.E. (1977) *Learning to Labour*, Farnborough: Saxon House.

—— (1981) 'Cultural production is different from cultural reproduction is different from social reproduction is different from reproduction', *Interchange* 12 (2–3): 48–67.

Wood, D. (1984) 'A neighbourhood is to hang around', *Children's Environment Quarterly* 1: 29–35.

Wright, S.P. (1991) 'Trends in deaths associated with abuse of volatile substances 1971–1989', London, St Georges Hospital Medical School.

Young, E. and Parish, T. (1977) 'Impact of father absence during childhood on the psychological adjustment of college females', *Sex Roles: A Journal of Research* 3 (3): 217–27.

Youniss, J. and Smollar, J. (1985) *Adolescent Relations with Mothers, Fathers and Friends*, Chicago, IL: University of Chicago Press.

Youthaid (1979) *Study of the Transition from School to Working Life*, London: Youthaid.

Zieman, G.L. and Benson, G.P. (1983) 'Delinquency: the role of self esteem and self values', *Journal of Youth and Adolescence* 12 (6): 489–99.

Zimbardo, P.G. (1977) *Shyness*, Reading, MA: Addison-Wesley.

Name index

Subject index